AN INTRODUCTION TO MEDIEVAL INSTITUTIONS

NORMAN ZACOUR

UNIVERSITY OF TORONTO

AN INTRODUCTION TO
MEDIEVAL
INSTITUTIONS

ST. MARTIN'S PRESS / NEW YORK

PREFACE

In writing this book I have tried to keep two problems in mind. The first is that of the teacher of a broad survey of modern European history who would like his students to spend a few weeks on the medieval background without being freighted with a cargo of names and events bound to remain meaningless. The many good historical narratives now available are too detailed, while the brief introductory paragraphs of works devoted to later history are over-simple and satisfy no one. In what follows I have avoided narrative history except for a few broad strokes in the first chapter by way of introduction. Instead I have attempted to describe some of the major social and political forms of medieval society, their growth and change, and their interaction where it seemed appropriate. I have invested these descriptions with sufficient detail to make them relatively meaningful without, I hope, overwhelming the reader for whom this will be a first essay upon the Middle Ages.

The second problem is that facing the student in a course in medieval history who must not only grapple with a narrative of exotic events but must place these within a social context the idiom of which, if I may phrase it thus, too often eludes him. Slavery, the presidency, the supreme court, capitalism, manifest destiny, or western expansion call up images and touch upon attitudes which for all their incompleteness and possible distortion at least allow for meaningful discussion and eventual refinement. Papal provisions, the *commenda*, the college of cardinals, Germanic kingship, or serfdom do not. Among students the tendency is strong to assimilate the strange to the familiar, to force medieval institutions into molds often fashioned as late as the eighteenth century or later, and to talk of church and state, king and nation, peasant and lord, capitalism and feudalism, with a disarming and thoroughly misplaced familiarity. It is my hope that the institutional approach adopted in the following pages will provide a useful framework into which the student of medieval history can fit the extensive data with which he will be confronted.

It not only takes a lot of people to make history, but also to write it. I can hardly claim much in the way of originality in a work of this nature, nor begin to acknowledge the many works to which I am indebted. I can, however, thank my colleagues Walter Goffart and Thayron Sandquist for reading and criticizing parts of this book, while reserving to myself full responsibility for factual errors and perverse opinions. I must also thank Mrs. Sandra van Niekerk for her assistance in preparing the manuscript.

CONTENTS

PREFACE / vii

I   CHRONOLOGICAL INTRODUCTION / 1
THE WESTERN EMPIRE / 2   THE GERMAN TRIBES / 3
THE CAROLINGIAN EMPIRE / 9   LATER INVASIONS / 10
GERMANY AND ITALY / 12   FRANCE / 18   ENGLAND / 23
THE FRONTIERS OF MEDIEVAL EUROPE / 28

II   AGRICULTURE / 35
THE LAND / 36   THE VILLAGE / 39   THE PEASANT / 41
THE SEIGNEURY / 44   CHANGE / 47

III   COMMERCE / 51
EARLY TRADE / 52   THE PLACE OF THE MERCHANT / 54
MONEY / 59   EARLY CAPITAL / 61   MARKETS AND FAIRS / 63
DEPRESSION AND DECLINE / 66

IV   INDUSTRY / 69
CRAFT INDUSTRY / 70   CAPITALIST INDUSTRY / 73   TOWNS / 78

V   FEUDALISM / 85
ORIGINS / 86   LEGALIZED VASSALAGE / 90   THE FIEF / 92
OBLIGATIONS OF FEUDALISM / 97

VI   G O V E R N M E N T / 101
CAROLINGIAN GOVERNMENT / 102   FEUDAL GOVERNMENT / 106
KINGSHIP / 111   KINGSHIP IN FRANCE / 114
KINGSHIP IN GERMANY / 118   KINGSHIP IN ENGLAND / 123
REPRESENTATIVE GOVERNMENT / 129

VII   L A W / 135
CUSTOMARY LAW / 136   THE COURTS / 141
FEUDAL LAW / 143   ROYAL LAW / 144   ROMAN LAW / 146
CANON LAW / 149

VIII   T H E   C H U R C H / 153
EARLY ORGANIZATION / 154   THE OFFICE OF BISHOP / 157
THE BISHOPRIC AS PROPERTY / 160   CATHEDRAL CANONS / 161
THE PARISH / 165   MONASTERIES / 166
MONASTIC REFORM / 170

IX   T H E   P A P A C Y / 177
THE BISHOP OF ROME / 178
THE POPES AND SECULAR AUTHORITY / 181
GREGORIAN REFORM / 186   THE PAPAL COURT / 191
COUNCILS / 195

X   E D U C A T I O N / 201
CHRISTIAN AND PAGAN / 202   SECULAR SCHOOLS / 205
CHURCH SCHOOLS / 208   CHARLEMAGNE AND EDUCATION / 210
THE REVIVAL OF THE TWELFTH CENTURY / 214
UNIVERSITIES / 217

XI   T H E   E A R L Y   M O D E R N   S T A T E / 225

SUGGESTIONS FOR FURTHER READING / 232

INDEX / 235

LIST OF MAPS

THE MEDITERRANEAN WORLD UNDER ROME AND BYZANTIUM / 6
INVASIONS OF EUROPE / 29
FEUDAL EUROPE / 107
INTELLECTUAL CENTERS / 215

AN INTRODUCTION TO MEDIEVAL INSTITUTIONS

To the memory of Elizabeth

I
CHRONOLOGICAL INTRODUCTION

THE WESTERN EMPIRE

A STRIKING FEATURE OF THE LATE ROMAN Empire, which had been plagued in the third century by revolt and regional secession, was its gradual division between east and west. This division, which in time reflected broad cultural and religious differences, was initiated by administrative and military arrangements from the time of the emperor Diocletian (A.D. 285–305). It shortly led to the establishment of two capitals, Constantinople in the east and Rome (and for a while Ravenna) in the west.

In theory there remained but one empire—but the administrative division into two parts, one mainly Latin, the other mainly Greek, often ruled by two emperors, made its contribution to a final separation hastened by large-scale German settlement especially in the western portions of the empire and reinforced by growing religious differences. Only the consequences in the west will be the subject of the following brief chapter, the historical context of medieval institutions.

2

THE GERMAN TRIBES

The Germans were no strangers to the empire. The military troubles and civil strife of the third century had required a rapid increase in Roman military forces. The old practice of relying solely on Roman citizens was abandoned, and large numbers of foreigners, including Germans, were absorbed into the Roman armies. There were increasing numbers of Germans living within the empire along its frontiers as farmers, and it was along these frontiers that they served in military districts. Many Germans rose to high rank in the imperial service.

This gradual absorption of Germans, however, proved to be only the prelude to a larger series of incursions beginning in the late fourth century. The Visigoths living in Dacia north of the Danube came into the empire as a body, refugees fleeing before the terrible Huns who swept into eastern Europe out of Asia. The Huns were nomads driven from their traditional grazing grounds in the Asiatic steppes by others stronger or more numerous than themselves. They fell first upon the Ostrogoths who inhabited the plains beyond the Dniester River. Next it was the turn of the Visigoths, who tried to stop them and were crushed. In a panic the Visigoths appealed to the Roman emperor, Valens, who allowed them entry into the empire in 376. Two years later, inflamed by their treatment at the hands of imperial officials, the Visigoths rose in rebellion; in the great battle of Hadrianople in 378, in which Valens himself fell, the imperial forces suffered a humiliating defeat at their hands. For several years thereafter the Visigoths, conciliated by the new emperor, Theodosius, lived as imperial allies on lands assigned to them in the Balkans. But after the death of Theodosius in 395, their situation became uncertain; and first in the Balkans and later in Italy, their newly elected king Alaric tried boldly to carve out a portion of the empire for his people and gain imperial recognition for himself. In neither the Balkans nor Italy were Alaric and the Visigoths successful, although the course of their wanderings was marked by military successes, the most notable being the sack of Rome in 410. It was further west, in southern France and Spain, that they would find a permanent home.

The west had already suffered invasions from other tribes. The Asdic and Siling Vandals, the Sueves and the non-Germanic Alans poured across the Rhine late in 406, almost completing the collapse of Roman government in Gaul. For the most part they plundered, continuing southward until, by 409, they had entered Spain. In return for a permanent home in southern France, agreed to by the Roman authorities in Italy, the Visigoths undertook to clear the west of the other invaders. The agreement gave two thirds of the land to the Visigoths, one third remaining in the hands of the Roman proprietors, a division based on the old Roman practice of quartering soldiers in the provinces. This, and Rome's formal recognition of the Visigoths as federates or allies, at least kept up appearances of Roman control, but in fact the Visigoths were virtually independent. From Gaul they exerted pressure against Spain, where the Vandals, attracted by North Africa, crossed the Straits in 429, leaving the Visigoths a clear field.

The Vandals were led to Roman Africa by their king Gaiseric, ostensibly as mercenaries in the service of a rebel official of the Roman Empire; but they soon overran the province and established an independent kingdom whence they preyed upon shipping in the Mediterranean and attacked the coasts of Sicily and Italy. Rome was sacked a second time in 455, the outrage ensuring the tribal name of the Vandals a place in history as a synonym for perpetrators of senseless destruction.

To the north yet another tribe, the Burgundians, took advantage of the general turmoil of the fifth century to push down the Main River and move northward toward the area of modern Belgium. They suffered a terrible defeat at the hands of the Huns, however, and the Roman government assigned them territories south of Lake Geneva in Savoy as imperial allies. Their history as an independent people was relatively brief, for they were soon defeated and absorbed by a far more powerful German tribe, the Franks.

During the first half of the fifth century, the west remained in turmoil. The Huns, after overrunning the Goths, established an empire in Hungary, ruling over a large collection of German subjects of many tribes, from which they continually threatened both the west and Constantinople. In 451 a large Hun force moved into Gaul, and though not defeated it was met and checked by a motley collection of Romans, Franks, Burgundians, and Visigoths. A second descent in 452, this time on Italy, came to nothing, and the death of their great king Attila in 453 led to a rapid dissolution of the Hun kingdom. This removed the pressure which had driven Romans and Germans in the west to cooperate for mutual defense and led to the release of many subject tribes. The most important of these was the Ostrogoths, who then moved into the Balkans as allies of the eastern empire. Although their king Theodoric obtained imperial recognition, the Ostrogoths remained a troublesome threat to the eastern emperor Zeno, who persuaded them to go to Italy. In Italy the remnants of political power had by this time passed into the hands of German mercenary generals who made and unmade emperors at will, the last Roman emperor in the west being a twelve-year-old boy deposed in 476. Thereafter Italy was in charge of an independent barbarian, Odovacar. Zeno had nothing to lose and much to gain from a contest between Theodoric and Odovacar. Theodoric reached Italy in 489; by 493 he was master of the peninsula.

Theodoric's rule of Italy demonstrated a strong respect for imperial forms and customs. His followers took a third of the Roman estates, leaving two thirds to the Roman proprietors. While all military offices were filled by Goths, all civil offices were reserved to Romans. The Goths in Italy were in effect mercenary allies of the empire, foreign soldiers without Roman citizenship, although they were the actual political masters of the peninsula.

Theodoric's policy was to preserve Roman civilization. To do this it was necessary, at the outset, to keep Goths and Romans separate. Each people lived according to its own law, its own customs, its own religion. Whether Theodoric might in time have established a basis for the ultimate merging of the two peoples can never be known, for his kingdom was destroyed shortly after his death in 526. Justinian, emperor of the eastern empire (527–565), undertook to recover the western provinces of the empire. He swiftly destroyed the Vandal state of North Africa in 533. The recovery of Italy from the Ostrogoths was a long drawn-out affair, however —only after some twenty years and more of hard fighting did the Ostrogoths disappear over the Alps, leaving an Italy ruined by ceaseless warfare. Justinian's reconquest of Italy was short-lived; he was hard pressed in the east and could not defend Italy from the incursion of the Lombards, yet another German tribe. The Lombards occupied the Po valley and much of the central portion of the peninsula, while Byzantium retained only a gradually diminishing hold in southern Italy, around Rome, and in the coastal districts of the northeast.

The success of the German kingdoms in the west depended in

SCOTLAND

IRELAND

NORTH SEA

BALTIC

ENGLAND

• London

ATLANTIC OCEAN

BELGIUM

ENGLISH CHANNEL

Rhine R.

G E R M A N Y

Weser R.

Elbe R.

Oder R.

Seine R.

Paris •

Meuse R.

Main R.

Plain of Bohemia

Loire R.

FRANCE

Danube R.

Vienna •

SWITZERLAND

L. Geneva

Alps

Save R.

Garonne R.

Lombardy Plain

• Milan

Drave R.

Santiago de Compostela •

ASTURIAS

Rhone R.

Po R.

Toulouse •

Pyrenees

Marseilles •

• Fraxinetum

Apennine

Ravenna •

ADRIATIC SEA

Douro R.

Ebro R.

Saragossa •

ITALY

Tiber R.

Mts.

Tagus R.

Toledo •

CORSICA

Rome •

SPAIN

LIMIT OF
MOORISH CONTROL
c. A.D. 1000

SARDINIA

TYRRHENIAN SEA

Amalfi •

• Naples

• Salerno

Seville •

• Cordoba

• Granada

M E D I T E R R A N E A N

Straits of Gibraltar

SICILY

MOROCCO

ALGERIA

• Hippo

• Carthage

☐ THE ROMAN EMPIRE
(c. A.D. 350)

THE MEDITERRANEAN WORLD

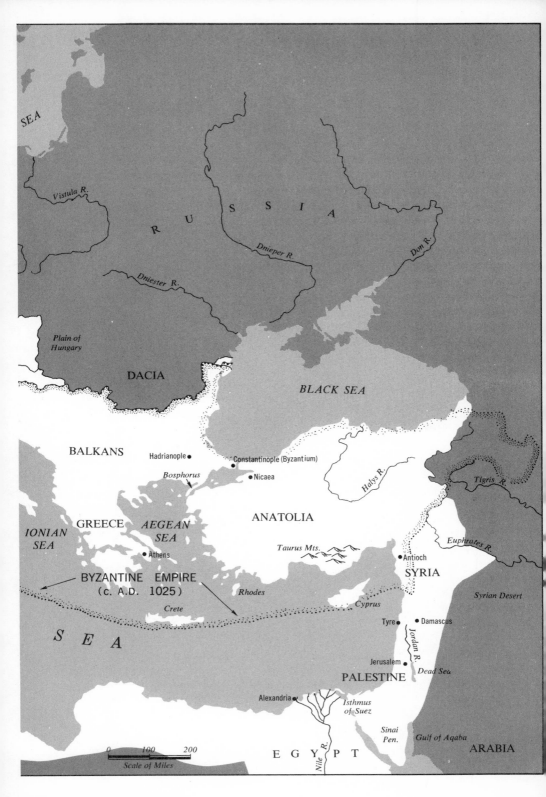

SEA

Vistula R.

R U S S I A

Dnieper R.

Don R.

Dniester R.

Plain of
Hungary

DACIA

BLACK SEA

BALKANS

Hadrianople ●

● Constantinople (Byzantium)

Bosphorus

● Nicaea

Halys R.

Tigris R.

GREECE

AEGEAN
SEA

ANATOLIA

IONIAN
SEA

Euphrates R.

● Athens

Taurus Mts.

● Antioch

SYRIA

BYZANTINE EMPIRE
(C. A.D. 1025)

Rhodes

Syrian Desert

Crete

Cyprus

S E A

Tyre ● ● Damascus

Jordan R.

● Jerusalem

Dead Sea

PALESTINE

0   100   200

Scale of Miles

Alexandria ●

Isthmus
of Suez

Sinai
Pen.

Gulf of Aqaba

ARABIA

E G Y P T

Nile R.

UNDER ROME AND BYZANTIUM

large measure on their ability to gain general acceptance among the subject Roman population. In the fourth century Christianity had come to the Goths, whence it had spread to many other German tribes; but it was a form of Christianity, Arianism, which at that very time was being proscribed as a heresy throughout the Roman Empire. The Germans who occupied the west were hated, therefore, not merely as barbarians but as heretical enemies of the true faith. Indeed, the Vandals were fanatic persecutors of Catholics. The Visigoths, a great power in Spain and southern France by the end of the fifth century, were far less severe, but did little to endear themselves to their Catholic subjects. In Italy Theodoric had been remarkably tolerant, but to no avail: at the first appearance of the emperor Justinian's troops in Italy, the Roman population quickly turned on the Ostrogoths. The Lombards came as pagans but lost any hope of an accommodation by adopting Arianism; when they later turned to Catholicism, a gradual fusion of Roman and Lombard began, but it was too late to overcome the antipathy of the papacy to the political authority of the Lombard kingdom.

The tribe with the greatest political future in the west was uncontaminated by heresy; the pagan Franks, occupying the northeast corner of France, accepted Catholic Christianity in the late fifth century. This was undoubtedly an important factor in their general acceptance by the Gallo-Romans, especially by the Catholic bishops who exercised considerable political influence, after they had driven the Visigoths out of France and subjected the Burgundians.

The Frankish kingdom possessed few other elements, however, that might have contributed to political unity. When their king, Clovis, died in 511, his kingdom was divided among four sons. While the crown was later reunited from time to time, the practice of treating the kingdom as private property in which all male heirs were entitled to a share contributed to bitter political rivalries. This was compounded by the disparate nature of the territories under Frankish domination, which stretched from the Romanized provinces in the south to the Germanic lands of north and east. The Merovingian kings—the dynasty of which Clovis himself was the most notable member—had little of the Roman administrative practices which might have contributed to their authority; and the sixth and seventh centuries, with the alienation of royal estates into the hands of a growing aristocracy, marked the inability of the monarchy to transcend its limitations.

Nevertheless, the kingdom remained intact, mainly because of the efforts of those who filled the office of mayor of the palace, an office which came to be monopolized by a powerful aristocratic family. In the eighth century a member of this family, Charles Martel, who had succeeded his father in 714, proved to be a strong and effective ruler. He expelled the Moslems from southern Gaul, broke much of the resistance in the kingdom to his government, and conducted campaigns against the pagan Frisians and Saxons. By the end of his life, he was so secure in office that he did not bother with the pretense of ruling through a powerless Merovingian king, but simply did without one. His son Pepin completed the process. In 751 he was elected king of the Franks, and the last obscure Merovingian was tonsured and thrust into a monastery.

THE CAROLINGIAN EMPIRE

The most impressive member of the new Carolingian dynasty was Pepin's son Charles the Great, or Charlemagne. Succeeding to the throne in 768, Charlemagne expanded the frontiers of his kingdom and asserted within its boundaries an unquestioned authority. He added Bavaria and Lombardy to his kingdom, began inroads into Spain, and extended his authority in the northeast. He waged eighteen campaigns against the Saxons before he could establish his political dominion and the Christian religion, which he considered inseparable. His realm was diverse, an empire in fact if not yet in name, since it included much more than the old kingdom inherited from the Merovingians. In the year 800, when he was in Rome, Charlemagne assumed the title of Roman emperor, which gave expression to his rulership over Germans and Romans alike. His government, however, remained at bottom a personal one based on his control of men. There were large diversities between the various regions of the kingdom which could not be overcome by royal legislation and administration. Political integration was only an ideal.

Charlemagne died in 814. Like his predecessors Charles was quite prepared to divide his territories among his several sons, but all but one had died before him. His son, Louis the Pious (814–840), strove to realize the ideal of a unified Christian empire in which secular government might be directed to ultimate spiritual goals, an ideal of churchmen in the service of the crown, but he was plagued by the disloyalty of his own sons. Civil war darkened Louis' later years, and continued after his death between his eldest son, Lothair, and his two younger sons, Charles and Louis. The Treaty of Verdun in 843, establishing peace among them on the basis of a tripartite division of the empire, foreshadowed the modern political geography of Europe. Louis and Charles got the eastern and western portions of the kingdom, the later Germany and France; Lothair retained a middle kingdom between them, stretching from the North Sea to the Mediterranean, including much of modern day Belgium and the Lowlands, Lorraine and Alsace, Switzerland, and Italy. When Lothair died in 855, his middle kingdom was further divided; whatever unity had existed under Charles the Great had been by now completely dissipated.

LATER INVASIONS

Political unity had disappeared not solely because of internal dissension. The west had come under heavy pressure from attackers in the north, the south, and the east, adding to the difficulties of the Carolingians. As early as the late eighth century, there had been Viking raids on the British Isles, and on the continent not long after Charlemagne's death. The raids increased in number and ferocity during the second half of the ninth century, gradually changing from summer plundering expeditions of the treasure-rich monasteries and churches to permanent occupation of fortified places on Frankish soil. The British Isles and the west Frankish kingdom bore the brunt of the attacks. The raids were not only enormously destructive but had the effect on the continent of enhancing, at the expense of royal authority, the reputation and power of those who could organize local resistance. The incompetent Carolingian ruler Charles the Fat (who for a brief period had reunited the eastern and western kingdoms) was deposed in 887. The two kingdoms were again separated. The west Franks elected a local leader, Odo of Paris, to take his place. The abandonment of the legitimate Carolingian line was premature, and on Odo's death in 898, there was a reversion to the descendants of Charlemagne. For the next hundred years, royal authority in the west was reduced to negligible proportions. Over a long period of time the Carolingians dissipated the royal estates and were unable to replace them with new acquisitions.

In 987 Hugh Capet, a member of Odo's family, from whom subsequent kings of France were descended, was elected. Hugh Capet had little on which to base any royal authority; his own estates were limited and only tenuously held; more and more men commended themselves to local lords, and the countryside began to bristle with strongholds defensible not only against Viking attack but also against the king; in short, the ground was being prepared for the development of feudalism as a major feature of social and political life.

The eastern portion of the Frankish kingdom had also abandoned its Carolingian rulers. Other than the German language, the east Franks had few elements to give them any unity, and they too were under serious military pressure. The Viking raids had not been as serious as they had been further west, but by 900 the Magyars had appeared on the eastern frontiers and many areas of the kingdom were devastated. When Charles the Fat was deposed in 887, the east Franks stuck with the Carolingian family for a successor, electing his nephew Arnulf, duke of Carinthia (887–899). Though a vigorous and able ruler, Arnulf found himself more and more dependent on the support of regional leaders whose growing independence was itself a serious threat to royal authority. With the frontiers unstable and unitary traditions only half remembered, in the tenth century Frankish Germany saw a strong tendency to break into regional areas called duchies. From the duchies the dukes excluded royal authority and brought the church into subjection.

The west had more than the Vikings and Magyars to put up with. In the sixth and seventh centuries the political geography of much of the lands surrounding the Mediterranean had been seriously rearranged by an eruption out of the Arabian desert of nomads unified by a new and vigorous religion, Islam. They appeared at the very moment when the Byzantine empire had concluded an exhausting war with the Persians. Quickly they overran not only the Persian empire but also several provinces of the Byzantine empire. Syria, Palestine, and Egypt fell swiftly; in the seventh century the city of Constantinople was itself attacked; and although the capital survived two serious sieges and would fend off another in the first quarter of the eighth century, several important possessions in the Aegean fell to Arab sea power. Further west, in the last years of the seventh century, the Arabs finally took Carthage. North Africa, which Justinian had won back from the Vandals, was lost forever. In 711 Arabs and Moslem Berbers crossed the Straits of Gibraltar and quickly occupied almost all of the Spanish peninsula, meeting little resistance from a weakened Visigothic kingdom. In a series of sporadic attacks, islands in the western Mediterranean, especially Sicily, were finally occupied.

By the ninth century the Arabs were attacking and occupying the mainland of the Italian peninsula. The emperor Louis, son of Lothair of the middle kingdom, who had inherited the Italian portion of his father's kingdom along with the imperial title, did what he could against the invaders. He was continually frustrated, however, by south Italian nobles and cities who frequently collaborated with the Moslems to secure their own independence. It was not until 915 that the Moslem stronghold on the Garigliano River was destroyed, ending the threat of a permanent Arab occupation in Italy.

Southern France also felt the effects of the Arab control of the western Mediterranean. Although their advance north of the Pyrenees had been stopped by Charles Martel in 732, they continued their forays into southern Gaul for some years thereafter. Later, Moslem pirates attacked and plundered the south coast at many places; and for a good part of the tenth century Moslems occupied Fraxinetum from which they attacked both to the east and the west of the Alps as well as levying tolls on those who passed their way between France and Italy.

GERMANY AND ITALY

The political collapse of the Carolingian empire left in its wake a host of petty local authorities whose efforts at self-preservation made impossible any renewed effort at consolidation. But the ideal of a universal Christian empire did not die; and first in the hands of the kings of Germany, later in the hands of the papacy, it would serve as an instrument for the establishment, at least in part, of a unity which seemed at once historical and ideal.

In Germany, the Carolingian line was finally abandoned when Conrad, the duke of Franconia, was elected king in 911. One of several such officers who had risen to power as a result of the disunity of the empire, Conrad spent much of his time as king struggling against the other dukes. Because he was not a Carolingian, he could claim nothing of the traditional rights of royal blood, and his failure to deal adequately with the Magyar incursions contributed to his weakness. His reign saw, therefore, a strengthening of the local authority of the dukes.

On Conrad's death in 918, one of them, Henry the Fowler of Saxony, was elected king.

Henry I was the first of the Saxon line of kings and emperors. His policy was directed mainly at acquiring as much as possible of the old middle kingdom for Germany. He dealt with the continuing Magyar menace by paying a yearly tribute until he was strong enough to defeat them (at the Unstrutt River in 933).

Henry's son Otto I, or Otto the Great, continued and strengthened these policies. As king of Germany he completed his father's work against the Magyars at Lechfeld in 955. This not only ended the Magyar menace in Germany but enhanced his prestige over rival dukes who had not been very successful in defending their lands. Elected to his father's throne in 936, Otto later (962) took the title of Roman emperor, providing the German monarch with a legal claim to the lands of Lothair and allowing Otto to extend his authority into Italy.

Otto's importance in the history of Germany can also be found in his relations with the church. Otto (and his successors) used the church as an agency of the crown in matters of local government, thus laying the groundwork for that close association of king and church so characteristic of medieval Germany and undermining the control of the dukes over the churches of their areas. Otto also made good his claim to the right to approve papal elections in the Carolingian tradition. It was a claim that reflected the growing practice in Germany and northern Italy of the king's appointment and employment of higher ecclesiastics as a basis for his government. Lacking a bureaucracy the king had little reason to hesitate between a clergy which was ready to enhance the role of the king as protector of the church and an aristocracy with strong local interests and a tendency to convert public office into inherited right. At least churchmen posed no threat of hereditary succession to the royal estates placed in their charge, and they exhibited far less local political ambition than the laity. The clergy, too, found the arrangement beneficial, for the exploitation they had suffered at the hands of local dukes and counts could not otherwise be avoided.

The arrangement was not satisfactory to all. The emperor's claim to the right of approval of papal elections was counter to local Roman interests. Pope John XII, who had crowned Otto emperor, repented his action and was supported by Roman interests. Otto invaded Rome, deposed John, and secured the election of a pope of his own choice. For the next few years he supported ecclesiastical reform and alliance with the Byzantine empire. But the Romans revolted and in 964 restored John XII to the throne. The pope died that same year, and Otto I again enforced his selection as pope. Again the Romans revolted. Not until Otto II (973–983) entered Italy in 980 could the papacy be brought back under the mantle of imperial protection.

There it remained until the death of Otto II's heir, Otto III (983–1002), who during his very brief majority (996–1002) had appointed a cousin, an enthusiastic reformer, as Gregory V, and after him his old teacher Gerbert as Sylvester II. Otto III's successor Henry II, the last of the Saxon dynasty, was the grandnephew of Otto I; during Henry II's reign (1002–1024) control of the papacy slipped into the hands of the Roman counts of Tusculum, who turned the office into a virtually hereditary possession.

Two brothers, Benedict VIII (1012–1024) and John XIX (1024–1032), were succeeded by a nephew, Benedict IX (1032–1044). Challenged by a rival claimant to the papal throne, Benedict eventually sold the office to yet a third aspirant, Gregory VI, and then changed his mind and claimed that he was still the pope.

Henry II's successor, Conrad II, was the first of the Franconian or Salian dynasty (and a descendant of one of Otto I's daughters, thanks to the German electors' loyalty to the dynastic principle). Upon Conrad's death in 1039, he was succeeded by his son, Henry III (1039–1056). In 1046 Henry III came to Rome and effectively deposed the three warring claimants, placing a German reformer, Clement II, on the papal throne. Clement II was succeeded, thanks to imperial protection, by a continuous series of reformers.

When Henry III died in 1056 he was succeeded by a minor, Henry IV, during whose minority a good deal of royal property and rights were expropriated by the German aristocracy, both ecclesiastic and lay. When Henry reached his majority, he had a lot of ground to make up. In so doing he antagonized many of the particularist interests in Germany and many church reformers who resented the way in which he handled the church in Germany. This resentment was strongest in the papal court where, in the years of Henry's minority, a new sense of independence and a vision of a church universally free from lay control had emerged.

At the very moment that Henry IV succeeded in crushing his opponents in Germany, Pope Gregory VII inaugurated a revolution by demanding that laymen give up appointing ecclesiastics to their offices—in effect, abandon control of the church. Henry had no intention of stripping himself of the only basis for his authority in Germany, especially in view of the aristocratic opposition with which he was constantly confronted. But if he had any thought that he could impose his will on Rome as his father had done before him, he was soon to learn better. His crude attempt to dispose of the problem by withdrawing his recognition of Gregory as true pope brought down upon him both excommunication and deposition. By absolving all Christians from their oaths of fealty to the king, Gregory gave ecclesiastical sanction to German rebellion. This great conflict of the eleventh century is usually called the "Investiture Controversy."

Gregory and his successors found assistance from many quarters. In southern Italy, in the early eleventh century, the Byzantine empire struggled fitfully to hang on in the face of rebellious nobles and Saracen invaders. The coming of adventurers from Normandy introduced a new element. Appearing as a threat at first, the new Norman regime was soon recognized by the papacy as an important ally in keeping the Germans at a distance. In northern Italy, too, there were many who feared the reestablishment of German imperial authority; in the growing towns of Lombardy the papacy could rely on popular support among the lower orders for its reform program. And, of course, in Germany itself there were many to seize any opportunity to check the pretensions of the monarchy.

The struggle between pope and emperor outlasted both Gregory and Henry. It was finally settled by the Concordat of Worms in 1122, a compromise which did nothing to clarify the serious issues about the relative authority of pope and emperor raised during the controversy. Instead, the king abandoned the formality of investing bishops with the spiritual symbols of their office while retaining effective control over their election, a recognition of the fact that they were temporal officers of the crown, holding crown lands and assisting the king in the administration of his kingdom.

The effect of the controversy was serious for both Germany and Italy. The loyalty of the church to the crown was in part broken; the continual civil war in Germany posed a serious threat to the monarchy; crown lands were dissipated and wasted; Henry V was forced to rely on the support of the aristocracy, which did not bode well for the future of royal authority; and the kings of Germany found it impossible henceforth to maintain their hold on Italy, which tended to break up into independent cities and regions.

In 1152 Frederick Barbarossa (Frederick I) acceded to the imperial throne. In the interval between the Concordat of Worms and his accession, a consolidation of political forces occurred in both Germany and Italy that seriously limited the ability of German kings to give political reality to their imperial title. Frederick fought with little success a half dozen campaigns in Italy in an attempt to reestablish his authority over Rome and the burgeoning towns of Lombardy. He was finally forced to recognize the claims of many north Italian towns to self-government and to concede their right to league together in their own interests.

His major success, ironically, came not through warfare but through a marriage alliance, which he effected with the king of Sicily, erstwhile ally of the papacy. Under the Normans, the Sicilian kingdom had acquired considerable wealth, stability, and unity; the kingdom, which had its origins in a collection of south Italian territories brought together by Robert Guiscard, was later joined as a single state to the island of Sicily which Guiscard's brother Roger had conquered from the Saracens. Within the kingdom, the king enjoyed a secure control over the church, being recognized as hereditary papal legate; in return he remained a staunch ally of the papacy in its struggles against the German kings.

In 1184 William II of Sicily (1166–1189), who had no male heir to succeed him, agreed to the betrothal of his aunt Constance to Frederick's son Henry. For the papacy the marriage was a disaster since the union of the German and Sicilian kingdoms, north and south of the papal states, threatened its independence. After William's death, Henry had a struggle on his hands to enforce his claim to the Norman kingdom, and it was not until 1194 that he was crowned.

His own death only three years later gave the papacy a chance to exploit the internal rivalries within both Germany and Sicily, with a view to keeping the two kingdoms separate. In Sicily there was chaos. Germans and Normans disputed the throne, which Constance had virtually no hope of securing for her infant son Frederick, whom she gave to Pope Innocent III as a ward. In Germany civil war broke out between the followers of the house of Frederick Barbarossa and those of a rival family, each of which supported their own candidate for the throne. Innocent gained many concessions in return for his recognition; but when the candidate he favored, Otto IV, finally secured his position in Germany, he quickly forgot his promises, renewed the imperial policy of his predecessors in Italy, and laid claim not only to Tuscany (part of which the papacy had recently absorbed), but also to the kingdom of Sicily.

Innocent could only turn to the young ward in his charge, Frederick II. In 1212 Frederick was sixteen, as lavish in his promises as Innocent could desire and eager for all the help he could find to regain his father's empire. Fortunately for him, Otto IV was defeated in a battle with the French in 1214, which reduced to negligible importance any resistance to Frederick's claims in Germany. Frederick effected his promises to the papacy by recognizing the independence of the enlarged papal states in central Italy and by giving up all control over the church in Germany, thus abandoning his rights under the Concordat of Worms.

With Frederick II, Italy and Sicily came first. The highly centralized nature of Sicilian government, allowing full scope to the royal will, was undoubtedly far more attractive than a Germany in which the princes and the papacy had effectively dismantled the authority of the king. Whether Frederick might have reestablished a vigorous royal leadership in Germany is questionable; at all events he did not try. Using Sicily as his base, he worked toward the extension of his authority over the Italian peninsula. This brought him into conflict almost immediately with the north Italian towns, which were determined to throw off imperial control, and especially with the papacy, which could only view such a policy as a renewed threat to its own independence. Frederick worked to reestablish imperial authority in northern Italy, thus threatening the papal states in the center. The papacy responded with ecclesiastical censures, blackening Frederick's reputation throughout Christendom while leaning ever more heavily on French support. Only after Frederick II's death in 1250, however, was the papacy able to get a French military expedition under Charles of Anjou, brother of the king of France, to invade Italy, destroy imperial authority there, and receive the kingdom of Sicily as a fief from the papacy. Henceforth Germany and Italy went their separate ways. The successive defeats of German kings in pursuit of their imperial ambitions proved fatal and destroyed whatever chances there may have been for a strong monarchy in Germany; in northern Italy, freed from the threat of imperial domination, the greater towns, especially Venice, Milan, and Florence, embarked on policies of territorial aggrandizement and rivalry; and the kingdom of Sicily, weaker under the Angevins (the dukes of Anjou) than before, soon lost the island of Sicily to the Aragonese, and itself succumbed to Spanish attacks in the fifteenth century.

FRANCE

In the tenth century the western portion of the Carolingian empire, the future France, was a congeries of principalities and lordships, with shifting frontiers depending on the momentary fortunes of their holders. Some of the greater lords, the counts of Anjou, for example, were able to create something of a compact territory of their possessions; but the lands of many others reflected in their inner dissolution the same forces of decentralization characteristic of the entire Carolingian kingdom.

From the time of Odo of Paris in the ninth century, his family (the Capetians) had disputed the royal office with the descendants of Charlemagne. Although the Carolingians were successful, the struggle was over a shadow monarchy, for by the tenth century the kingdom was but a name. The later Carolingians had few resources or supporters to withstand their opponents; when Odo's grandnephew Hugh Capet was elected king in 987, after the Carolingian Louis V had died without a direct heir, he took over an office almost empty of content. Like other lords of the time, Hugh had his own domains but these were neither contiguous nor extensive. To buy support he even had to abandon some of his possessions; for example, Paris itself along with Melun went to one vassal, the county of Dreux to another. Some of the spaces between the Capetians' scattered territories were filled in by Hugh's successors.

Paris and Melun reverted to the crown in the early eleventh century, the royal domain becoming a narrow strip extending from Senlis in the north to Orleans in the south. The process of acquisition did not stop there; in fact the history of the Capetian monarchy down through the Middle Ages is a history of the continued extension of royal territories. But for a long time the royal domain remained overshadowed by the growing principalities of others who, like the Capetians, added to their possessions by conquest, marriage, or the promise of military aid.

At the outset the Capetians were usurpers, with little in the way of tradition or legality with which to secure their authority. The dynasty was fortunate, however, in remaining unbroken; and whatever latent weakness there was in an elective kingship was gradually overcome by the practice, from Hugh's time on, of anointing and crowning the king's eldest son during the lifetime of his father. As independent as the west Frankish nobility might become, they were thus denied the chance of exploiting the possibilities of royal election. The Capetians also enjoyed the support of the church. Consecration with holy oil gave them a special character, a priestly character, marking them out from other laymen and granting them a sanctity that enhanced their prestige and contributed to the permanence of their dynasty.

Hugh Capet's descendants inherited no imperial ambitions from the Carolingians. They exerted only meager efforts to extend their influence beyond their own small possessions. As kings they were conceded only a theoretical suzerainty by men so distant or so strong that the concession was almost meaningless. Not until the reign of Louis VI (1108–1137) could the king exert sufficient local control to end the brigandage and lawlessness which troubled his own domain. It was only then that the kings of France were free to look beyond their immediate frontiers. When Louis VI arranged a marriage between his son, who would succeed him in 1137, and Eleanor, heiress to Aquitaine, Poitou, and Gascony, an immense territory came under the immediate administration of the king at one stroke, and a host of territorial lords throughout the south were brought into direct contact with the crown for the first time. This large acquisition was lost, however, when Louis VII divorced Eleanor in 1152; and the loss became doubly embarrassing when Eleanor immediately married Henry Plantagenet (Henry II), who thus was able to combine his wife's vast holdings with his own which included the counties of Maine, Anjou, Touraine, the duchy of Normandy, and the kingdom of England.

The creation of this quasi-empire by the king of England conditioned the policy of the French monarchy throughout the remaining centuries of the Middle Ages. It was a policy directed toward the extension of royal authority throughout the principalities and counties of France in the guise of feudal rights. In the face of the large continental resources of the kings of England, caution was a necessity, but the French monarchy had frequent recourse to arms when the occasion warranted. When Richard the Lionheart (Henry II's son and successor as king of England) was absent on a crusade, Philip II (1180–1223) took the opportunity to attack and take some parts of Normandy and Touraine; and during the reign of King John of England (Richard's brother), Philip was successful in winning the whole of Normandy, Brittany, Touraine, Maine, Anjou, and part of Poitou. The French royal domain was thus increased fourfold.

During Philip's reign also, a movement began to the south that laid the groundwork for the extension of royal authority there. A crusade preached by the papacy against heretics in southern France in 1209 was answered by northern French nobles under the leadership of Simon de Montfort. After Simon was killed in the siege of Toulouse in 1218, his son Amaury found it impossible to carry on alone and turned over his claims and rights to the king. Thus, what had started as a crusade against heretics became in part an opportunity for northern French nobles to obtain land and political authority in southern France and resulted finally in the French crown's direct control over a large part of southern France.

Much of the thirteenth century was spent in absorbing the new acquisitions, developing the administrative machinery to manage them, and reducing the new kingdom to obedience. There were serious rebellions against royal authority, especially during the minority of King Louis IX (1226–1270) when his mother, Blanche of Castile, acting as regent, had to combat a baronial coalition which attempted to seize the person of the young king and to limit the authority of the crown. Her energetic defense of her son's rights had the support of townsmen and churchmen who would have suffered seriously if the feudal reaction had succeeded and saw in a strong kingship their only protection. Blanche made a large contribution to the eventual development of absolute monarchy in France, as did her son Louis IX, whose reputation for piety and justice contributed as much to the growing stability of his kingdom as did his strong demand for obedience and discipline. Louis was willing to leave the possessions of the king of England in peace, provided his own suzerainty was recognized, but this marked at best a long pause before a final settlement. The continued growth of the royal domain and the extension of royal authority in France soon created an atmosphere in which semi-independent baronies such as Aquitaine to the south or Flanders to the north appeared to be exasperating anomalies. In the course of his reign Philip IV (1285–1314), pursuing the recognition of his rights throughout his kingdom, went to war with Edward I of England; and late in his reign he was involved in a series of campaigns in Flanders.

Up to Philip IV's reign, royal relations with the papacy had on the whole been remarkably free from tensions. Some of the early Capetians were more than conventionally pious, and the dynasty depended on the support of the church, which was of no little importance. But the Capetians were as avid to control bishoprics and monasteries as any secular lord, and for much the same reasons: to benefit from their revenues and from the patronage they provided. Philip I was castigated by Gregory VII and other reformers for his unwillingness to abandon his rights, but the heavy involvement of the papacy with Henry IV (of Germany) kept France relatively free from the troubles that afflicted Germany. Before Philip's reign was over, the principle of free elections of bishops and abbots by the church was established. While lay lords, including the king, continued to authorize, postpone, or otherwise influence elections, the practice of lay investiture came to an end. From this settlement dates a long period of cooperation and mutual assistance between papacy and crown. It was to France that more than one pope would turn for help or refuge in time of trouble; it was in France that the papacy found a warm response to appeals for crusaders to the Holy Land; and it was France that gave military assistance against Frederick of Sicily and the kingdom of Aragon in support of papal policy in the thirteenth century.

However, the increasing scope of royal government in France placed on the crown large financial burdens which could no longer be supported out of ordinary revenues. One source of assistance was the papal tithe. This was an extraordinary tax levied by the papacy on the holders of church offices to support unusually expensive enterprises. Papal financial agents in the thirteenth century estimated the annual income for each office, deducted the expenses involved in its administration, and established an amount (the *taxatio*) upon which the tax—sometimes a tenth, frequently a little less—could be based, to be collected over one or more years as the case might be. While the papacy was often prepared to allow the French crown to collect the tax, this was only at the price of submitting royal projects to papal approval or undertaking projects initiated by the papacy; thus in 1285 a disastrous expedition against Aragon, undertaken by Philip III at the wish of the papacy, was defined as a crusade in order to allow the church in France to be taxed.

The French crown was coming, therefore, to count on ecclesiastical taxes to help defray the extraordinary expenses of warfare. Philip IV continued to seek such concessions from local church synods in France, only to find that Pope Boniface VIII (1294–1303), anxious to protect the church from lay encroachment, forbade all clerical subsidies to lay rulers without the prior authorization of Rome. The opposition this aroused, and Boniface's own problems in Italy, quickly led him to a series of modifications, allowing that the church might grant subsidies for the defense of the kingdom provided that papal consent was first obtained; and finally that if the need were pressing, collection of such subsidies could be made immediately "without recourse to the Holy See." In effect, "defense of the kingdom" took its place beside the crusade as justification for the taxation of the church.

The quarrel, though brief, had serious consequences. Philip had in effect taken a major step toward bringing the French church into dependence upon himself. A second quarrel with Boniface over the king's right to try a bishop in the royal courts, thus limiting further the independence of the clerical order from secular control, ended in a crushing defeat for the pope. In Anagni, Boniface's native town, some of Philip's followers attacked the pope and briefly held him prisoner, intending to drag him off to France to stand trial. He was soon released by the townsmen and made his way to Rome where he died a month later; but not even the grave could save him from the continual hounding of Philip, who sought to have him tried *post mortem*. The numerous charges of heresy and other heinous offenses against Boniface could hardly stand close examination; their value, however, for the royal propaganda machine was inestimable. Philip was able to bully Clement V (1305–1314) into measures which Clement would have preferred to avoid, and to reduce the papacy to a subservience unheard of since the eleventh century.

From Clement's pontificate until 1378 the popes resided in the city of Avignon which, although technically beyond the limits of the French kingdom, brought the papal court under French influence. From Clement V to Gregory XI (1370–1378) all of the popes were from central or southern France. The composition of their court increasingly took on a French character, and throughout the period relations between the papacy and the French crown remained close. Philip IV's attack on Pope Boniface did not, therefore, inaugurate any long period of conflict between crown and papacy; nor, except for the pontificate of Clement V, did it usher in a period of royal domination over the papacy. The Hundred Years War with England, which broke out in 1337, forced the French crown to rely heavily on the papacy for moral and material support, and, in turn, gave the papacy an opportunity to play its traditional role of international arbiter and advocate of peace. As far as France was concerned, a good case can be made for the assertion that the popes in Avignon, far from being dependent on the French crown, frequently exerted a strong influence over royal policy.

ENGLAND

Left undefended by the Romans in the fifth century, Britain did not escape the invasions of German tribes. In the first half of the century, Angles, Saxons, and Jutes attacked the southeast coastline of the island and soon penetrated far inland on their raids; by the middle of the century the tribes had begun the process of permanent settlement, reinforced by a continuous immigration from north Germany. Christianity, the religion of the conquered Britons and the only remaining link with the world of the old Roman Empire, left the invaders untouched. In 597, however, Pope Gregory I sent a mission to England under the monk Augustine, who established himself at Canterbury. Within a century the conversion of the pagan Anglo-Saxons was virtually complete. A Christian church on the Roman model, relatively uniform in practice and under a centralized episcopal organization which looked to Rome for leadership, contributed much to an ultimate sense of unity among the several small conflicting kingdoms which had developed after the settlement. In the mid-ninth century, the Viking raids almost extinguished the Christian culture of the Anglo-Saxons. One of the small kingdoms, Wessex, under King Alfred, emerged as the only political power capable of withstanding the threat and giving to Anglo-Saxon society a political unity hitherto lacking. The large areas lost to the Vikings in East Anglia, Northumbria, and the northeast Midlands were gradually recovered by Alfred and his successors and absorbed into a unified kingdom; and although a recurrence of Danish attacks after 980 culminated in the victory of the Danish king Canute, it was a unified kingdom that he and his sons ruled from 1016 to 1042.

The restoration of the English line in the person of Edward the Confessor did not last long; during his reign, control slipped into the hands of magnates, one of whom, Harold, claimed the kingdom on Edward's death. But William of Normandy, to whom Edward had promised the crown, crossed the channel with a small army in 1066, defeated Harold, and quickly established his control. Unlike the earlier Saxon and Viking invasions, this was no great migration but only a military victory followed by the quick replacement of the Anglo-Saxon with a Norman king and aristocracy. The immediate effects of the conquest on many parts of English society were therefore slight, but the conquest gave William an opportunity to create a kingship of unprecedented authority. He had his followers to reward as well as a conquered land to govern; he was able to do both by granting his followers lands and estates taken from the Englishmen who had resisted him, on conditions of military service far more favorable to the crown than he or others on the continent had hitherto been in a position to exact. He saw to the building of castles throughout the country, garrisoned and maintained at his expense, and allowed his followers to do the same to defend their own lands; on more than one occasion he resorted to a mercenary soldiery, hired on the continent, to strengthen his hand.

The coupling of Normandy and England under one ruler lasted through William's lifetime; on his death, his eldest son Robert received Normandy while his second son William Rufus was crowned king of England. But it was not easy to separate the two, since the barons who had followed the Conqueror to England possessed estates on both sides of the channel and owed allegiance to both rulers. There followed a protracted struggle between the brothers for undivided control of their father's domains, which continued after William Rufus' death and the succession in England of a third brother, Henry I. In 1106 Henry I finally destroyed Robert's army, took and held his brother prisoner for the rest of his life, and imposed on Normandy his firm control.

Whatever stability Henry was able to impose in both England and Normandy was threatened by his lack of a legitimate male heir; his son was lost in a shipwreck, and Henry's plan to guarantee the succession to a daughter, Mathilda, did not sit well with a large number of barons who had no liking for a female ruler. Mathilda's husband, Geoffrey, count of Anjou, sought through his wife to extend his authority over Normandy and England but was met with much opposition. In Normandy he was ultimately successful; but in England a war went on intermittently between those who supported Mathilda and those who had assisted in the crowning of Henry I's nephew, Stephen of Blois. The war was indeterminate, the course of it marked by lavish concessions to churchmen and nobility by both sides. The country was troubled by the breakdown of the administrative and judicial machinery of the crown, and whole regions were torn by years of anarchy. Stephen finally agreed to accept Mathilda's son as his heir. When Henry II came to the throne in 1154, he already held Normandy, Anjou, and Maine through his father, and Aquitaine through his wife.

By 1175, having successfully broken the remaining resistance to his rule, Henry II's authority was uncontested in England. He was able to restore or continue administrative and judicial reforms which laid the basis for secure royal government and a relatively uniform legal system common to the whole country. His holdings on the continent remained vulnerable because of their size and distribution and because of difficulties of communication and the lack of centralized control. Henry's sons, of which he had too many, eyed one another jealously in anticipation of their personal inheritances; the kings of France—first Louis VII but especially his son Philip II—did everything possible to exacerbate their distrust of their father's intentions. In his last years, Henry was again plagued with rebellion, this time by his sons Richard (The Lionheart) and John, aided by Philip of France. Both Richard (1189–1199) and John (1199–1216), who succeeded their father in turn, had to defend their continental possessions against the persistent hostility of the French crown; and John's inability to retain the undivided loyalty of his continental barons, coupled with his troubles with the papacy, allowed Philip II to conquer the northern portions of John's continental holdings. Many of the nobility in Guienne and Gascony, which remained to John and his successors, tended to play off their immediate lord, the king of England, against the king of France; hostilities continued to break out when either side thought to gain an advantage. Louis IX of France (Philip II's grandson) was genuinely interested in peace, and provided his feudal rights were respected, he left the English possessions alone. But his successors entered upon a series of conflicts with their overmighty English vassals lasting until the middle of the fifteenth century. The so-called Hundred Years War (1337–1453) was marked by some remarkable successes of English arms, allowing the English not only to maintain their possessions on the continent but also, for a while, to control the French government itself. In 1415 the English defeated the French at Agincourt. The English occupation of northern France after this and the marriage of Henry V of England to the daughter of Charles VI of France seemed for the moment to promise a union of the two crowns. However, the inspiration of Joan of Arc and the uniting of the hitherto discordant French parties against the foreigner made it impossible for the English to establish their authority; by 1453 the English had been cleared out of northern France as well as out of their possessions in the south. Only Calais on the English channel remained of their once great continental holdings.

From the time of the Norman Conquest, royal relations with the papacy had been marked by bitter quarrels. William the Conqueror, though anxious to reform the church in England in the spirit of the movement then making its way on the continent, was just as anxious to guarantee his rights as ruler against the intrusion of papal authority. To Pope Gregory VII he was willing to concede the payment of Peter's pence, a customary contribution of the church of England to the popes, but he would in no wise recognize the pope's claim to overlordship over England. Furthermore, no papal decrees were considered valid in England without royal sanction, and no royal officials could be excommunicated without the king's consent. The independent line William followed was bound in time to run afoul of strengthened papal claims, but for the time being the papacy had its problems in Germany and William was at least actively repressing many of the abuses characteristic of the church in England.

William and his archbishop of Canterbury, Lanfranc, saw eye to eye in the matter of church reform and administration; but the Conqueror's sons William Rufus and Henry I both had to deal with Lanfranc's successor, Anselm, whose opposition to the royal investiture of bishops led to bitter quarrels until the question was settled in 1107. Later, the disorders of Stephen's reign (1135–1154) allowed a large measure of independence to the church, which looked increasingly to the papacy for leadership. Henry II's immense task of reconstruction, including an attempt to define his rights over the church on the basis of earlier custom, led him to quarrel with Thomas Becket, archbishop of Canterbury, which ended only when Thomas was murdered in 1172. The crime was expiated by Henry's recognition of an enlarged papal influence over the church in England and an increased independence of churchmen from secular control. Henry's son John also quarreled with Innocent III over the appointment of an archbishop of Canterbury, resulting in the king's eventual capitulation.

By the thirteenth century, therefore, the exclusion of papal influence and leadership in the church in England was far from complete; the crown had been forced to accept in large part the right of direct communication between popes and English bishops, as well as the independence of the clergy in England from the operation of the royal courts. Still, to judge from the complaints of the clergy in the thirteenth and fourteenth centuries, the crown continued to enjoy considerable success in limiting the operation of ecclesiastical courts in England, especially in cases having to do with church benefices. From the crown's point of view, advowson, the right to present a candidate for a church benefice, was a question of property and lawful ownership, to be determined by royal rather than church courts. And the strict interpretation of royal rights during the vacancy of a bishopric allowed the king to exercise the function, ordinarily reserved to the bishop, of filling church offices in the diocese. With the growth of the royal bureaucracy, coupled with the severe limitations of the king's revenues, this often proved a convenient way of rewarding royal officials out of ecclesiastical revenue. Church complaints against such encroachments increased, and on the whole found a sympathetic ear in Rome. But the papacy, too, was beset by the problems of supporting an increasing army of officials; it too was in the process of reserving to its own disposal more and more church offices, with varying success depending on local resistance. In England, while opposing royal encroachments in principle, the pope often enough accepted them in practice, in effect collaborating with the crown in a division of spoils on a scale sufficient to disturb ordinary patrons—bishops, canons, and the lay aristocracy—all of whom saw their privileges threatened. There was, therefore, a steady growth in England of hostility to the exercise of these papal "provisions," reinforced by a conviction common in the fourteenth century that the French popes of Avignon were actively assisting the enemies of the English. The resentment found continual expression in parliament; the Statutes of Provisors (1351) and Praemunire (1353) excluded the papal right to confer benefices and denied the access to the papal court of those who had received papal provisions. These were ominous signs that the universalism of the papacy had reached its limit.

THE FRONTIERS OF MEDIEVAL EUROPE

Subject to attack and invasion into the tenth century, in time the west grew able to withstand or absorb its invaders and in turn to extend its own frontiers. Expansion took place along the eastern frontier of Germany, in the Spanish peninsula, and in the eastern Mediterranean. The long and bloody history of German expansion at the expense of pagan tribes to the east began in earnest under Charlemagne, who carried on a brutal conquest in conjunction with the work of Christian missionaries. Although the Magyar incursion momentarily arrested the eastward drive, it was resumed after Henry I and Otto I of Germany had checked the Magyars and opened the way to settlement of the land between the Saale and the upper Elbe, where Brandenburg was founded. A large number of fortifications were soon established, each a church center, a fortress for defense, and a jumping off place for later advance. Colonists were attracted to the frontier by grants of special privileges in return for draining marshes, clearing forests, and settling the land. Slav uprisings, which periodically wiped out many of the

INVASIONS OF EUROPE

German frontier settlements, slowed the process but could not stop it; and both in the north across the Elbe and in the south along the Danube, where Vienna was founded in the eleventh century, German colonists continued to move. The settlers were lured by new lands, newly discovered silver mines, and, not infrequently, the hope of escaping heavy dues paid to landlords in the older communities in the west. Merchants and traders soon followed in the van; and of course the new settlements marked the constantly expanding frontier of Roman Christianity. By the twelfth century Hungary was subject to a virtual invasion by westerners, who formed important communities, especially in the mining regions. Silesia became predominantly German; Bohemia, where resistance to things German remained strong, nevertheless saw a continued increase in German cultural influence throughout the Middle Ages; even remote Poland, as isolated as it was, could not escape the influences of German settlement, especially German monastic foundations.

It was a different story in Spain, where a large and powerful Moslem state with its capital in Cordoba dominated the peninsula. The Moslems had not, however, overrun Spain completely; the northwest corner remained untouched, providing a small center of Christian resistance under the princes of Asturias and Leon. Another small area of Christian influence was carved out during the first decade of the ninth century with the creation of a Frankish March, a frontier county south of the Pyrenees; during the collapse of the Carolingian empire, the counts of the region gradually acquired independence. A third area, in the western Pyrenees, provided yet another center of ultimate resistance to the Moslems, where the Basques, traditionally hostile to both Arab and Frank, took Navarre from the Franks.

Until the eleventh century the internal affairs of the petty Christian states remained in turmoil; momentary victories against their Moslem neighbors to the south were frequently offset by internal rivalry and political dissolution. Directly and indirectly, the caliph of Cordoba was able to interfere by negotiation with disloyal or disaffected vassals in the north and by other forms of intervention in the relations of northern lords. Only when the caliphate weakened in the eleventh century and Moslem Spain split into some twenty-three rival petty regions was it possible for the northern principalities to grow. It was from Leon and Castile, Aragon and Catalonia that later expansion southward took place; Navarre, pinched between the latter two, remained small. Such expansion as took place, however, reflected no particular cooperation among Christians against Moslems; it was merely territorial expansion against weak neighbors, whether Christian or Moslem. In the eleventh century, however, the spread of monasteries in Spain gave to these intermittent conflicts the character of a Christian mission, and the advent of the crusades at the end of the century turned them into a holy war, which did not end until the fifteenth century with the expulsion of the last Moors from Spain.

The crusades to the Holy Land, which began in 1095–1096, gave a great stimulus to expansionist tendencies already present in the west. Pilgrimages to the spots where martyrs had died for the faith had grown immensely in popularity; the notion that a martyr about to die for the faith could remit one's sins had gradually given rise to the popular belief that the spot of his martyrdom possessed something of the same power. Rome had become one of the most important attractions to pilgrims anxious to visit the place of martyrdom of the apostles Peter and Paul; in the ninth century the belief that the burial place of James, one of the apostles, was at Compóstela in northwest Spain made that another of the favorite goals of western pilgrims. Above all, Jerusalem, where Christ had been crucified, remained for all Christians the most important place of pilgrimage. By the eleventh century large companies of Christian pilgrims were traveling westward each year down the Danube, through the Balkans, Anatolia, and Syria to Jerusalem. In the last quarter of the eleventh century, however, the Turkish conquest of Asia Minor and the Holy Land seriously disrupted the pilgrimage routes; and cries for help from a beleaguered Byzantine empire which, despite religious differences, was nevertheless Christian, prompted a large response from the west. Urban II preached the first crusade at Clermont in 1095, pleading with western warriors to stop their internecine warfare and turn their arms to the aid of their coreligionists in the east. In effect he inaugurated a movement with a long future, which began as an expedition of succor and quickly changed into a series of wars of conquest.

The crusade had a broad appeal, both to those who were moved by piety and to those who sought adventure. The conquest of Jerusalem and neighboring territories along the Levantine coast opened a new frontier to which many flocked to seek their fortune, and gave an immense stimulus to Italian commercial towns (such as Pisa, Genoa, and Venice) already actively wresting control of Mediterranean shipping from the Moslems of Spain and North Africa. Although some of the major crusades that followed the first have been singled out by historians and enumerated, there was in fact a constant flow of crusaders to the east and, as a result, a growing interchange of goods, personnel, and ideas between east and west. The very idea of the crusade acted as a stimulus to those who, in Germany or in Spain, sought to enlarge their territories at the expense of non-Christian neighbors, and provided the basis for large-scale cooperation in the prosecution of wars of conquest under the universal banner of Christianity. St. James of Compostela now became the crusading saint of Christian Spain; and French knights from Gascony, Toulouse, and Aquitaine animated the Spanish war of conquest in the spirit of a crusading movement which had its origin and found its most fervent expression in France. The answer given by a Castilian king to one who sought his aid in the east was "We are always on crusade here, and so we do our share." The Teutonic Knights, a military religious order which, in the late twelfth century, won a place in the east comparable to that of the Hospitalers and Templars, played a larger role by far in the extension of German culture in eastern Europe than it did in the crusading states of the Levant.

In the popular mind, the schismatic Greek was just as great an enemy as the infidel Moslem; and the twelfth century expeditions to the Holy Land increased rather than allayed the suspicion and hostility of Latin for Greek and Greek for Latin. The great fourth crusade of 1201–1202, which set out from Venice ostensibly for the Holy Land, was easily diverted into an attack upon Constantinople and resulted ultimately in the fall of the Byzantine capital and the occupation of a large part of the Balkans and Greece. The long-range effect of these western raids into the eastern Mediterranean was so to weaken the Byzantine empire that it could no longer act as a European buffer against Asian attack. From the fourteenth century on, the Turks penetrated the European continent, captured Constantinople in 1453, and then attacked the west through Hungary. Henceforth the crusades became a defensive war to stave off invaders rather than a holy expedition to the shrines of Christianity.

The expansion of Europe to the east was checked; the search for new possessions and eastern goods for which European tastes had been whetted was now to be redirected. But the Europe which turned to reach out around Africa and across the Atlantic had come a long way from the primitive society of the early Middle Ages. It carried to new worlds highly developed ideas about social and political organization, the origins and development of which lay deep within its own experience. It is to some facets of that experience that we must now turn.

II

AGRICULTURE

THE LAND

THROUGHOUT THE MIDDLE AGES FARMING WAS the most important economic activity in Europe, absorbing the time and labor of nearly all its inhabitants. The land and its fruits made up the major form of wealth. The ownership or control of land determined in large part the structure of society and the distribution and exercise of power.

Although the produce of particular fields and gardens was severely limited, medieval agriculture was surprisingly rich and varied when viewed in its totality. Medieval agriculture had inherited from the ancient Mediterranean world most of its techniques and crops, introducing a few innovations in them as needed; by present standards, of course, it remained primitive. One problem that besets modern agriculture—how to increase yield proportionate to increases in population—was of no great moment in the early Middle Ages since the population had declined during the late Roman Empire and did not increase significantly until the eleventh and twelfth centuries. Consequently the basic forms of agriculture came to be developed under static conditions, with no real demand for intensive cultivation.

By the eleventh century the growth of population, slow at first, more rapid as time went on, ultimately led to an increase in food production, but not without considerable dislocation. In some areas of relatively dense settlement, agricultural productivity could not keep pace with the birth rate. Local population growth, with more children to divide the family holdings, led to the breakup of holdings among more and more petty farmers, thus perpetuating inefficient production and a continuous depression. Agricultural production in such areas significantly increased only as fragmented holdings were brought together into larger and more efficient units by purchase or other means or as superfluous agricultural labor was used to bring more land under the plow by clearing, draining, and other forms of reclamation.

Not that the medieval cultivator lacked the knowledge to improve his yields. He knew the value of manure, but there was never enough. To raise sufficient numbers of animals to produce larger amounts of manure would have taken too much land for grazing and left not enough for grain. In fact, throughout the Middle Ages there was constant tension between cattle grazing and grain growing, because increased demand for food for human consumption led to the extension of field crops usually at the expense of grazing land. This was not always the case, of course; climate and terrain often dictated where pastoral occupations would drive out farming.

The shortage of fertilizers necessitated the old practice of fallowing the land, leaving it unused that it might renew itself. The primitive two-field rotation, in which one field was sown for a year and the other fallowed, meant that half the available arable land always lay unproductive. In areas favored by temperate climates this gradually gave way to three-field and sometimes four-field systems, allowing more cultivation and a greater overall yield each year. In the three-field system, which became increasingly common, one field was planted in the fall, another in the spring, and the third left fallow, thus keeping two thirds of the land in production at any one time instead of one half. The system also spread the risk of crop failure and distributed the available agricultural labor over more of the year. But there was a limit to how far yields could be increased in this way. Only a few very favored areas could afford to abandon fallowing altogether. In much of Europe, especially in the south where summer heat and insufficient moisture made a spring crop unlikely and much of the north where a fall crop was hopeless, the old two-field system prevailed. Fertilization with wood ash was practiced in some places with short-term success, but this led in time to deforestation over wide areas, itself a serious economic loss. Marling, the periodic liming of the soil, was an innovation of the ninth century where lime was available; burning stubble for ash was another practice to improve fertility. These were all pragmatic measures, undertaken with no understanding of soil chemistry, true also of the increase of special crops for animal fodder, such as clover which stored nitrogen from the air instead of taking it out of the soil.

Other medieval farming techniques also betrayed ancient origins, although again there were some modifications and slow changes. The heavier soil in the more temperate zones of Europe called for a heavier plow than the light *aratrum* of antiquity. In the ancient Mediterranean world, the constant enemy of agriculture was lack of moisture. This forced the development of the dry-farming technique of light plowing (often bare scratching) and pulverization of the soil surface by cross-plowing, which breaks the capillary action by which sub-soil moisture is drawn up and dissipated by the hot sun. In the north, however, the problem was often just the opposite: that of draining sub-soil moisture in low-lying wet areas. Deep plowing and ridging for drainage required a heavy wheeled plow. While it had not been uncommon for plows to be pulled by man power, the heavier plow in a heavier soil required animal teams, usually oxen. With the introduction of the horse collar, horses could be harnessed to a plow without choking; in some areas horses came to be the preferred source of power for speed and efficiency, although not all agreed. Walter of Henley, an overseer of an English manor in the thirteenth century, insisted in his handbook on husbandry that oxen were a good deal cheaper to keep and that a mixed team of oxen and horses worked faster than horses alone, provided the ground was not too stony.

Farm implements remained primitive; in the field, plow and harrow, sickle or scythe; in the garden, spade and hoe. Iron, though relatively rare and expensive, was sometimes used for the cutting edges of tools. A flail replaced the older beating stick for threshing, although in many places the grain was still beaten out by horses' hooves. After threshing, the grain was tossed from side to side in a barn or thrown up in the open air for the wind to blow the chaff free.

A wide variety of grains—wheat, barley, oats, and many other coarse grains—were known, as well as a large number of leguminous plants for animal and human consumption, flax and hemp for textile fibers, and many garden vegetables. But in no one place was there much variety; and it was long before there was any northern acclimatization of such plants as asparagus and melons, spinach, and new varieties of other vegetables. Only after the growth of town populations had created a sufficient demand was there an expansion of gardening for the marketplace, and the wide variety of vegetables and fruits taken for granted today had to wait upon slowly changing taste. In general local conditions of climate and soil, lack of communication which might have introduced new seed, the heavy hand of local tradition, and the absence of stimulus to produce a surplus for sale made the diet in any one place un- relievedly monotonous.

In general, in western Europe then, as in North America until relatively recently, when faced in time with increased demand, agriculture took the easier road of extensive rather than intensive cultivation, clearing forests, draining swamps and marshes, beating back the sea, and bringing under the plow greater and greater amounts of land. Technical innovation remained rare, not merely because of the innate conservatism of the farmers themselves, but because it was unnecessary. Extensive agriculture of this kind met other needs as well: it helped to absorb the increased rural popu- lation that could find no place in existing agricultural communities and served as a means of colonizing vast, sparsely populated tracts of the European continent.

THE VILLAGE

Communal organization was an important aspect of medieval agriculture, largely determining the methods of farming and the extent of production. The peasantry usually lived in villages rather than on their own lands. Such arrangements were not universal; in some parts of Europe, there were found separate homesteads. But in the main, reliance on cooperative labor imposed on the peasantry a communal life in which the major decisions of the agricultural year that closely touched the lives of all were made by all, a life in which innovations springing from individual initiative were rare. The village exercised its own sanctions over the peasant through locally chosen village officials and the operation of customary law, all the more difficult to modify because it was customary.

The arable land available to a village community for cultivation was divided into two—sometimes, and more often as time went on, three—separate fields; the fields usually lay open for domestic animals to graze on and to fertilize with their droppings, except during the growing season when the fields were fenced. Each field was divided into long strips. The peasant used several of these strips, but they were scattered in each of the fields so that no individual had a contiguous holding. The scattered nature of a peasant's holding made it difficult for him to remain independent of the village community and reinforced the handling of village affairs on a cooperative basis. It is not certain that all the strips in a given field were worked in common; the peasant might work alone, but it is more likely that he needed the help of a few neighbors before he could garner the fruits of his scattered holdings. The hard tasks of plowing, harrowing, and reaping—especially on the heavy alluvial lands of northern Europe—and the need for large teams of oxen or horses, which no one peasant could afford, meant that villagers often had to pool their resources and work together in the fields and meadows.

The division of the arable fields into strips was not a universal arrangement; the Anglo-Saxons took it to England, but where the native Celts were left in possession of the soil, the fields remained roughly divided into rectangles. In general, however, strips were the characteristic feature of arable fields in much of northern Europe, in England, France north of the Loire River, eastern France, and western Germany.

Arable land was not the peasant's only resource. Wasteland and meadow land, local water in stream, pond, and lake, and especially the products of the forest supplied crucial needs of man and beast alike—fish, game, grazing for cattle, food for pigs, building materials, fuel, and a host of other wants. There was no way that these resources could be divided. They were held in common, each peasant enjoying, in accordance with the custom of his village, rights in all these resources, usually in proportion to his arable holding. The common holdings of the village provided a large proportion of a peasant's livelihood, and since this was often at a bare subsistence level, helped to maintain a precarious economic balance that could be too easily upset.

The ultimate end of this agriculture was self-preservation. The inhabitants of primitive agricultural communities, little villages of simple huts surrounded by garden plots and the great fields beyond, sheltered themselves, clothed themselves, and fed themselves from the products of their fields and commons, painfully wrested from an often perverse Nature. In the decay of towns and markets following the disintegration of the Roman Empire, the decline of trade and transportation, the drop in population, and the general uncertainty—to say nothing of the chaos—in the years following the reign of Charlemagne, the west reverted to this subsistence economy tied close to the soil. There were local markets, of course, and some exchange of goods; but these were incidental to the main task of subsistence. Buying and selling were not the ends of agricultural production, but occurred only with the accidental circumstances of surplus or shortage. Only with the return of some semblance of political order in a relatively settled and peaceful era could there come a revival of economic intercourse as a purposeful occupation, and with it some incentive to provide agricultural products beyond the needs of the village itself.

THE PEASANT

Because of the nature of agricultural life in Europe, there were always serious limitations on the independence of the peasantry. The services and dues owed by primitive cultivators to their local chieftains in pre-Roman times, the public duties demanded by the Roman imperial government, which in time were usurped by large private landowners, the compulsions of the primitive village's community decisions, all these were limitations which make it unlikely that a peasantry completely independent in the management of its land ever existed. Still, there were many so-called free peasants whose obligations to some local magnate or chieftain, usually to labor on his land, did not extinguish or seriously limit their personal status, their rights to buy and sell, to seek justice in the courts, to come and go as they pleased. Many such peasants possessed their own land; many others were tenants, holding their lands of some large landowner, often on a sharecropping basis.

During the late Roman Empire, the condition of the farmer changed drastically. The holders of large estates, facing a general shortage of slave labor for their own lands, pursued the practice of settling their slaves on part of the estate to cultivate it, subject to very heavy restrictions and obligations. These slave holdings quickly became hereditary without opposition from the landlord, who was thus assured sufficient labor. While the ex-slave thus slowly acquired some of the characteristics of a tenant farmer, the free tenant was in fact losing much of his freedom and beginning to look like an ex-slave. Legislation during the late empire had fixed all farmers to the soil, forbidding them or their children to abandon their holdings. Unable to move, the tenants quickly fell under the control of local landed magnates, which the weakening central government could do nothing about. Where once the relationship between tenant and landlord had been easily dissolved and the obligations of the tenant easily thrown off, his dependence on the lord now became perpetual, sanctioned in fact by public law. As the state grew weaker, local magnates usurped public functions, such as tax collection and troop recruitment, gradually obtaining rights of government over their tenants to go with their already extensive economic control. The freedom of tenant farmers was therefore only nominal.

The position of independent farmers was no better. The conditions of insecurity in the early Middle Ages forced small peasant proprietors to seek the protection of local magnates. Such small proprietors turned their land over to the landlord and received it back as tenements burdened with various obligations. The process was not always voluntary, for there was no public authority to protect the peasant from being forced into a dependent and ultimately servile relationship. The independent cultivator was usually too weak to withstand the demands of a strong neighbor in the district, and making the best of a hopeless situation "commended" himself and his posterity to the other person, thus robbing his descendants of any choice. This loss of choice, the very antithesis of freedom, came to be the mark of the servile cultivator. Frequently whole villages or parts of villages elected or were forced into this kind of subject relationship.

The suppression of the free peasantry was reinforced by their growing assimilation with the ex-slaves of the lord's estate. Both were cultivators of the soil; both held land of the lord; both owed labor and other services to the lord; both were tied to their occupations for life; the posterity of both was committed to the same status. Thus there occurred a gradual merging of slaves, tenant farmers, and peasant proprietors into a single, relatively undifferentiated mass of half-free workers, the "serfs." Carolingian documents usually designated them *mancipia;* but by the ninth century, the term *servus* began to be used, first as a category of unfreedom, but later, with the general assimilation of unfree and free, as a generic term classifying all those agricultural and domestic workers who could not claim free legal status. The line was not easy to draw, and in many parts of England, for example, it was only with the growth of common law in the twelfth century that the lawyer's need for a simple classification, "free or unfree," completed the degradation of most peasants as serfs. The differences in original status were often reflected in the differences in their obligations to their lords, some lighter than others; but in the course of time the tendency grew strong to eradicate variations and to simplify and make uniform existing differences in status and obligations.

This process did not go on everywhere or at the same pace. In some parts of Europe, in southwest France and in Saxony, for instance, there remained an extensive free peasant proprietorship. The land of such proprietors was described as "allodial," that is, held without obligation to a lord. And in other areas serfdom did not spread widely or else died out early, as in Normandy in the late eleventh century. Nevertheless, in many areas where the peasant was reputedly free, he was in fact subjected to conditions, depending on local custom and the presence or absence of strong government, which often left him distinguished from his less fortunate servile fellows only by the amount or nature of the service he owed rather than by his complete freedom from service. Certainly, the amount of land unburdened by dues remaining in the hands of peasant proprietors was not important enough to exert any influence on the development of social institutions.

THE SEIGNEURY

The most characteristic institution of medieval agricultural society was what has come to be called the seigneury, or manor—"the union of power over men with power over land."[1] The seigneury was a collection of land and men over which a lord exercised economic and political rights. The peasant holdings comprised only part of the land of the seigneury, for the lord had land of his own, the produce of which came directly to him. This included the lord's arable land but also rights in the commons which he often extended at the expense of the peasants. Since the lord's rights over the various components of his seigneury had often been obtained at different times and under different circumstances, they frequently varied considerably from one part of his domain to the other, although there was a strong tendency for the lord to obliterate the exceptions.

The seigneury not only lacked uniformity, it frequently lacked contiguity. It was often in scattered pieces, a village here, a part of a village there, and it was not unusual to find a seigneurial lordship exercised over some members of a village in which others were free. Where this obtained, a struggle frequently followed between the lord and the free villagers over their respective share in the commons, resulting in some formal sharing by which the lord got part of the commons for himself. This could be dangerous for the villagers, a step toward their ultimate complete subjection to the lord.

The seigneury, then, is not to be confused with the village. In some cases the two institutions were coterminous, an entire village comprising a seigneury. On the other hand, a whole village might be divided among two or more seigneuries. Even so the village as such did not lose its corporate character. It persisted as a society with its own sanctions over its inhabitants, whether these were subject to one lord, several lords, or no lord at all. The apportionment of collective rights of grazing, fishing, and fuel gathering, the compulsory arrangements of cooperative sowing, fallowing, and harvesting, the regulation of crop and field rotations, and the local

---

[1] M. Bloch, in *Cambridge Economic History*, 2nd ed., Vol. I (Cambridge, 1966), p. 265.

election of village officials continued in practice as autonomous actions of the village community. Even where an entire village was subject to one lord and under the lord's "ban"—his right to issue orders and punish those who disobeyed—this might not mean very much in the face of the vigor of village life and custom. Whatever made a village more coherent tended to serve as an obstacle to the lord's power. Thus in communities where a larger amount of cooperative effort was needed than in the kind of settled village life we have been describing—in the pastoral areas of the Alps and Pyrenees, for example, where there was not much arable land to be parceled out in individual holdings, in the Lowlands where the draining of marshes demanded cooperative effort on a vast scale, or in newly settled areas of heavy forests where a good deal of cooperative labor was needed to bring the land under cultivation— the power of the lord was noticeably less than elsewhere.

Nevertheless within most seigneuries that power was difficult to withstand; and the lord's ban allowed him to usurp rights in the commons, extend his control over the economic activities of his peasants, and establish juridical rights over the village community through his control of the seigneurial court, simply because there was no power sufficient to stop him. The economic monopolies established by the lord whereby the peasants were forced to use his mill, oven, wine press, and so forth exclusively, and to pay for such use, betray by their very name, "banalities," their origins in the exercise of the lord's ban, his legal superiority supported by the threat or exercise of force.

For the lord the chief economic advantage of the seigneury lay in the peasants' labor services and the payments, usually in agricultural produce but often in money also, which they made to him at certain times of the year, both varying according to local custom. Thus on one of the manors of the abbey of Peterborough in England, the villeins or serfs holding a virgate (thirty acres) each had the following to do:

And these men plough in the spring from each virgate 4 acres for the work of the lord. And besides this they provide ploughs for the work of the lord four times in the winter, and three times in the spring, and once in the summer. And these men have 22 ploughs with which they work. And all these men work for the lord 3 days in each week. And besides this they render each year from each virgate by custom 2 shillings and 3 halfpence. And all the men render 50 hens and 640 eggs. . . . And there are 8 cottars each of whom has 5 acres and they work (for the lord) 1 day each week . . . and each one of them gives 1 penny for a he-goat (if he has one) and 1 half penny for a nanny-goat.[1]

Sometimes the labor could be varied as well as onerous. The holder of a virgate in the manor of Elton, Huntingdonshire, had this to do:

From Michaelmas [September 29] to the beginning of August he works for 2 days in each week and ploughs for a third, except at Christmas and Easter and Pentecost. And from the beginning of August to the Nativity of St. Mary [September 8] he works for three days each week. And from the Nativity of St. Mary until Michaelmas he works every day except Saturday. In winter he ploughs half an acre, and sows it with his own seed; and he harrows and reaps it, and also another half-acre in August. And he performs carrying services at his own expense. And he makes 2 mitts of malt from the lord's corn and the sixth part of 1 'milla'. He makes payments for rights on the common; and he pays 13 pence as 'heusire'. He pays also 4 pence at Michaelmas, and 1 half-penny for wool. And he shall go errands: if he goes outside the county he shall be quit of his week's work except for ploughing. And in August he gives 1 carrying service of timber, and 1 work at fencing and he performs 2 carrying services of corn in August. And each 5 virgates give 4 pence for fish, and each 2 virgates give 1 cart of thatch, and they make the thatch. When the winnower comes there, all shall go to the court and thresh the corn from day to day until the 'farm' is made up. And if there is such hard frost in winter that he cannot plough, then he shall work on Fridays instead of ploughing. And when the farmer calls for boon-works in August he shall come to them with his whole household, and he shall then be fed by the farmer.[2]

Labor service varied enormously throughout Europe, from a few days a year to the three days a week in the above examples, and there was usually a marked difference within any given seigneury between the amount due from a free tenant and that due from a serf. Where, as in some seigneuries, there were variations of servile

---

[1] *English Historical Documents*, Vol. II, 1042–1189, D. C. Douglas and G. W. Greenaway, ed. (London: Oxford University Press, 1953), p. 829.

[2] *Ibid.*, pp. 832–833. Reprinted by permission of Oxford University Press and Eyre & Spottiswoode Ltd. The "farmer" here is one who has rented land from the owner, and enjoys the dues normally owed by the villeins.

status, this was often reflected in variations of labor services also. Periodic payments at certain times of the year—of eggs, butter, cheese, fowl, grain, and sometimes money—formed another source of the lord's revenue derived from his peasants. But the lord also demanded, and frequently could not be stopped from obtaining, rights of common which in the course of time became exclusive: nearly everywhere in Europe, for example, the hunting of wild game in wastes and forests became the monopoly of the nobility, an extension of their rights of common. Such extensions later worked great hardship on rural populations. This was especially the case with "enclosures," the fencing of part or all of the commons for the exclusive use of the lord and the eviction of peasants not only from the commons but even from their arable land in order to convert the whole into sheep pasturage, a process which in England began to gather headway in the thirteenth century. Enclosure was aided by the revival of Roman legal ideas respecting ownership, whereby common rights came to appear illogical and the lord was able to reestablish his full proprietary rights. Enclosures often permitted improvement of the land or its more economical use, but in depriving the peasant of an important source of his livelihood without adequate compensation, they often upset the delicate balance of the village economy.

Within the seigneury, some of the many obligations and demands to which the peasant was subjected came to be sure marks of servile status. These were the head tax (*chevage, cens*), the fine paid to the lord in order to marry a son or daughter off the seigneury (*formariage, merchet*), and the fine paid to take up or "inherit" one's tenement (*mainmorte, heriot*). Serfs were often required to contribute to the lord in times of emergency. This contribution, the *taille*, was eventually reduced by custom to a regular and fixed payment.

CHANGE

It is difficult to describe social institutions without making them appear more static than they really are. In the case of medieval agriculture, however, this is not a great danger. While rural society was not completely stagnant, change was virtually undiscernible to the contemporary. Because of the uncertainty bred of long centuries of adversity, the need for subsistence and security permitted little opportunity for dynamic growth.

However, two forces were slowly taking shape which would combine to bring about substantial changes in the basic forms of rural life: a steady decline in the political authority of local magnates with the growth of central governments, and the development of commerce, itself a sign of more widespread security and a harbinger of profound economic changes to come. These developments will be discussed in more detail below; however we may note here that their effect upon the landlord and his relation to his land and his peasants was widespread and important. Many things forced the landlord to cast about for new sources of revenue: the evolution of a merchant class, the growth of towns, the increased availability of a wider assortment of goods, and the need for more money to facilitate the exchange of goods and to satisfy the new tastes of a new age. To the extent that he could, he attempted to convert the various dues and services owed to him into cash payments to meet the demands of an exchange economy. Where it seemed profitable and feasible, the lord might increase his personal activity on the estate by extending his demesne (the manorial land he used rather than rented) and, as some did in England, using the enlarged demesne to raise sheep for wool export, a more profitable pursuit. Frequently, however, the estate was threatened by loss of labor as peasants made off for better opportunities elsewhere. To hold on to labor it was necessary to offer better terms. This often coincided with the lord's own immediate interests. By relieving peasants of servile obligations in return for fixed annual payments, the lord allowed the old serf to become a new tenant. The peasant received legal freedom; the lord received money. Often the lord went further, renting out his own demesne on a fixed lease. These changes meant that the peasant could spend more time on his own holding, possibly rent more land, and enjoy more personal freedom. He was certainly encouraged to produce more for an increasing market. So the manorial economy of self-subsistence gradually gave way to an exchange economy in which the peasant deliberately raised a surplus for the market.

In the process it became increasingly difficult to distinguish between the free and unfree peasant. A tendency grew to transpose the distinction from persons to land—to speak of free or unfree land instead of workers, that is, land either lightly burdened or heavily burdened with dues. While many of the old servile obligations continued to be met, they no longer implied that the peasant himself suffered any legal disability.

All of these tendencies were strongly reinforced in the fourteenth century by the Black Death, the deadly bubonic plague which swept through Europe in 1348 with devastating effect. The loss of life was high everywhere, although in the several recurrences of plague in subsequent years it was the crowded town and city which suffered more than the countryside. Generally it was the weaker elements of the population who were swept off—the old and the very young. The effect was, nevertheless, to reduce available labor and push up wages, giving labor an improved bargaining position. Landlords in England, therefore, tried to enforce the old services, now preferable to commutation and the hiring of expensive wage labor. Labor, on the other hand, was bent on commuting services into money payments and working for wages; the result was a marked decrease of services and the substitution of money rents for old tenures. There was also a sharp decline in demesne land since it was becoming too costly to work. The lord came to prefer letting out his demesne and living off his rents. His estate, at one time supplying him with all his necessities and therefore the center of his interests, now ceased to play as important a role in his life as before. He might still be the landlord; he was no longer the lord of the land.

III
COMMERCE

EARLY TRADE

MOST EUROPEANS LIVED ON THE LAND, GROW-
ing food to eat rather than to sell, but trade was not
nonexistent. Besides local barter, commerce persisted
over great distances throughout the early Middle Ages
despite great handicaps. The historian's older belief that the Germanic invasions in the fifth century brought commerce to a standstill
in the west has been abandoned because of new evidence. Not only
foreigners—Syrians, Jews, and Greeks—but native westerners were
active in commerce; and there is evidence of markets, fairs, and
active seaports.

Inadequate as our sources are, they nevertheless reveal what we
might expect about this early commerce—a tenuous trade in high-
priced luxury articles, the least likely trade to suffer from political
dislocations or interruptions. Spices, silks, furs, and slaves continued
to find their way to buyers over long distances. From the tenth
century on, however, there was a growing exchange of bulky commodities also, especially in the north through the lands bordering
the Baltic and the North Sea. This exchange included foodstuffs

such as grains, fish, and meat, timber resources such as lumber, pitch, and potash, and an increasing trade in raw wool, conjointly with the early development of the greatest industry of the Middle Ages, the manufacture of woolen cloth. In time there grew an extensive trade in wine. In the Mediterranean, a great highway of commerce since antiquity, merchants were handling ore, timber, and other bulky goods. The total impact of this commerce, however, was uneven and relatively light, and it was continually checked in its growth by the long series of disastrous invasions to which Europe was subjected before the eleventh century. Only slowly thereafter did local and international commerce grow more complex, affect more and more people, and gradually force broad changes in the organization of western society.

Italy's role in the growth of western commerce was a large one because of its central position between the eastern Mediterranean, the southern areas of the European continent, and the coast of North Africa. Although earlier sources indicate a predominance of Greeks and Syrians in control of the limited trade in the west, as that trade grew Italians soon took their place. They enjoyed the advantages of coastal cities with good harbors, whose only recourse after the invasion of Italy by the Lombards in the seventh century was to rely upon the sea for subsistence. Rome and Naples, Ravenna on the Adriatic, later the Tyrrhenian cities of Amalfi, Gaëta, and Salerno, and Bari on the Adriatic all became in turn important seaports and commercial centers. By the ninth century, a community of fisherfolk on the tiny islands at the head of the Adriatic was beginning to foreshadow the later powerful commercial city of Venice. These communities, under cover of the vague political suzerainty of the Byzantine emperors, strove to remain independent of the Lombards in Italy. They trafficked with the Moslems of Egypt, Syria, and North Africa, treading a delicate line between two forces, Arab and Byzantine, often at war with one another. By the eleventh century Venice was preeminent in the commerce between east and west, not merely because of the decline of her rivals in southern Italy but also because of careful diplomacy between her nominal suzerain Byzantium to the east and the Carolingian emperors to the north, ensuring Venice primacy as the intermediary in east-west commerce.

On the west coast of Italy, Pisa and Genoa cooperated in a critical venture to drive the Moslems from much of the Mediterranean in the early eleventh century. It was an effort born of commercial enterprise but reinforced by hatred of the "infidel"; and its success, marked by the expulsion of the Moslems from Sardinia in 1015 and the eventual sack of Mahdia on the North African coast in 1087, was a large step toward gaining commercial superiority in the Mediterranean from the Moslems. The communities of Venice, Pisa, and Genoa also profited much from the crusades, and in return for their assistance they received extraterritorial rights and commercial monopolies in those Levantine ports which fell into the hands of the crusaders. Venice had a peculiar advantage because of her long-standing alliance with Byzantium. Her merchants enjoyed freedom from customs duties in Constantinople and had their own quarter there. Their strong competitive position allowed them eventually to dominate much of the carrying trade of the eastern Mediterranean. Even after relations between Venice and Byzantium deteriorated in the twelfth century, the fourth crusade, which attacked and captured the city of Constantinople in 1204, put Venice in commercial control of Constantinople as well as the shores and islands of the Aegean. In time the Genoese, too, were able to enjoy extensive privileges in the Byzantine Empire, emerging as a potent rival to the Venetians in the commerce of the Mediterranean.

Italy rose quickly to commercial primacy in the west, however, not merely because of the rapid and early development of active seaports but also because the feudal disintegration that plagued northern Europe after the collapse of the Carolingian empire was less severe in Italy. Relative stability in large parts of the peninsula allowed the development of commercial intercourse between seaport and hinterland and an uninterrupted growth of commercial experience.

THE PLACE OF THE MERCHANT

Under the influence of the church, medieval Europe elevated the concept of labor to remove from it connotations of degradation that had clung to it since antiquity. The different occupations of man were frequently ranked into a hierarchy of dignity in which intellectual as well as agricultural and industrial labor took an honored place. But what was to be thought of the merchant, who grew nothing, added nothing to the general store, but only bought something to sell it unchanged for a higher price? The desire for profit had all the earmarks of the sin of avarice. Was money not the root of all evil? The acts of buying and selling, even if neither good nor bad in themselves, presented so many temptations for fraud as to make the merchant's occupation extremely hazardous for the soul. Canon law enshrined Pope Leo I's declaration in the fifth century that it was difficult to distinguish honest from ill-gotten gain and that "in commerce between buyer and seller it is easy for sin to enter in." No merchant, it seemed, could please God. No one could buy or sell without cheating. Business, the act of buying cheap and selling dear, had deceit at its roots. In sum, merchants were an abomination. In all of this we may discern the suspicious nature of an agrarian society, reinforced by biblical injunctions which elevated spiritual aims over material goods. Christ's words were continually recalled: "It is easier for a camel to pass through the eye of a needle than for a rich man to enter into the kingdom of God."

The continued growth of commercial activity, however, soon required a more complete assessment of the role of the merchant in society. When one invested labor and expense in one's enterprise or ran the risk of danger to one's person or property, one could hardly be condemned out of hand for receiving something over and above what one had paid for the goods. Those who addressed themselves to the morality of this kind of economic activity—and it was always treated as a moral question—soon established a legitimate place in society for the merchant. Indeed, with the recovery of Aristotle's works in the thirteenth century, the merchant's contribution to a society marked by division of labor, an Aristotelian view, was seen clearly as essential to the very continuance of that society. The merchant's profit could therefore be justified on the grounds that he not only underwent expense but also performed a labor which by the precepts of true justice should have its due reward. But if the exchange of goods was a positive service, the uneasiness about the merchant himself was not easily dissipated. Both lawyers and theologians were moved by strong motives of justice to examine the acts of the merchant and pronounce upon their legitimacy.

Much of this discussion revolved about the question of gain in commercial transactions. Even though what the merchant did was legitimate because of the labor, expense, and risk to which he was subjected, there was still need to establish how much he was due in return. In effect, the discussion of the merchant's gain, or "profit," was no more than a discussion of the factors which were to determine prices. But while most modern economists are content to describe how prices are established, medieval moralists set out to determine what the price ought to be—as they put it in their concern for justice, the "just price," the measure of the true value of a thing. Not that the discussion was pursued without reference to current economic practice. Medieval lawyers, heirs to the precepts of Roman law, continued to accept the idea of freedom of bargaining whereby the price was established through negotiation. But they provided redress for gross injury, called *laesio enormis*. If the seller received, through some error in establishing the true value of a thing, less than half the "just price," he was entitled to legal action for recovery of the article or an additional payment. In similar fashion the action was extended to protect the buyer. While medieval law, therefore, permitted the establishment of prices through the operation of what we would now call supply and demand, it nevertheless assumed that there was a price which was just and that such a price could be determined—although it provided for legal redress only when departure from that price was so great as to constitute a gross injury. Lesser mistakes had no legal redress. To be sure, canon lawyers recognized the moral problem surrounding the question of intent: if the merchant intended to sell at a price higher than the just price, he sinned; but since intent had no legal proof in an ordinary court of law, a human judge could take cognizance only of gross injury. Intent would have to be left to the divine judge, that is, intent was a question of conscience.

As for determining what the just price was, this was to be done by a judge on the basis of the current price of the article, bearing in mind the time and place of the sale. It could be done on the advice of "good men," those with experience of market conditions who could make a relatively objective and acceptable decision. In other words, the just price was the current price, the "going" price.

Theological writers added another dimension to the discussion. For St. Thomas Aquinas, "if the price exceeds the quantity of value of the thing, or conversely if the thing exceeds in value the price, the equality of justice is destroyed." It was this view of equivalent justice that was the peculiar contribution of theologians. The "commutative justice" of Aristotle, whose works were highly influential after the thirteenth century, defined as the equality of things given in exchange, simply made explicit what earlier ecclesiastical writers had already said, that justice was the desire to give everyone his due. Applied to commercial transactions, the seller who received less than the true value of the thing sold was not given his due. He suffered damage, as did the buyer who paid more than the thing he bought was worth. In neither case was there an equality of things exchanged.

Where the lawyer was content to leave deviations from the just price to the conscience, the theologian went further. He insisted that the seller sinned if he sold at more than the just price, even if only through a mistake. Human law might allow error; divine law did not. When it came to a question of determining precisely what the just price was, theologians fell back on the answer given by the lawyers—the current price of an article, having in mind the time and place of sale. But while legal redress could be had only for gross injury, the theologians' insistence that the just price be observed in the interests of justice produced an immeasurable effect. The intent of the merchant, and the extent of the injuries he may have inflicted on others, could be examined in the "internal forum," in the confessional, if not in the external court of law. Where secular law might demand restitution only in gross cases, spiritual absolution demanded restitution in all cases. The last wills and testaments of merchants, their account books and personal letters, and their acts of public and private charity reveal a long history of troubled consciences and continual efforts to make amends, reflecting the influence of the moral teaching of the church in economic matters.

Theological writers approached the question of profit through their concern with usury, which came to be seen as one of many kinds of economic transaction. The prohibition of usury was a teaching of the church throughout the Middle Ages, reinforced by an almost completely agrarian economy in which borrowing was nearly always for consumption. The prohibition was based on biblical and patristic literature, as well as the canons of early church councils.

In part the economic conditions of medieval Europe, and the changes in these conditions, frequently explain the interest shown in the question. Thus the legislation against usury under Charlemagne, repeated during the ninth century by local church synods, seems to reflect an effort to preserve petty farmers from absorption by the large landholders who were the usual lenders. But it would be a mistake to look on the gradual evolution of theories of usury as merely rationalizations of contemporary needs. Despite some correlation to be observed between economic conditions and the condemnation of usury, the teaching of the church was essentially a theological one. Usury ("where more is received than is given," as it was defined in a Carolingian capitulary) was a sin of avarice, a lack of charity, and a failure to love one's brother.

It was hard to accuse someone of a lack of charity, however, when he loaned money at usury to a merchant who used it to make a substantial profit in some commercial venture. With the growth of commerce, therefore, usury came to be discussed within the same context of law and justice as the just price. In the process, usury was extended to transactions which were not outright loans. For example, in the late twelfth century Pope Alexander III declared that selling on credit at a price higher than the cash price was usury. Thereafter theologians frequently dealt with problems of usury disguised in commercial transactions, that is to say credit operations. Usury came to be regarded not merely as a sin of avarice but as a sin against justice. This most important change of view grew out of the contemporary examination of the nature of private property. The rightness of private property was justified on the grounds of social need, and the rights of individual ownership of property were based on natural law. Usury was unjust, therefore, in the same way that theft was unjust, because it deprived an owner of what was by natural law his. This view had an important bearing on legal practice: where one guilty of avarice atoned to God alone, the usurer, like the thief, could be forced by the courts to make restitution. Finally, the close examination of economic practices led to what was in fact an embryonic science of economics, which attempted to classify economic activities, define money, describe the factors affecting prices, establish a theory of economic value, deal with problems of interest and rent, and establish the rights and duties of property.

MONEY

Even in the early Middle Ages there was an "aristocracy of money," a small class of influential men whose wealth and local power were based on money, its minting and its exchange. This fact illustrates that it was possible for some specialized workers, in this case members of the gild of moneyers, not only to maintain their personal freedom but even to rise to the nobility against the general trend of the times. With the extension of feudalism, which will be discussed at greater length below, the moneyers, whose skills were of prime importance, did not lose status; they received office by a feudal investiture in return for an oath of fealty; unlike feudal vassals, however, they exchanged specialized labor rather than military service for money payments. Many of them were extremely wealthy by contemporary standards, deriving their income from the profits of minting, trade in gold dust, money changing, and investments in commerce and land.

This aristocracy of money was at its peak not when money was in wide circulation but when it was rare—when, in fact, the moneyers were almost the only holders of money. But they remind us that the use of money to facilitate exchange goes well back beyond the Middle Ages. The amount of money in circulation may have been small because the volume of exchange was relatively small. Most economic activity aimed at wresting subsistence from nature, a process in which money played no part. One frequently finds the economy of the early Middle Ages labeled "natural economy," therefore, as contrasted with a later "money economy," to the emergence of which all kinds of revolutionary changes in European history are often attributed. But there is little to justify this chronological distinction between a natural and a money economy. The internal economy of the seigneury, which did not engage in commerce, had little need of money and seigneurial obligations were most often met in kind; nevertheless money still remained the usual means of exchange when exchange took place, as well as the means of meeting obligations incurred in the leasing of agricultural land. A money economy existed throughout the Middle Ages. The only chronological distinction to be made is the *volume* of money transactions; before the eleventh century, this volume was relatively slight, increasing rapidly thereafter as a result of many interacting forces which turned more and more individuals from domestic self-subsistence to the marketplace. Even when produce was used in exchange instead of money, one need not conclude that a collapse of trade in the early Middle Ages had produced a "natural economy." It was merely a sign that the high cost of coin in a period of money scarcity led to a good deal of hoarding; "a merchant who hoarded precious metals and left grain 'in circulation' merely followed the law of Gresham."[1]

The growth in volume of money transactions was beset by many problems, all of which stimulated techniques and institutions for their solution. We shall never know to what extent the chronic shortage of gold and silver in the west hampered commercial growth because of the growth of credit which offset the shortage. There was the problem of standardization of coins, complicated because minting privileges were frequently dispersed in the hands of many secular and ecclesiastical authorities producing a host of different coins with only local currency. This condition gave importance to the money changer, an expert in determining the worth of different coins on the basis of their content, who facilitated the exchange of one local currency for another and, therefore, trade between one region and another. Finally there were the complications of counterfeiting and coin-clipping, the frequent legislation against which was a measure of their prevalence, and the debasement of coins by those who enjoyed the monopoly of the mint, as unsettling to merchants then as inflation is now.

The insufficient quantity of money in circulation would make the development of large-scale commerce by the twelfth century difficult to understand except on the assumption that credit operations were habitual. Indeed there is plenty of evidence to support such an assumption. The major creditors of the early Middle Ages had been abbeys and monasteries, known repositories of wealth. Their loans were usually for consumption, to offset the effects of local famine, to pay a ransom, to equip some local lord for a crusade. Such loans sometimes took the form of mortgages, whereby the lender drew the income from the property which had been pledged. Such credit operations as these were infrequent, however,

---

[1] Robert Sabatino Lopez, "An Aristocracy of Money in the Early Middle Ages," *Speculum*, Vol. XXVIII (1953), pp. 1–43.

and there is no evidence of credit institutions as such in the early Middle Ages. But with the growth of commerce we find credit operations on every hand—the purchase of goods to be paid for later when they were resold (sale credits); the lending of money to merchants and others, usually at usury; the investment of money in cooperative commercial ventures; and credit operations in foreign exchange. As a result, instruments were developed to facilitate the extension of credit; one of these was the bill of exchange, which was merely a promise to pay at a later time and at another place than where the debt was contracted, sometimes in local currency, sometimes in a foreign currency; another was the institution of banking, which was primarily a lending institution in the Middle Ages. The fairs of Europe, at which so many merchants congregated periodically, soon became clearing houses for instruments of credit; and as a result a regular money market developed in which financial obligations were frequently met through the exchange and cancellation of bills of exchange. As for banking operations, these were essentially loan operations frequently controlled by large merchant houses, usually Italian. Italian primacy in banking was merely a reflection of Italian primacy in commerce. Medieval banks did not deal in negotiable currency nor did they circulate notes; they were merchant banks in which the operations of trade and money lending went hand in hand.

EARLY CAPITAL

The early merchant's life was perilous and his business full of risks. He not only had to face the lawlessness of the countryside to get his wares from one place to another, but he also had to operate in an atmosphere of general hostility and distrust. Inevitably he sought safety in numbers, coming together with others into fraternal organizations later called "merchant gilds." Merchants traveled in groups and pooled their resources to hire protection and pay for facilities and security. Although they might be independent of one another, they were soon collaborating in commercial ventures, sharing in the costs and the profits of each enterprise.

Cooperation for protection and the reduction of costs led to techniques of accumulating capital for larger and more profitable enterprises. The early merchant had only a small capital with which to work. By pooling his small resources with those of others, he could participate in larger ventures otherwise inaccessible. The accumulation of capital was not always easy. The problem was not so much the absence of capital as the absence of techniques for its conversion to commercial needs, of "liquefying" it. One way of getting capital was through the sale of land or its revenues; this was done quite early in some north Italian communities. Indeed the heavy real estate dealings of merchants throughout the Middle Ages reflect not only the social aspirations of the newly rich to enter into the aristocracy of the countryside but also a method of investing reserve capital and liquefying it later when needed.

The advantages of cooperation between merchants led to the development of partnerships in which the Italians were in the forefront. Such arrangements allowed for the attraction of funds even of those not engaged in commerce. The *commenda* was a partnership in which a traveling partner contracted to carry goods from abroad for sale in home or neighboring markets while an investing partner put up the capital. The traveler got one quarter of the profits, the investor three quarters. There were other arrangements whereby the traveler put up some of the capital and took a larger share of the profits. Sometimes the investing partner was a merchant, himself active in the direction of business. But often the *commenda* brought together the small capital of many petty investors, widows and orphans, priests and nuns, shopkeepers and artisans, who played no role in the direction of transactions but merely made an investment in the hope of a good return. The advantage of this kind of contract was that the investor had only a limited liability— he might lose his investment but no more, whereas in an ordinary partnership all the partners were liable for the debts of the partnership and might be ruined through mismanagement or misfortune.

The "sea loan" was another way of getting capital for the large overseas ventures in which Italians were increasingly active. Here the investor loaned money to the merchant in order to finance the venture. But this was not an ordinary loan; it was repayable only if the voyage was completed safely. If it failed through shipwreck or piracy, the merchant was protected. In other words, the sea loan possessed an element of insurance—the insurer put up the money prior to a possible claim and recovered it if no claim was made. Of course, the risks run by the insurer were high. They were offset by the high rate of interest he received. It should be noted that the merchant was insured only against loss at sea, not failure in business. If the ship arrived safely at port, the loan had to be repaid regardless of the profit or loss of the enterprise.

Yet another way of sharing risks and pooling capital for large-scale enterprises was the apportionment of the cost of shipping. Early ships in the Mediterranean were small and were owned by individuals alone or in simple partnerships with a few others. Ship-owners were not usually great merchants themselves. They were shippers, distinct from the merchant class. But by the second half of the twelfth century, as ships grew in size, there was a corresponding change in the pattern of ownership. In Genoa, for example, ships came to be owned by several persons, each possessing one or more shares (*loca*) in a vessel. The total number of shares, even tiny fractions of shares, was dispersed in the hands of many part-owners, and in fact came to be handled as any other form of property, being used to secure loans, pay wages, purchase goods for export, or meet other obligations. This type of investment in shipping served several purposes: it was an excellent way of spreading the risks of shipping; it allowed large merchants to invest capital in parts of several ships and thus spread their own risks while participating in several ventures at once; it made possible the building and operation of larger ships, too costly for individuals to finance; and of course the *loca* provided a means of investment to persons other than merchants, thus tapping additional sources of capital. Only in the late thirteenth century, with the accumulation of large fortunes by families, individuals, trade associations, and banking houses, did the system cease to be necessary. Then smaller groups of wealthy men could safely build, own, and operate their own vessels.

MARKETS AND FAIRS

The growing commerce within Europe (in north and central France, much of Christian Spain, western Germany, England, and the Lowlands) stimulated the characteristic institution of local commerce—the market. In the market agricultural produce was the only kind of commodity, and the locality was usually determined by a legal grant from emperor, king, or other lord. In the early

Middle Ages there had also been fairs—that is to say, larger con-
courses of merchants coming over great distances to meet periodically. There is evidence of markets and fairs in Merovingian Gaul
and Visigothic Spain and, in some places, clearly defined trading
quarters.

It was only with the increased commercial activity of the
eleventh century that the fair developed as the most striking and
most important feature of medieval economic organization. Flanders, lying athwart the trade routes adjacent to the North Sea and
north European river systems, saw a lively growth of fairs. The most
important development came in the twelfth century in certain favored areas when, as international traders moved from one fair
to another, cycles of fairs developed covering the entire calendar
year and providing an unbroken international marketplace of remarkable stability.

The largest and most important of these was the cycle of fairs
in the lands of the count of Champagne. Not only was Champagne
well situated where merchants of north and south could conveni-
ently meet; but the enlightened self-interest of the counts helped
attract traders by providing services for commercial records, convenient facilities, secure roads to and from the fairs, peace, and impartial administration of commercial justice at the fairs themselves
(to say nothing of the suspension of the laws against usury). The
revenues of the lord of the fair, the count of Champagne—from
tolls, taxes, the administration of justice, and dues from standard
weights and measures—suggest the community of interest between
the growing merchant class and existing political authority.

There had been numerous early markets and fairs in Champagne,
but they had existed primarily for traffic in local produce. With
the growth of commerce, these fairs grew in importance because
the large population in the area provided a market potential attractive to foreign merchants. The institution of a regular, annual
cycle of fairs in the late twelfth century led to the predominance
of some over others and made them the most important institution
of international commerce in the Middle Ages. The cycle in Champagne consisted of six fairs, each lasting about seven weeks, held
in four towns: two at Troyes, two at Provins, and one each at
Lagny and Bar-sur-Aube. The first, at Lagny, opened in January;
the last, the "cold fair" at Troyes, closed in December. Each of

the fairs was strictly regulated as to the times of opening and closing and what could be sold on which days; time was allowed for setting up stalls at the outset and for settling debts at the conclusion.

Unlike the markets, the fairs were essentially wholesale operations: merchants from all over Europe carried their goods to sell, and, in turn, bought the goods of other merchants to take back for sale in home markets. The articles exchanged were of great variety and in fact provide a catalog of the wares of medieval Europe: woolen cloth, silk, leather, fur, linen, some cotton; goods sold by weight brought by the Italians, such as spices, wax, sugar, alum, lacquer, dye woods; and some iron, grain, and, of course, an abundance of wine. The merchants came from every direction—from all parts of France, Spain, the Lowlands, Germany—but above all from Italy, whose contingents were of such importance that they even managed to obtain special rights at the fairs, having their own courts and their own consuls to represent them.

In the thirteenth century the Champagne fairs gradually began to change. Because of the foreign exchange that they stimulated between outlying areas, the fairs had become an important money market where money-changing began to take precedence over trade in goods. Further, merchants were becoming less peripatetic, preferring to deal directly with markets through correspondence with others; and gradually they gave up the arduous tasks attendant upon travel and transport to and from the fairs. By the mid-fourteenth century the Italians had abandoned Champagne, having developed more efficient and direct means of tapping distant markets. The great international fairs declined with the inauguration of direct sailing from Italian ports to the English Channel and the North Sea in the early fourteenth century, although other influences worked in the same direction. The industrialization of Italy saw a large cloth trade develop there; consequently, there was less dependence on Flemish woolen cloth, which had been the major item of trade in Champagne. Even the money-changing business of the fairs was dislocated by the fluctuations following the substitution of gold for silver as an international currency from the last half of the thirteenth century. European fairs continued as regional markets with the associated function of entertainment centers, but their day as the chief institution of international commerce was over.

DEPRESSION AND DECLINE

The commercial expansion of medieval Europe did not continue unchecked. In the thirteenth century there were already signs of slowing down, of saturation, and in the fourteenth century depression and decline became more marked. There is clear evidence of a reduction in population, which explains the abandonment of land, the shrinking numbers in the towns, the general decline in demand for and in production of food, and the slackening in commercial and industrial growth. By the fourteenth century more frequent and more widespread wars, especially the Hundred Years War, and the Black Death helped to disrupt an already faltering economy. Not only did a good deal of marginal land go out of production, but the proportion of agricultural goods going into interregional and international trade declined as well. Fewer mouths needed less food.

The slow economic decline was marked by periodic fluctuations which disguised the general movement. The last half of the fourteenth century was a period of relative abundance for some; food prices remained relatively stable, and the rapid reduction in the number of workers occasioned by the plague had a buoyant effect on wages. But signs of a general decline were abundant everywhere. The great wool trade between England and the Lowlands slowed drastically, and only some of this decline can be attributed to increased cloth manufacturing in England. The great wine trade between Gascony and England was seriously disrupted. Gascony was the scene of many military campaigns in the Hundred Years War; not only were the vineyards often laid in ruins, but French occupation of Gascony periodically disrupted and finally destroyed commercial relations with England. In the Mediterranean, commerce was also in the throes of serious dislocation. The Mongolian expansion into Asia Minor, the quick collapse of the Mongol empire, and the expansion of Ottoman Turkish invaders from Asia Minor to southeast Europe disrupted east-west commerce. The century-long collapse of the Byzantine empire in the face of Turkish aggression, culminating in the fall of the city of Constantinople in 1453, seriously upset the commercial life of those Italian cities that had for so long dominated the sea lanes of the eastern Mediterranean.

In general, throughout the fourteenth century the margin of

profit and interest shrank. While the decline in population enlarged the amount of money per capita, producing many signs of abundance, this prosperity was more apparent than real and in any event did not last long. As profits fell, there were increased attempts by the authorities to hold down wages, resulting in hardship and civil strife, especially in industrial communities. The attempt to check overproduction was reflected by the ways in which gilds became much more rigid and restrictive, holding down the numbers who might share in markets which were becoming more and more limited. With the restriction of commercial opportunities, many merchants invested their money in land rather than in commerce, retired from business, and entered the aristocracy.

IV
INDUSTRY

CRAFT INDUSTRY

IN THE MIDDLE AGES THE LIMITED DEMAND FOR services and manufactures provided by local lords and ecclesiastical establishments could be satisfied by the servants of the seigneury, some of whom specialized in one of a few basic crafts. But the expansion of population and growth of commerce led to an increased need for and supply of all kinds of goods, not only foodstuffs but manufactured articles as well. Gone for many were the days when the simple needs of the everyday agricultural life could be met by home or seigneurial industry—when one made and repaired one's own farming tools, coarse clothing, and the thatched roof over one's head. The addition of a mercantile population living in towns which were not economically self-sufficient rapidly produced a growing number of artisans and specialists in food-processing, cloth-making, building and construction work, the manufacture of household articles, implements for storage and transportation, and a host of other services and goods. The larger markets of the medieval town stimulated specialization of economic function; and more and more people found that they could meet their wants more satisfactorily by, in effect, selling a special skill, be it woodworking or leather-making, and in return buying what they needed from others better equipped to provide it.

The nature of industrial development and organization was often determined by whether its products entered into local or international trade. Commodities for local consumption were usually provided by petty artisans working in small shops with relatively little capital investment. These small producers, when there were enough of them in any given occupation, organized themselves in associations called "craft gilds," which sought to regulate the employment of skilled workers and apprentices, control the supplies and therefore the prices of the raw materials of their trade, standardize workmanship, maintain retail prices for their products, and promote piety and fellowship among their members. Such craft gilds became important only from the thirteenth century on, and not even then in small communities or in towns given over for the most part to international commerce, such as seaports, or to a single great industry, such as the textile towns of Flanders where manufacturing was carried on primarily for export. It was in the medium-sized towns, those not dominated by any single industry and those in which industrial production was carried on mostly for local consumption, that craft gilds were to be found in large numbers. Here the demand was large and stable enough to maintain sufficiently large numbers of individuals in any given trade to make the formation of a gild useful and profitable to its members.

While the association of artisans in any given craft allowed for the promotion of their common interests, it did not in itself alter the pattern of production and the sale of products. Industry remained essentially an individual or family operation. The small shop, employing one or two journeymen and apprentices and selling directly to the consumer over the counter, remained the backbone of town industry in the Middle Ages. The techniques of the trade were handed down from master to apprentice with little opportunity for innovations. The market, being local and stable, exerted no pressure to produce in large quantities.

Craft gilds, where they were strong enough, frequently tried to control the supply of the raw materials of their craft and to maintain within the town a monopoly control over the trade in which they were engaged. In these efforts they were rarely completely successful. Local nongildsmen, neighboring villagers, and other outsiders frequently enjoyed some limited rights to penetrate the town market. Gilds enjoyed a virtual monopoly of raw materials and retail sales only when the sources of supply were limited and adequate substitutes unavailable, as in the case of gold- and silversmiths and a few other trades. Where, however, the commodity was woolen cloth, for instance, the supplies of which were usually abundant, or where the commodity was such that substitutes for it might be found, the gilds were usually far less monopolistic. It was the same with foodstuffs, where the community at large tended to ensure that its welfare would not depend wholly on the monopoly of a gild.

To allay hostility among the townsmen, the gilds were forced to adopt regulations respecting the standards of workmanship within their respective trades. In some crafts, especially those dealing with foodstuffs, gildsmen were frequently under the strong suspicion of benefiting from fluctuations of prices—of taking advantage of the fact that they dealt in the necessities of life. The perennial problem of inadequate and irregular food supplies occasioned by poor transportation, poor storage facilities, and recurring local famine frequently produced violent price fluctuations; the gilds were continually suspected of creating these fluctuations or at least of exaggerating them for their own profit. Even though all gilds sought to raise prices, therefore, or at least to keep them from falling, town suspicions ensured that their success was not great.

Another area of gild concern was the supply of skilled labor, which was controlled through an apprenticeship system. The gilds determined the number of apprentices that a member could use in his shop, their age, the length and nature of their training, and their upbringing. The gilds were frequently accused of abusing the system by limiting unduly the number of apprentices used, but such limitations when they occurred were often dictated by considerations other than the desire to keep the number of their members down—death, runaways, the intimate nature of the family workshop and the difficulty of absorbing more than a very few apprentices, the tendency of the wealthier gildsmen to take more than their share, and, before the fourteenth century, the continual shortage of labor.

The protective devices of craft gilds could not be maintained if the craftsmen had to depend on sources of material and on markets beyond their control. This explains the general hostility of local gildsmen to interregional trade, their distrust of the international merchant, and their constant attempts to regulate the supplies and costs of raw materials and the output and prices of finished products in the limited market of the town. Further, the gild, in its many regulations, sought an ideal equality among its members by reducing competition among them to a minimum. The obsession with equality had the effect of imposing a very conservative attitude toward change. Members tended to resist improvements which, requiring capital outlay, would have given greater advantages to the richer members and reduced the others to the status of employees. There was a good deal of opposition to the merging of different gilds in mutually supporting crafts, which might have led to innovations and increased production. There was resistance to bulk purchases by gilds, which might have reduced costs. Many regulations were adopted to reduce competition within the gild, concerning the hours of work, prices charged and the amount of labor that each master could use.

But despite all this, equality remained an elusive ideal, and over a period of time large disparities appeared. While towns grew, the gilds grew with them. But by the end of the thirteenth century the great economic expansion was over; and in many towns the gilds, through various devices, closed their ranks to newcomers, frequently converted gild membership into family affairs, and took on all the airs of an aristocracy. Economic disparity between gildsmen grew too; while some waxed rich, and therefore important, others were often engaged in marginal businesses or slid into the ranks of the wage earners.

CAPITALIST INDUSTRY

Because of their influence on town government, craft gilds enjoyed considerable power in those towns large enough for them to develop. In the smaller towns and villages, they were of little importance although handicraft industry was carried on there in much the same way. Further, in those few areas dominated by a single great industry, the craft gilds were consistently subordinated to the merchants who controlled the exchange of the product concerned. It is true that the old merchant gild, the early association of those engaged in trade, frequently withered away in the medium-sized towns where trade organization came to reflect the different occupations of the townsmen. But in those places where all or nearly all of the industrial production depended not on local but on distant markets, the merchant remained of first importance—and the gild of which he was a member an institution of great power. Of course, there were craft gilds also, but the craftsmen were in fact wage earners in a vast industrial complex.

Such an area was Flanders, where by the eleventh century a growing population could no longer support itself on the land. This in part explains why so many from this region were to be found in far-flung enterprises such as the crusades, large emigrations to the east, and the rapid growth of towns to which many flocked in large numbers. It was an area in which old social forms broke down more rapidly than elsewhere, where economic insecurity became chronic, and where release from anxiety often came in sudden, violent action. Flanders had been an area of cloth production in the early Middle Ages. The Viking raids of the ninth century, far from disrupting it, undoubtedly encouraged it, for the expansion of the Northmen on both sides of the English Channel created new demands and facilitated the exchange of cloth over wider areas. By the twelfth century Flemish merchants were selling woolen cloth in Italy or to adventurous Italian merchants who had come north of the Alps, and the cloth of Flanders soon came to be an important staple not only in northern Europe but in the east-west Mediterranean trade as well. Its wide popularity was a measure of its relative excellence.

Flanders soon outstripped its local sources of raw wool, and of course it had to sell its finished product on a world market. Therefore the merchant who had contacts abroad and sufficient access to capital and credit came to control the first and the last crucial stages: the purchase of raw materials (wool, dye, potash, and other materials used in the processing of cloth, importing them from England, France, Spain, the Baltic countries, and even the Near East via the Italians) and the disposal of the finished cloth in all these regions, frequently through the operation of the great fairs of Flanders and Champagne. Many of the intermediate operations in the manufacture of cloth were performed in the homes of the craftsmen—the cleaning, carding, spinning, and weaving. Often the work was done by women, and for the most part the tools were simple and inexpensive, although weaving called for large looms. Fulling was an arduous task, requiring no great skill but a good deal of energy and some equipment. Dyeing and finishing demanded far greater skill and expensive tools. The very nature of woolen manufacture dictated an organization quite unlike that to be seen where individual crafts controlled all phases of production from the acquisition of raw material to the final retail sale. It was a capitalist industry in fact. The artisans here did not, could not, deal with the consumer directly. The combination of so many processes required some central direction, which was supplied by the capitalist, that is to say the merchant with capital who bought the materials, put them out to different crafts for different operations, and marketed the finished product. Sometimes he might actually invest in and thus control directly some of the intermediate steps, with his own dye house, fulling vats, looms, and frames. In these establishments there could be no pretense of craft independence; the workers were direct employees. But even when the merchant put out work to independent craftsmen, the latter, although owning their own tools, came to be by the very nature of the industry completely dependent for their welfare on the operations of the merchant and were often in effect little better off than wage earners.

The control of the industry by the merchant gild was extremely effective, and all dealing in raw materials and finished products was carefully reserved to its members. This control was exercised through the town corporations in which the merchants were most influential. The towns legislated for all aspects of the industry, especially techniques of production, standards of size, weight, and quality, hours of labor, and wages. As a result the social and economic cleavage between workers and merchants grew. This was not critical in good times, but it was disastrous in bad. The cloth industry, dependent ultimately on international sources and markets, was peculiarly sensitive to international affairs. The growth of a native cloth industry in Italy in the thirteenth century, the decline of the international fairs of northern France, the development of cloth-making in England which consumed much of the best raw wool, the political rivalry between England and France with Flanders caught in between, the taxation of wool by the kings of France and England as an economic weapon against one another —all this produced in Flanders serious disruptions in the industry and exacerbated the tensions between workers and merchants.

The conditions of workers in Italian cities where cloth-making was important were no different. Again, control by the entrepreneur led to the suppression of a working class which, dependent upon the fluctuations of the international market, often suffered unemployment and bad pay with little hope of obtaining that political power which they hoped could be used to better their lot. The *Arte della Lana,* the great gild of wool merchants in Florence, not only controlled all aspects of the industry but even participated as a corporation in the manufacture of woolen cloth, investing funds and emerging as the dominant partner if not the outright owner of many of the craft shops engaged in the operations of the industry. In these the craftsmen were out and out wage earners.

Conditions were not always so bad in other industries which had an international character, such as mining or the building industry. Unlike cloth-making, mining was not a town industry— quite the opposite; and while the workers in cloth had frequently to struggle against town governments dominated by an increasingly aristocratic merchant oligarchy, miners searching for the silver-bearing ores of the highlands of southern Germany or central Europe, or the deposits of iron ore scattered throughout Europe, were attracted to their work by princes and other lords of the countryside whose claim to dispose of the "wasteland" of their domains was expressed as a claim on mineral rights. The search for minerals, their extraction, and the conversion of ores to metals were consequently thrown open to all comers in large areas of Europe, especially the principal region of German colonization in central Europe as far as the Balkans. To get colonists one had to offer conditions at least as good as those to be found elsewhere; and around the mine faces there grew communities of workers whose status was quite unlike that of the peasants on the older agricultural estates. The miners enjoyed a good deal of self-government and dealt with the lord's representatives through their own officials in matters relating to the mining operation itself. In the older, more settled parts of western Europe the mining communities were often more exclusive, and the right to seek minerals or to work in the mines was restricted to people living in the area. Even here, however, the social status of the miner was as high as that of the townsman. Mining was a rigorous and not very attractive occupation—to find and hold skilled labor the inducements had to be as great as those elsewhere.

Just as feudal conditions—the need of lords for money and their feudal claims on wasteland—stimulated the mining industry, so too feudal conditions stimulated the building industry, although in a different manner. The independence and authority of feudal lords depended on their having a place of defense, and the growing competition among them, and between them and the centralizing authority of the monarchy, stimulated the construction of thousands of fortresses, large and small, all over western Europe. The institutions of Christianity also played a large role in building: every parish had its church, every see its cathedral. Monasteries multiplied, each with its church, cloisters, and other buildings. The desire for greater comfort, at least among those who could afford it, also helped to employ an increasing number of workers in stone, wood, and plaster, the results of whose skills can often be seen and admired still.

In the early Middle Ages building was mostly of timber. An important change in the industry occurred when builders began to use stone, especially in the construction of castles and churches. Changes in material went with the increasing size and complexity of construction, which called for large accumulations of skilled craftsmen in one place, frequently far from towns. Now the town was the home of the craft gild. In the towns themselves there were building craftsmen, but they were often too few in number to form separate craft gilds except in the largest towns. Building workers moving from one construction job to another, often over great distances, were therefore not organized as town artisans were. Their characteristic organization was that of the mason's lodge, one of which was to be found in connection with every large building under construction. The lodge was primarily a workshop which soon took on social functions as well, creating among the workers a sense of solidarity. There gradually evolved lodge customs which were relatively uniform throughout the west because of the migration of workers from one place to another.

From the ranks of building craftsmen came contractors—those who obtained a contract for construction, controlled in one way or another supplies of materials, and hired others to do the work.

Other craftsmen could rise in wealth and status by getting positions as foremen or master builders on the permanent staff of some great lord, prince, bishop, or monastery. But the great majority remained wage earners. Their mobility and the lack of opportunity to acquire or control the materials of their trade put them in the position of having only their labor to sell. Furthermore, unlike craftsmen in towns working in small shops and dealing directly with the consumer, builders were employed in large numbers in conditions approximating those of a large industrial establishment and thus were more easily governed by a discipline unknown to the ordinary artisan.

TOWNS

From the foregoing, the importance of towns in the growth of commerce and industry in the Middle Ages is apparent. Towns could have little place in a purely agricultural world, and it is only with the concentration of populations in pursuit of different economic ends with different resources that towns become significant. The inhabitants of towns are consumers; they do not grow their own food but consume that produced in the countryside. They are also producers, and it is in the towns of western Europe that most industry and trade flourished.

There were such towns in antiquity, but with the decline of Rome the institution of the town virtually disappeared. The old Roman *civitas* often became an administrative ecclesiastical center in the Middle Ages, but the old lay elements—the merchants, the craftsmen, the persons of wealth—disappeared. Ancient towns survived longest in southern Europe, especially in Italy, but the seaports were gradually paralyzed by the contraction of trade, losses through piracy, the effects of the breakdown of civil administration, civil war in the provinces, and the continual invasions and depredations of hostile peoples. In the west foreign merchants, Syrians, Jews, and Greeks, might still be found in decreasing numbers; but by the ninth century, although cities existed, they had no economic functions of significance and were in fact small administrative centers encompassing very few freemen, populated mostly by servants of the lord or bishop. The economy of such centers was closely tied to the surrounding agricultural land.

It was the introduction of mercantile elements which led to a reinvigoration of these centers. This occurred earliest in Italy in the coastal regions of the Mediterranean and in northern Europe along the rivers Scheldt, Meuse, and Rhine. These were the areas first to be stimulated by mercantile activity. Security and safety demanded that settlements grow in or near existing fortifications, so that the early merchant in locating himself took into account not only obvious geographical advantages such as roads, river transportation, bridges, and fords but also local defensive features. Where the old walled city was too small, the merchants tended to spill outside, and as their quarters grew larger, these were fortified in turn. Not only was the early administrative center frequently revived in this way but also new towns were founded where there were none before.

The close connection between commerce and the growth of towns helps to explain an aspect of town life that has led to considerable debate among historians, namely, the free institutions of the medieval town, in which some of our most cherished liberties seem to have their roots. There were many things besides its walls which marked off the town as an island of freedom in a sea of unfreedom. Early towns needed freedom from two things: from feudal restrictions under which the trader could not operate and from the effects of monopoly. The expansiveness of the economy helped to offset the latter; but the fact that towns were usually located on land within the domain of some lord, lay or ecclesiastic, who often sought to treat its residents in much the same way he dealt with his other subjects, frequently created problems. In some cases the townsmen's holdings were considered analogous to seigneurial tenures, and the lord's jurisdiction was exercised through his seigneurial court. But in most cases the town-dweller paid rent to the lord for his holding, thus escaping the implication of personal servitude. Townsmen who drew their livelihood from commerce tried to avoid any control by the seigneurial regime; frequently they compounded with the lord, commuting the many obligations which he claimed from each of them into one annual payment, contributions toward which they levied among themselves. Usually the lord was sufficiently hard up to welcome the promise of a regular annual income; but in some cases, especially when the lord was a bishop or an abbot mindful of the stricture that church lands were not to be alienated, resistance to the townsmen's drive for independence and free tenure was frequently stubborn, and more than one town was driven to fight for what it could not buy. The need to organize such resistance, to finance defenses, to arrange among themselves equitable assessments, all contributed to the development, in fact if not yet in law, of towns as independent corporations.

The liberty enjoyed by medieval towns was a liberty peculiar to craftsmen and merchants, though from the outset it affected the countryside. The early town attracted many of servile status from the surrounding rural areas, becoming a haven for those who sought to throw off the restrictions of servitude; in the passage of time the terms of seigneurial service had to be modified to meet such competition. The saying that "town air makes a man free" had a good deal of substance, and generally residence in a town for a year and a day was sufficient to rally to one's defense the entire body of townsmen against any lord seeking to exercise his old prerogatives.

Before the fourteenth century most towns had a relatively egalitarian society. This did not mean, however, rampant individualism. The town depended not only on the existence of trade but also on the control of its conditions. As a collection of consumers and producers, it consistently sought to increase its trade and to improve its terms. The expansion of trade, however, while broadening opportunities for some, posed serious threats of competition both from abroad and from within, causing the townsman as producer to adopt many defensive tactics. There was also the problem of defending the townsman in his role of consumer, that is, of obtaining sufficient supplies of consumer goods and raw materials at reasonable prices, of ensuring a fitting distribution of goods in the town, and of preserving standards of quality.

The cooperation of townsmen in the pursuit of these common goals was often complicated by internal divisions. Frequently, as we have seen, the interests of the crafts ran counter to consumer interests. Then, too, a growing patriciate, whose position had been acquired through early mercantile success, often sought to derive wealth through fiscal and political control, for example, through taxation and the power given by their social standing. Their use of the machinery of town government in their own interests often clashed with the interests of craftsmen. Despite these complications, however, the town was united in keeping out the foreigner and preserving the local market for the local resident. And despite latent internal tensions, the general effort to defend the local consumer gave scope to the social and ethical principles propagated by the church and created the appearance of a rough social equality which strengthened the sense of community.

No matter what the internal rivalries, therefore, the general economic policies of medieval towns were directed to the profit of town producers and the defense of town consumers. Generally these policies took the form of buying as cheaply as possible, selling as dearly as possible, and monopolizing wherever possible the control of both these features of trade. There were different ways of doing this. Foreign merchants were often required by legislation to pass through the town where they could be taxed or forced to sell their goods at fixed prices or where their continued journey might be made conditional on terms imposed by local traders who frequently required that they bypass rival towns. The regulation of foreigners was motivated, of course, not only by a desire to increase town profits but also by the desire to insure a cheap and abundant supply of consumer goods, to protect local industry, and help pay the cost of town facilities and defenses for which the local trader was taxed and for which the foreigner, since he also benefited from them, ought to be. Genoa and Venice owed much of their growth to their success in forcing merchants from other regions to use their facilities, and to their insistence that neighboring cities give up certain activities. In 1166, for example, Genoa forced Narbonne to cease transporting pilgrims from many of the port towns of the south coast of France where Genoa was able to establish a shipping monopoly.

Towns were often in competition with one another to control trade routes, dominate sources of commodities, and monopolize markets. Much of the history of such competition may be written from the naval struggles between Genoa and Venice in the twelfth and thirteenth centuries, the struggles between Florence and her rivals Pisa and Lucca and her eventual control of much of Tuscany, and the expansion of Milan at the expense of neighboring cities in northern Italy. The extension of the political power of the cities into a greater and greater hinterland, especially in Italy where the political authority of the emperor had broken down, was merely the political expression of the towns' drive for commercial and industrial monopoly. Where central political authority was strong, or was in the process of growing strong, towns had no such political future; the city-states of northern Italy found no counterpart therefore in England, France, or Spain. There, what hopes the town might have of regulating economic activity on behalf of local residents found expression only in local legislation.

It was the general welfare of the town itself which forced towns-men to act in corporate fashion, to accept town regulation of all economic activities, and to subject their individualism to corporate policies. Before the last half of the thirteenth century, the economy was not yet saturated; that is to say it could always use more traders, more capital, more goods, and more services than were actually present. Population grew, consumption increased, and op-portunities for economic expansion were many. Roughly speaking, therefore, regulation was not so much restrictive as ethical. It sought not so much the advantage of the few over the many as an equitable distribution of economic benefits to all. When, however, in the late thirteenth century the economy of Europe began to show signs of saturation, the regulated nature of town life was turned to other, narrower ends. Economic saturation did not mean economic crisis. It meant a gradual change in the balance between the goods society produced and those it could consume. It was also marked by a more widespread distribution of productive and commercial capacities than had existed before, with the result that the earlier dependence of large regions of Europe on a few highly developed areas was lessened. Therefore opportunities of exchange declined while at the same time competition grew. The early days of large quick profits were gone, and the medieval merchant was soon forced to operate more efficiently or go under. In towns where there was already a large body of economic legislation, it was in-evitable that he would take the easiest course. Where the merchant class dominated the town, it could use its political and fiscal con-trol of town machinery to maintain profits by converting its public influence and power to private ends. Regulations which had pro-tected the town itself now protected a privileged section of the town at the expense of the town consumers. This kind of protec-tion had several general features: a restriction in the number of those allowed to share in important branches of trade; the main-tenance of high consumer prices in those goods imported by local merchants; the depression of production costs on items to be ex-ported, usually by holding down wages. These were not new measures. The control of trade and prices was a continual and accepted practice on behalf of the welfare of the community. The novelty here is that it was adapted to the welfare of only a portion of the community. Earlier, for example, the emergence of craft gilds had been slow because of the legislation protecting town consumers from the effects of craft monopoly. Now the controls over craft gilds, especially in the large industrial towns, were enforced by the merchants in their own interests.

V
FEUDALISM

ORIGINS

TO SEEK THE PROTECTION OF OTHERS MORE powerful than oneself or conversely to derive satisfaction or benefits by extending one's protection to others are tendencies to be found in all ages, even our own. These tendencies became a prominent feature of social organization in the early Middle Ages, however, because the newly founded Germanic kingdoms failed to provide adequate protection for their subjects, who were driven to look elsewhere for it. The result was a rapid extension of independent arrangements which answered the need so well that they eventually determined the nature of the major legal and political institutions in western Europe.

After the collapse of Rome the establishment of German kingdoms on western soil was not accompanied by any reestablishment of widespread political security. While one's membership in a family group might provide a body of relatives to whom one might appeal when one was wronged, the kind of rough justice such an arrangement provided, with its blood feuds or payments for manslaughter could hardly contribute to an era of peace and justice. The Germanic kingdoms inherited from Rome some of the ideals but inherited little if any of the machinery of central government. Beset by rivalry within and invasion from without, they could provide no redress for a populace suffering the cruel consequences of lawlessness and warfare. Everywhere, therefore, the weak sought out the powerful to allay their insecurities, and everywhere the powerful sought the support of followers to maintain their prestige, their fortune, their property and even their safety. We have already seen the process at work: the petty tenant farmer and the small peasant proprietor sought the protection of local magnates by turning over their land and receiving it back as tenements.

The rapid growth of private arrangements whereby one person commended himself to another presented no great novelty in those areas that had been part of the Roman or Romanized world; in such areas the old Roman patron-client relationship (*patrocinium*) had never completely disappeared. There is no direct connection between this ancient Roman institution and the later practice of personal commendation. The wealthy Roman, surrounded by a claque of hangers-on who swarmed about him from the moment he rose in the morning until he retired at night, accompanied him in the streets, applauded his speeches in the forum, and accepted gratefully his handouts of food and other presents, is a far cry from the medieval ruffian and his household of servants and drinking companions. But the Roman institution of patronage had struck firm root in Gaul since it approximated earlier customs in which local chieftains had surrounded themselves with groups of personal retainers. The growth of ties of personal dependence, of commendation, could hardly therefore have appeared unusual to contemporaries.

Germanic influences, however, were strongly at work. The development of commendation was encouraged by an old German practice whereby a powerful man extended to some weaker neighbor his personal protection (*mundeburdum*). The royal *mundeburdum* was especially desirable, for an attack upon one thus protected was an attack upon the king himself. Those who enjoyed such protection were a favored group indeed, usually comprising young men of good families seeking to get on in the world. The search for protection was not then restricted to the lower classes of peasants. At all levels of society men commended themselves to others more powerful than themselves.

The ceremonial act of submission on the part of one individual to another was a simple one—the act of "homage." One man clasped his hands together, placed them between the hands of another, and made a short statement acknowledging himself to be the "man" of the other person. The two then kissed each other, symbolizing their friendship. This simple ceremony of homage only appears in the documents from the second half of the eighth century but in such a form as to indicate that it had probably been in use for some considerable time before this. It seems to have been a ceremony of Germanic origin, but it quickly spread throughout all of Europe. It was through this act of homage that the "vassal" was created. The word "vassal" (Lat. *vassus* or *vassallus*) was only one of many used indiscriminately to refer to the servant, but it soon came to be used almost exclusively. Its root was Celtic; its connotation was derogatory and condescending—something like "young boy." A man's followers then were his "boys." He protected them; they served him. In the beginning the service might be honorable or menial, but this vagueness would not long remain.

The results of personal commendation were that many lost their freedom. It was probably not too great a price to pay in return for the chance to stay alive, but freedom nonetheless remained a prized possession. An early document reads:

Inasmuch as it is recognized by all how I have too little by which I might feed or clothe myself, I therefore petitioned your piety, and your good will granted to me that I might deliver and commend myself to your protection . . . that you ought to support and sustain me as well in food as in clothing . . . , and as long as I shall live I ought to render to you service and obedience compatible with my free status. . . .[1]

The German warrior-peasant who followed his chieftain into territories of Rome had been a free man, whether he fought or

---

[1] Cited by R. S. Hoyt, *Feudal Institutions* (New York, 1961), p. 7.

farmed. In the course of time, however, as the personal status of the peasantry was depressed, the notion of freedom came to be attached to the other attribute of the early Germans—fighting. The military expenses which faced the peasant, especially as cavalry became increasingly important and a horse became an indispensable part of one's equipment, made it all but impossible for him to meet the full obligations of a free Frank—but if he abandoned his military obligations he abandoned, in fact, his last hope of personal freedom. Those who sought the protection of a lord in return for agricultural service sank in status; those who did so, however, in return for military service preserved their personal liberty.

The institution of vassalage lent itself to a situation of pressing importance. This was an age when war was regarded as the normal pursuit of the career of every leader and the foundation of every position of political authority. The need for warrior followers was constant. The custom of maintaining groups of household warriors in their service already existed among powerful individuals. This custom had its roots deep in early Germanic society when warrior chiefs often surrounded themselves with companions whom they led into battle and on plundering expeditions and, in the intervals of rest, treated with hospitality and long drinking bouts. The custom spread to Romanized Gauls with the settlement of Germans in the Roman territories, and there was scarcely a member of the aristocracy who did not come to have his own private band of soldiers.

Among the early Franks there had been no standing army apart from a few guards whom a king or a magnate might collect about him. There was little enthusiasm or experience among peasant recruits, and for that matter the peasant could hardly afford the increasing cost of warfare. As the troubles of the Merovingian epoch grew, everything conspired to make it more and more necessary to find professional warriors. It happened that the ties of personal dependence to be found in the growing institution of vassalage were easily adapted to meet the need for military followers. Soon the word "vassal" came to bear the specific meaning of armed retainer, even though its early connotation was akin to slave. The very promotion of the word is a reflection of the promotion of the person to whom it was applied. The original social status of many of the lord's servants must have been low indeed. Many of them were landless, footloose adventurers, having no stake in society other than the strength of their arms. The decay of earlier military organization gave them an increasingly important role; and as their importance grew, so did their social status.

Thus vassalage, which had been a generic institution within which one obtained labor and service of undifferentiated kind, soon became narrowed to that institution by which one equipped oneself with what amounted to a private army. At the time when the peasant masses were slowly losing their personal freedom, a new caste was being formed of men characterized by the profession of arms and the exercise of military command.

LEGALIZED VASSALAGE

These developments had gone without official recognition, but with the collapse of the Merovingian monarchy and its replacement by the Carolingians they became an integral part of the legal and political system of the Frankish kingdom, from which they spread to other parts of western Europe. The Carolingians themselves, as members of the aristocracy, had played a large role in the destruction of the Merovingian monarchy, contributing in the process to that dissipation of central authority for which the seventh century is so noted. Once in control, however, the Carolingians sought to reestablish order. To do this through a reconstituted central government was virtually impossible. The machinery for such a government no longer existed. Economic conditions made impossible the establishment of a large retinue of paid officials. Uncertain communications and insecurity on the roads made it hopeless for any central government to try to rule a large territory directly and effectively. But the system of vassalage was well developed and promised a means of government which must have appeared quite natural. Under Charlemagne and his successors, therefore, royal enactments sought to ensure that every man had his lord and that under certain safeguards these personal contracts remained binding upon the parties at least for the duration of their lives. Thus, no one was to leave his lord unless his lord tried to kill him, committed adultery with his wife, stole his property, tried to reduce him to slavery, or refused him due protection. And even when entitled to renounce his lord, he was obliged to find another. In this way the lord could be made officially responsible for the appearance of his underlings in court or on the battlefield and could be used for other purposes of the crown in distant provinces. In all this, of course, it was important that the crown tie the lord to itself. This it did by the distribution of gifts—frequently gifts of land—in return for which those who had been so endowed swore an oath of fealty to the crown. In a sense what was really happening was that the old group around the king, his companions in arms, was being enlarged to include new followers, the powerful throughout the kingdom. These were now bound to the crown by the same tie of vassalage as the king's own household was. Since most of their time was spent far from their master, the conditions under which they lived were necessarily much different from those of household warriors. In fact each of them was the center of a more or less widely scattered group of dependents whom he was expected to keep in order.

The system of vassalage was also used to tie court officials closely to the crown. These were now more frequently recruited from men who, before their appointment, had already served the king as vassals. Soon there was no office in the Carolingian court, no great command, no countship whose holder was not obliged to bind himself as vassal to the monarch. Thus the Carolingians depended less on a theoretical sovereignty, which in any event had done nothing to preserve the state, and more on the faithfulness of their personal retainers, their vassals. The new caste was characterized not only by the profession of arms but by the exercise of political office as well.

The example of the ruler was bound to have its effect among those of lesser status. Counts bound to themselves officials of lower rank, bishops and abbots the laymen on whom they relied to assist them. Powerful individuals, whoever and wherever they were, strove in like fashion to draw into their orbit increasing numbers of petty lords who in turn acted in the same way toward those still weaker than themselves. Everywhere, from the monarch down, personal contract between individual and individual took the place of public sovereignty in the operation of government. In the ninth century the increased chaos and insecurity attending the collapse of the Carolingian state speeded this development.

THE FIEF

From the outset the institution of vassalage had its economic aspect. Powerful men, while exercising authority over others, sought to increase the amount of property they might control; vassals, while putting themselves in the protection of others, looked for some reward for their service. The economic aspect of vassalage was restricted, however, by the general economic condition of the times. The lord might reward his vassal with occasional gifts— a horse, arms, clothing, and other accouterments—and by housing him under his own roof and feeding him at his own board. These were characteristic rewards of the early household warriors. But there was another way of rewarding the follower: by making him a simple grant of land from which he could support himself while he remained in the service of the lord but which would revert to the lord as soon as that service ceased. It was much easier to distribute men among the available land resources than to bring the fruits of those resources to the men. It was more convenient to make the vassal responsible for his own subsistence while giving him the means to do so. During the Carolingian period, the distribution of land among vassals steadily became a characteristic feature of the institution of vassalage at the very time that vassalage itself was being rapidly extended.

Vassalage thus gave rise to a form of land tenure, temporary in nature, not too dissimilar to the "precarious" tenure which had become increasingly common during the uncertainty and insecurity of the early centuries of medieval Europe. Precarious tenure, the *precaria*, was a grant of land, usually for rent, so called by reason of the prayer (*preces*) which the recipient made to the grantor when begging him for the benefit of a gift of land. The land was to be held at the pleasure of the grantor, hence the modern connotation of the word "precarious," because the tenure could be terminated at the will of the lord. In time, however, it became customary for the *precaria* to be granted for a specific term. The church made special use of this form of tenure, granting land in response to specific requests or, as frequently became the custom, receiving title to land from pious donors and granting it back to them to be held on precarious tenure, usually for the lifetime of the donor. These donations were not always made from motives of pure

piety. Behind them often lay a debt to the ecclesiastical establishment, usually a monastery, which held a mortgage on the debtor's
land. At all events, the *precaria* was a convenient way for the
church not only to keep its lands under cultivation without permanently alienating church property, but also to acquire title to
additional property without ejecting the donor. The growth of
precarious tenure was also encouraged by the practice of receiving
title to the small property of some hard-pressed peasant and granting it back with additional land from the holdings of the lord
himself. This made the *precaria* of greater mutual advantage to
both lord and tenant, the former enlarging his title and assuring
the regular cultivation of more of his land, the latter increasing the
amount of land he actually worked and thus increasing his assurance of subsistence. In the circumstances, then, the practice of
handing land over to a vassal as temporary remuneration for temporary service would hardly seem out of the ordinary.

As the term *precaria* came to be reserved, however, for grants
involving the payment of rent, another term, *beneficium,* which had
no suggestion of prayer or supplication and therefore seemed more
honorable, was applied to those grants made in return for service.
The trouble with the term "*beneficium*" was that while its generic
connotation was "benefit" or "boon," allowing it to be used to
describe any kind of grant, ecclesiastical writers were coming to
use it in a special sense to describe ecclesiastical offices. Therefore,
while it continued to be used for grants to vassals by writers who,
being literate, were usually churchmen, what they really had in
mind was what the uneducated were already calling the "fief." This
was a word which had traditionally meant movable property, such
as arms, clothing, horses, and sometimes food. These were the very
items with which household vassals were rewarded. When the vassal came to be granted immovable property, land, the word "fief"
likewise made the shift from movable to immovable property and
in the end ousted *beneficium* completely. Fief, like *beneficium,* connoted a property granted in return for service. It had to be service
of a specialized kind, for example, of specialists who minted coins,
painted churches, supervised other tenants, made gold or silver
ware. Increasingly, however, it was thought of as the normal reward
of a vassal for military service, and it was this for which the word
was finally reserved. The history of the fief, like the history of

vassalage itself, is that of an institution originally of a very general character gradually acquiring a narrow application in association with a particular social caste.

Since the vassal was an honorable person, he did not soil his hands by labor on the land. When he received a fief, he could expect to find on it tenants who paid rent and gave labor services. Over these subjects he came to exercise political authority as well as economic power. Though fiefs were usually distributed among vassals from the original possessions of the lord, it was not always so. Sometimes a man brought his land as a gift to another, entered his service as a vassal, and then received the same land back as a fief. In this way much of the allodial land of Europe was brought into the feudal system. Where the individual was a peasant, the land was returned to him burdened with rents and labor services. But where the person was of higher social status and of warlike habits, he did his homage, swore fealty, and received back his former possessions as an honorable vassal's fief.

Just as the act of homage symbolized the subjection of man to man, so the act of investiture symbolized the economic basis of this relationship. Again, the ceremony was simple. The lord handed the vassal an object which symbolized property—a small stick, a clod of earth. It was a ceremony which took place immediately after, not before, the act of homage and the oath of fealty. The ceremony which created the bond between man and man was a necessary preliminary to that which dealt with reward.

By the end of the thirteenth century the class of household vassals had almost disappeared, owing to the almost universal use of the fief as a reward for service. By this time, however, an important change in the nature of the fief had occurred. As a reward for service it was supposedly revocable when that service ended. Since vassalage lasted usually until the death of one of the parties, the grant of the fief would normally terminate at the same time. This practice was destroyed, however, by the strength of the notion of inheritance, which was impossible to withstand.

Already under the Carolingians the great offices of state—the seneschal, butler, marshal, and the like—had shown a tendency to be passed from father to son. The more important official families, whose members administered regional districts, the counties, frequently acquired other territories besides those assigned to their care by the crown. These they held independently, acquiring thus a basis for political power in a given district during a period in which the authority of the crown declined drastically. It became increasingly difficult to eject such officials from control of their offices. In 877 Charles the Bald provided that counts while campaigning in Italy with the king should be succeeded by their sons; and while the provision was presumably of a temporary nature, it amounted, in fact, to a recognition of the hereditary principle. Inheritance therefore was not uncommon during the development of feudalism from the ninth century on; and by the eleventh century, the heritability of the fief itself was well on the way to being generally recognized. In Germany it was given added impetus: the emperor Conrad II (1024–1039), anxious to break the power of the great territorial lords, sought to make an alliance with the vassals of those lords by extending to them the right of inheritance by an imperial edict in 1037.

Now, nothing appears more contrary to the nature of the fief—a temporary reward for temporary service—than its heritability. Take the case of the succession of an infant son or a woman, which threatened to deprive the lord of those military services for which he granted the fief in the first place. To turn over a military holding to a child or a woman was illogical; yet dispossession seemed cruel. Inheritance, therefore, posed a series of problems the solutions of which modified the entire feudal structure. Minors came to be recognized as heirs, but until such time as they could perform their military duties, the lord frequently turned the revenues of the fief over to someone who could. Later he kept the revenues, constituting himself the guardian of the heir and thus using his rights as a feudal lord to enlarge his income. The problem was not so easily dealt with when the heir was a woman—the daughter or the widow of a deceased vassal. A woman was considered incapable of bearing arms, of carrying out the military services due from a vassal; but it was soon recognized that her husband could do so in her stead. It was therefore imperative that the lord control who that husband might be, and everywhere lords attempted, with considerable success, to control the marriages of their vassals' daughters and the remarriage of their vassals' widows. This also provided the lord with a source of revenue, for he was often able to sell his ward or take from her a large payment to abandon his right to marry her off to whomever he chose or, indeed, to sell that right to another. In sum, the pressure to convert the fief into inheritable property and the ways in which the lord's rights were exploited for financial ends reveal how military service and close personal ties between lord and vassal were ceasing to be of importance.

Inheritance created another problem, for although in theory the fief was indivisible, in fact the equal claims of several heirs soon led to its partition. This could be a matter of serious concern to the lord. Along with the absence of any clear principle of discrimination among heirs, it explains the many different practices adopted to prevent disintegration of the fief and the lord's loss of the services due from its holder. Frequently, the lord decided which of the heirs ought to inherit; sometimes the father selected his own heir with the lord's approval; sometimes joint heirs were invested with the fief collectively; in many places, notably in Germany, the division of holdings among multiple heirs was recognized. Inheritance presented a special threat, however, to the more important families whose power was based on a large accumulation of territories. The division of their lands among several heirs would bring about the fragmentation and loss of their political authority. Thus primogeniture (the principle that the eldest male heir solely can inherit), which had made great headway in France and especially in England, came to Germany also.

The transformation of the fief into an item of family property led to its treatment as an economic commodity. This was hastened in other ways. Inheritance being viewed in earlier days as a favor, the new vassal often showed his gratitude to the lord by a gift. In a society based upon custom, voluntary acts, when they became habitual, were quickly transformed into obligations. Naturally, vassals sought to reduce and regulate this obligation which became in the process a succession tax on the fief, called "relief." Furthermore, vassals were inclined to sell or pawn their fiefs or parts of their fiefs whenever they needed money, and in a period of an increasing exchange economy this happened often enough. At first sight, to treat the fief in this way seems an absurdity, but since inheritance was becoming common there was little inclination to oppose other kinds of alienation provided there was some recompense. The early fear that alienation might reduce the ability of the fief to render military service had allowed the lord to insist that his permission be granted first, and since nothing in the Middle Ages was granted without a payment in return, alienation of fiefs became common in time on the payment of what amounted to a tax on change of tenancy. Nothing demonstrates better than these taxes on transference how the fief was becoming commercialized and how far the decline in importance of the intimate personal relationship between lord and vassal had proceeded. Feudal obligations were ceasing to be personal; often converted into items of revenue, they were transferred to the estate, passing with it to its inheritor or purchaser as the case might be.

The erosion of the personal element of feudalism was becoming evident in yet other ways. It was taken for granted in the early days that a vassal could have only one lord, but as early as the tenth century it was beginning to be usual for members of the military caste to become the vassals of two lords or sometimes even more. This was the result of exploiting feudalism for economic purposes. In order to extend one's possessions, one merely sought from this or that lord more land in return for the promise of service. To distribute one's homage among several lords, however, was bound to lead to contradictions. If two lords of the same vassal went to war against one another, which of the two was the vassal obliged to serve? No matter what the arrangements (and they were many) to avoid conflicts of loyalty, the effect was to empty homage of its primitive content. Nor was there much to be gained by creating a kind of superhomage, known as "liege" homage, whereby one lord above all others was designated as the lord to whom one's service was primarily due. This might have been an attempt to preserve the close personal relationship of man to man, but the forces which depersonalized homage had much the same effect on liege homage. Soon every lord was "my liege."

OBLIGATIONS OF FEUDALISM

The obligations of the vassal to his lord and of the lord to his vassal were at the outset ill defined, amounting in a vague way to service in return for protection. Inevitably a need was felt to define more precisely what was involved. Inevitably, too, definition had the effect of limitation. In the course of time the verbal exchange in the act of homage was reinforced by a written contract, frequently in some detail, stipulating the precise terms of the relationship. On the side of the vassal the first and most important duty was military service. He was bound to serve in person, with full military equipment, accompanied usually by one or two squires, and leading with him his own vassals if he had any. Presumably he was to serve his lord as long as he was needed. All of this soon came to be limited. Personal service remained an obligation but like so many other obligations could be avoided by the payment of a fine, the amount of which was soon fixed. The number of followers the vassal had to bring was in the course of time also fixed, and need have no relationship to the number of vassals he actually had. As for the length of service, a traditional period of forty days a year soon became standard in large parts of Europe; if the vassal was needed for any longer period than that, he had to be paid.

Besides military service, which could include either fighting in the field or garrisoning some stronghold, the vassal had the duty of attendance at the lord's court, a solemn session held more or less regularly. This was at once a court of law, a war council, and a ceremonial occasion at which the lord's prestige and power were made manifest. Here the vassal was called upon to give his judgment in matters of feudal law, to counsel his lord when called upon to do so, and, by serving in some symbolic office such as cup-bearer or steward, to contribute to the visible status of the lord whom he served. Although it is true that the vassal did not dislike court service as much as military service since it carried with it some advantages, it did make large demands upon his purse and soon was limited in many ways.

Another obligation, at first vague but soon to take on clearer features, was the vassal's duty to render aid to his lord. This was first thought of as military aid, but a time came when the vassal was expected to reach into his pocket as well. Gifts that vassals made to their lords in times of great emergency came to be a kind of feudal exaction, but although custom made them compulsory it also specified the occasions when they could be demanded and how much they were to be. Standard "aids" were those for the lord's ransom if he were taken prisoner, for the knighting of his eldest son, and for the marriage of his eldest daughter, the latter two being affairs of increasing expense. Sometimes other aids could be successfully demanded, for example, for a crusade, a costly business indeed, or when the lord himself had been taxed by someone above him.

When we come to investigate the obligations of the lord to his vassals, we find little clear definition. These obligations certainly included the duty of giving aid and protection when needed (which came to mean the vassal's property as well as his person) and treating the vassal honorably as a member of the same social class. The lord also owed the vassal justice, meaning that the lord was not only to treat the vassal justly but was to open his court to the vassal to arbitrate the disputes in which the vassal was often embroiled, most frequently over vague and ill-defined land boundaries. The matter of rendering justice, however, was often a source of friction, especially when the dispute was between the vassal and his own lord, in which case the vassal had little hope of a fair hearing. His only recourse was defiance, a formal breaking of the feudal tie, which was often the first act of outright war. The dispute might be settled by force, and not infrequently the vassal was strong enough to defy his lord with impunity. In these circumstances, however, what happened to the fief? If the lord was at fault and the vassal was able to make his defiance good, the right of the unworthy lord usually passed up the feudal scale to his lord in turn. This was how the kings of France reached down and brought into direct dependence upon themselves the sub-vassals of some of their overmighty vassals, encouraging the sub-vassals to revolt against their immediate lords. In some areas, especially in northern Italy, a successful break in the feudal tie led to the fief being converted into allodial property, held without feudal obligation to any lord—an indication of the weakness of feudal ideas south of the Alps. Where the vassal was unable to withstand the force of his lord, his fief was forfeited and given to another. In most cases, however, disputes between lord and vassal were patched up by concession on one side or the other and the feudal relationship reestablished.

Certainly, the personal ties of man to man for service and protection were never sufficient to control entirely the greed, envy, pride, independence, brutality, and violence which led lord and vassal to ravage one another's land, destroy one another's villages, and slaughter one another's peasants. But they did allow for a systematic arrangement of land tenure, the administration of justice, and a form of organized government which, though simple, was often effective.

VI
GOVERNMENT

CAROLINGIAN GOVERNMENT

DESPITE THE MANY EVIDENCES OF LOCAL DIVERsity, under Charlemagne there was a real empire with a unity maintained for the most part by a system of local administrators reporting directly to the emperor. The chief local officer was the "count," who had to be chosen with great care because even in the older territories subject to the Franks, to say nothing of Italy or the new-won regions of Germany, there were too many memories of local independence. Generally the count was a member of an important Frankish family, raised and educated at the royal court. The area of his administration was the county, of which there were several hundred throughout the empire. The count represented the emperor in the fullness of his power in governmental, financial, judicial, and military matters. In theory he could be removed from his office and replaced at will, but in fact his tenure was often relatively secure. Some counts held office in the same county for twenty to thirty years. They often amassed large private holdings in addition to the estates granted to them by the crown as a reward for their services. The count was closely dependent upon the king, who limited his initiative in many ways, by issuing him frequent instructions, by requiring him to attend court and render accounts of his office, by sending into his county special agents to investigate local affairs, and by playing off count against bishop in matters of local government.

In a state in which civil and religious affairs were closely bound together, it was natural that the bishop would also play a large role in local administration. In Charlemagne's day, the bishop was for the most part an imperial official and an important instrument of political unity. His election as bishop, therefore, rested with the emperor, who had to rely on him to act as an agent of public authority. Through his bishops Charlemagne also controlled the lower clergy.

This simple system of local government was maintained by constant inspection carried out by yet other officials, the *missi dominici*. These were usually two men—one lay and one ecclesiastic—whose mission was temporary and brief: a few weeks each year in a territorial circumscription comprising a group of counties. "Let the *missi* make a diligent investigation whenever any man claims that an injustice has been done to him by anyone," Charles ordered in 802, and went on at great length about what ought to be looked into or done regarding the church, the army, land tenure, serfdom, fealty to the crown, administration of justice, criminal law, protection of the poor, "so that all these good things may be well done to the praise of omnipotent God." Like the counts, the *missi* too amassed estates and converted their temporary functions into permanent, hereditary ones as did Robert the Strong, an ancestor of the later Capetian kings of France, who established himself between the Seine and the Loire.

There is little in all this to remind one of the Roman imperial government. Central government was in the emperor's hands, with a small household to assist him. Royal incomes were derived for the most part from royal estates, numerous villas that Charlemagne possessed, especially in the north along the Meuse and the Rhine where his family had taken its rise. Direct taxation was all but forgotten. The old Roman head tax and land tax were by now abandoned. The only direct tax was not really a tax at all but an annual gift that had become obligatory, to be paid by the greater subjects of Charlemagne at the annual May assembly, an obligation which they in turn passed on to their peasants. The only other direct levy of any importance did not go to the crown: this was the tithe given to the church, the payment of which was enforced by an emperor who could see no separation between ecclesiastical and lay affairs. There were some indirect taxes: customs and tolls at ports and taxes on markets and fairs; but the economic decline reduced their importance. Of the various economic monopolies enjoyed by the Roman emperors, the only one still retained by the crown was the striking of money. Where in the seventh century some eight hundred mints had operated in Gaul, Charlemagne was able to monopolize all minting himself.

The administration of justice was also an important source of revenue. It was fairly uniform in spite of the great diversity of legal codes. Justice was administered by the counts who associated with themselves a professional class of local men, the *scabini,* whose function it was to say what the law was, leaving to the count the duty of pronouncing sentence. Since the incomes of the court went to the count, his zeal in the pursuit of wrongdoers is readily understandable.

This administrative and judicial regime was not applicable everywhere. More and more church territories, monastic and diocesan estates, were granted "immunities" whereby the bishop or abbot, as the case may have been, replaced the officers of the crown in matters of administration, tax collection, and justice. "No public functionary," reads one document, "may enter the territory in question, neither to render justice, nor raise taxes, nor take oaths of allegiance, nor demand hospitality . . . nor constrain any whether free or unfree" (which last may have meant raising militia). In effect administrative responsibility rested with the immunist who had for all purposes replaced the public official. Since the immunists were for the most part bishops and abbots, they were generally careful not to antagonize Charlemagne to whom they owed their appointments. In fact the emperor was moved, since the churchmen were frequently more reliable than the counts, to be generous with them and in many grants of immunities to turn over to them other things, such as royal incomes from imposts and even the right to exact military service in some cases. Since the ecclesiastical position of the immunist, however, often made it impossible for him to perform all the administrative and judicial functions required of him, the emperor was frequently obliged to attach to him an "advocate," a layman to perform his lay functions.

The unity of this regime was maintained by a vigorous and powerful ruler, opposition to whom was out of the question. But the empire was very much a personal thing, and its dissolution began after Charlemagne's death. It was a dissolution completed by the inability of the empire to defend itself from external attack, but it grew out of latent centrifugal forces which began to manifest themselves shortly after Charlemagne died. The untrammeled authority of the crown was soon limited by ecclesiastics in Gaul who not only subjected royal rule to divine law, a law to be interpreted by the bishops, but also made royal rule subject to an explicit promise to rule justly. This concession, obtained in 843 from Charles the Bald, one of Charlemagne's grandsons, illustrates that the moral leadership once exercised by Charlemagne himself had passed by this time from royal hands into those of the higher clergy. The bishops of Frankish Gaul felt it their mission as interpreters of divine law to guide the action of kings by their advice, of which they had plenty. Of even more immediate effect, however, was the breakup of the Carolingian "fisc," the great agglomeration of imperial estates upon which imperial power was based. The struggle between Charlemagne's grandsons was over the possession of as many royal estates as possible, but in their search for supporters they had to grant away much of the prize. The divisions within the Carolingian family drove the magnates, who looked in vain for royal leadership and protection, to pursue their own interests. The result was a dispersion of the royal fisc among the landed aristocracy and with it the basis of the crown's capacity to rule. Although the imperial office persisted after the division of the empire among Charlemagne's grandsons, it was an empty title. Not only was the empire itself fragmented, but within each of the portions royal wealth, and therefore royal authority, was dissipated. Those who had exercised authority on behalf of the crown now continued to exercise it on behalf of themselves. Counts and other imperial officers not only succeeded in making their offices heritable, they also expropriated what they could of the royal estates entrusted to them while clinging to the powers they had exercised in the name of the king. The model was not lost on others, who seized similar powers outright. Immunists everywhere acted in their own behalf, and the immunities once enjoyed almost solely by ecclesiastics were successfully usurped by many laymen. In Germany, especially, the "advocate" was frequently able to turn his office into a hereditary one; the lands of his advocacy, supposedly belonging to the church, he converted into a private estate within which he exercised all the functions of government to the extent that he could.

FEUDAL GOVERNMENT

The fragmentation of the Carolingian empire and the great difficulties facing Charlemagne's successors within the parts of the empire in which they claimed royal power meant that the essential work of government could not be carried on without using local lords for administration, justice, and defense. This was especially true in the western portion of the empire, the future France; here feudalism developed rapidly in the face of an ineffective and nominal sovereign, great counties became virtually independent of the crown, and lesser lords grew increasingly independent of their counts. The regional independence of Burgundians, Aquitanians, Gascons, Bretons, Angevins, and Flemings reflects the fact that even under Charlemagne there remained a lively awareness of local differences and a good deal of autonomy and individuality.

There were, however, many attempts to gather lands together in more or less large agglomerations. In France from the tenth century to the twelfth several large principalities emerged, reflecting a collection in the hands of a single magnate of counties, fiefs, allods, rights over royal monasteries and churches, together with personal and family possessions; the collections manifested a tendency to military expansion at the expense of neighbors. In Germany the great duchies of Swabia, Bavaria, Saxony, and Franconia threatened for a time to become permanent political entities, reflecting as they did a certain amount of ethnic solidarity and local particularism. But their future was clouded; the crown, which had most to lose, threatened them from above, and from below the forces of decentralization operated here as in France. The greater princes could control or govern their possessions no more securely than kings. Partitions, immunities, usurpations—all the forces which tore kingdoms apart—continued their work. In France, despite all efforts, the rulers of larger principalities came to exercise real power only over lands that belonged to them personally; in fact they were forced to relinquish more and more authority to others over whom they tried to exercise some influence, often not very effective, by

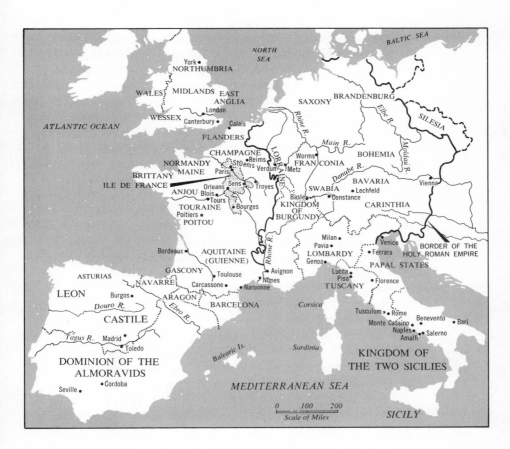

FEUDAL EUROPE

accepting them as vassals. It became impossible to distinguish the descendants of Carolingian officials who had at least some legal basis for their claims to power from the many new men of no known ancestry who were strong enough and lucky enough to carve out for themselves a place of power, and even in some cases to usurp for themselves the title of count.

Unlike more recent times, there was no debate about the role of government; the ruler was expected to ensure the spiritual salvation of his people, to defend them in their bodies and property, to give them justice and peace. But the activities of those who exercised political power revealed their insecurity. They were primarily concerned with keeping what they had, holding the loyalty of their supporters, and, moved as much by considerations of honor as desire for power, adding to their possessions by conquest. In a word, their activity was governed by warfare. As a result, feudal government, as limited as it was in objective, was not always effective. Violence was every person's constant companion. It had come with the invasions and flourished with the impotence of government. It was deeply entrenched in the customary law of the blood feud. Violence, or the threat of violence, lay behind many of the property transactions at a time when peaceful commerce was practically nonexistent. An entire class had come into being through its exercise, and in an age which saw human existence as merely a transitory stage before the awful infinitude, there could be little respect for human life.

Yet the agony was felt by everyone, and there grew out of this troubled epoch a persistent demand for peace. Since the great princes were powerless to guarantee it, organized though abortive efforts to establish peace and order developed outside the scope of regular government and inspired and led by churchmen. In the late tenth century bishops meeting in church councils not only condemned the killing of Christians in general terms but specifically called for the exemption of the weak and unarmed from the violent consequences of warfare. This was the "Peace of God," an idea which spread from central France throughout much of the west, although affecting Germany rather late and Italy hardly at all. Gradually the classes of people to be covered by the Peace of God were extended to include clergy, merchants, and peasants; the Peace of God also embraced possessions such as mills, vineyards, and livestock. So, too, special days called the "Truce of God" were set aside on which violence was prohibited. Just as at one time Charlemagne had outlawed the blood feud on Sundays, now there were bans for Easter, the greater feasts of the year, and then finally the three days of the week leading up to Sunday. At first taking the form of synodal legislation, in which bishops made solemn pronouncements which were ignored by the offenders, the Peace and Truce of God were soon demanded of men in the form of oaths, often refused, sometimes given only to be forgotten.

The root of the problem lay in the fact that the only existing coercive power that might have enforced the Peace and Truce of God rested with those who were most guilty of violence. Soon groups of people began to take matters into their own hands, forming sworn associations binding one another to good behavior and then taking on the responsibility of dealing with brigands and others who offended against the community. But such leagues were themselves a threat to the traditional powers, for they contained an element essentially hostile to the existing social order. For example, in the late twelfth century in south central France there grew up around an obscure carpenter, Durand of Le Puy, a large movement dedicated to the destruction of the region's brigands. It briefly enjoyed the support of all classes of society, but it soon turned on the established authorities, lost the support of the nobility and the church, became an outcast and undisciplined mob, and was hunted down and finally destroyed. Later writers expressed horror and disgust at this "dangerous presumption," this "rebellion against their betters," in which there was shown "no fear, no reverence, of their superiors."

Peace movements such as this, eloquent reminders of the insecurity of life in the Middle Ages, could do nothing to repress disorder permanently. But peace and internal security could serve political purposes, and kings and princes, though they had nothing to do with the peace movements, sought to turn them to advantage. There was much to be gained by having a peacemaker's reputation. The close connection between the maintenance of peace and the extension of central political authority was not lost on some; in Germany progressively detailed laws about peace, issued by the emperor, played a part in the imperial attempt to maintain control of Germany. In England the early peace gilds, with their rough popular justice, were recognized by the crown, which used them in preserving order to its own ultimate benefit.

Political centralization was accomplished not by the abandonment of feudalism but by its adaptation to the needs of government.
This adaptation was related to the decline in the old personal relations between lord and vassal, man and man, and to the systematic
inheritance of fiefs. Lords grew increasingly interested in revenues
rather than in personal services; vassals sought to reduce their obligations, to accumulate land, and to transmit to their heirs enlarged
and more secure inheritances. Those who lost most in the process
were local lords; those who gained most were the rulers of large
territories. Money, replacing feudal service, aided in the work of
creating states. Those who had the resources or could borrow to
hire mercenaries to replace the old feudal levies enjoyed a distinct
advantage. Further, there was a deliberate rationalization of the
feudal hierarchy, especially at the hands of churchmen, which produced a systematic description of feudal relations in the form of a
pyramid with the king, the duke, the count at or near the apex.
This helped to bring nominal vassals into practical submission and
to force small, hitherto independent, holders of allodial land into
the feudal system in dependence upon this or that great prince.
Then, too, the increasing insistence, again under the influence of
the church, that justice flowed down from the top of the pyramid
allowed the king and the greater princes to intervene in local matters, to encourage appeals to their courts, to undermine the independence of their vassals, and thus to extend their authority. As the
ties between local lords and their vassals grew less personal and
therefore weaker, it was easier to bring the latter into direct dependence upon some more central authority. Finally, employing
officials to carry out administrative functions rather than continuing
to rely on the assistance of a feudal court composed of vassals led
to the professionalization of political administration—the keeping
of records, the orderly preservation of precedents, and a narrow
passion for legality, all of which served to increase the prince's
income and extend his authority.

The government exercised by a feudal prince remained as simple
in form as it was limited in object. In his immediate possessions he
enjoyed the ban, a right of command which in some cases he was
able to extend into the territories of his vassals. His rights were
limited, however, by the age-old belief that law, to be enforceable
and therefore binding, had to be made with the agreement of those
whom it affected. This notion antedated feudalism, going back to

the popular traditions of primitive German tribal life, but it was given feudal form by the lord's court in which he consulted his vassals. As the prince's governmental tasks grew more detailed, depending upon the size and stability of his principality, there was a tendency for his court to operate with a more restricted membership of officials and a few barons and bishops, by whom most of the work of administration was performed. The court was enlarged infrequently by vassals whose attendance was required only periodically and whose function was essentially formal, with little to do with the business of day-to-day government.

Administration was in the hands of a few great officers—the seneschal, chamberlain, constable, butler—their names betray the origins of their offices in household services. These were for the most part laymen, unlike the chancellor who was an ecclesiastic. They held their offices as fiefs which they frequently succeeded in keeping in their families. Their duties, not particularly specialized, consisted primarily in the supervision of justice and administration, military command, and household finance and organization. Often these offices became honorary, while deputies did the actual work. At the local level there were also officials who helped to exploit the lord's domain, supervise local administration, and collect revenues. Their names varied: provost, bailli, seneschal, chatelain. They too were usually vassals bound to the lord by an oath of fealty and trying, with much less success than the high officers at court, to convert their offices into hereditary fiefs.

KINGSHIP

From the foregoing it is apparent that feudalism provided not only a somewhat systematic arrangement of personal relationships, land tenure, military organization, and rough justice but also, in the course of time, some semblance of organized government. We cannot say, however, that the feudal system appreciably modified abstract ideas of the state or theories of government. The idea of kingship remained strong, and while in practice the authority of the king might meet with serious checks, there was no questioning of the office itself. It was sanctioned by long tradition, by the blessings of the church, and by the convenience with which it lent itself as a capstone to the feudal structure that had emerged in the west. The sources of his authority, the extent of his power, his relations with his subjects might all be topics for debate, but the necessity of having a king, the ideal of a single ruler over the body politic, was never doubted.

European kingship was a Germanic institution. The Germans who invaded the Roman Empire were led by chiefs or kings. The office, being elective, had a popular basis; and while the choice of the king was usually restricted to members of a particular family popularly thought to have been descended from a god, election was not merely the confirmation of a hereditary right nor was primogeniture by any means the rule. The choice was made on the grounds of "throne-worthiness"; it was in fact a real choice, usually exercised by the magnates and confirmed by popular acclamation. The king was called to his office because of his ability as a military leader.

From the outset, however, the office contained a transcendental element arising from the king's presumed divine origin. This element was later enlarged at the expense of the idea of the king as an elected magistrate. In this the church was extremely important for it was the bishops who, while seeking to influence the ruler, contributed most to a theocratic view of kingship as a divinely ordained office with ethical duties enjoined by God. The king's guardianship over the community was bestowed by God, not the people, and to God alone was he responsible. In the eyes of the church, secular government became an image, a reflection, of divine government. The model for the king's rule was God's rule. The royal office, created by God, was a perpetual one, independent of the will of the community.

This theocratic view of kingship contributed a great deal toward freeing the royal office from its traditional checks. To view the king as God's vicegerent on earth, to see him anointed with holy oil in the manner of a priest or bishop, was to elevate king above people, to destroy the popular basis of kingship, and to raise the royal office above the law itself. It would become increasingly difficult to justify resistance to a king who answered to God alone. Furthermore, the prevalence of the idea that all authority descended from above meant that those of lesser rank than the king could be viewed as exercising their authority only on his behalf rather than from personal right. It was an idea which, if translated into practice, would allow the king to demand the subjection of lords and princes no matter how great—would allow him, in other words, to convert his feudal suzerainty into a true sovereignty.

Different and conflicting influences—Germanic origins of a popular monarchy, feudal practices, theocratic ideas—made the position of the king somewhat ambiguous in medieval society. For a long time the development of royal authority was held in check by its popular origins. The Germanic notion of law as the sum total of the rights of all individuals,[1] and the idea that the king's purpose was to realize the law by which he himself was bound, made it difficult for any doctrine of monarchical irresponsibility, of royal absolutism, to emerge, even though it was implied in the theocratic view. A strong notion of the inherent right to resist the king long remained, based on the idea of one's duty to protect the law, that is, to defend one's personal rights. This right of resistance antedated feudalism; but it was easily assimilated to the feudal right to defy one's lord when denied justice. When looked upon as the head of a feudal hierarchy in which the members were bound to one another by mutual obligations, the king took on the character of a feudal lord whose rights and powers were limited by the feudal contract. Even the elevation of his position by the church, raising him above the people and deriving his origins from God alone, did not necessarily free him from all limitations. The king might now be a supreme judge and answer to no man, but if he did not rule in accordance with divine will he was a tyrant against whom resistance might be legitimate. The king was king not through any merit of his own but by the grace of God. He enjoyed divine favor only by obedience to the divine will.

Nevertheless, theocratic kingship, much developed by ecclesiastic writers of the twelfth century, had many points of conflict with current ideas of feudal kingship. The feudal king was expected to fulfill the obligations and duties of a good lord, to give his vassals justice, and to govern with their consent. This was a far cry from the theocratic functions of a king who suffered no human limitations. Tension between the two ideas was continually present, conditioning political developments all over Europe, leading ultimately

---

[1] See Chapter VII.

to royal absolutism here, the destruction of monarchy there. From the last half of the eleventh century all generalization about kingship breaks down, and we must look at particular examples to see the varied course of its development.

KINGSHIP IN FRANCE

The experience of the French crown illustrates how feudalism could be used as the basis for the eventual creation of a strong monarchy. After the collapse of the Carolingian empire, the tenth to the twelfth centuries witnessed the establishment in its place of several great feudal principalities ruled by powerful dynasties as well as a host of relatively independent lesser counties and districts. The early Capetians, who succeeded the Carolingians, had an immense task before them. They themselves were lords of a restricted "France," a small strip of territory around Paris. Even within the royal domain proper they had difficulty in maintaining control, and much of their effort in these earlier years, like that of their greater vassals, went into a struggle against the petty lords of their own lands over whom it was difficult to exercise any restraint.

There was therefore no question of trying to establish any kind of authority over the feudal principalities, many of which were larger, wealthier, and in some cases more effectively administered than the royal domain itself. There were more immediate problems to solve. In the face of a persistent elective principle it was difficult for the early Capetians to establish the right of primogeniture for the crown, and only by having his oldest son crowned during his own lifetime was each king able to contribute in the course of several generations to the idea of a hereditary monarchy. There was danger, also, in the jumbled conditions of feudal tenure. In the confused exchanges of lands it was inevitable that the king would obtain fiefs which had been subject to some lord or other. In other words there was a constant danger of the king's becoming someone's vassal, which had to be avoided at all cost if his position at the apex of the feudal hierarchy was not to be jeopardized. Then there were his relations with the German emperor to be considered. Until the twelfth century the kings of Germany and France were considered independent monarchs of equal rank. But the growth of imperial pretensions under Frederick Barbarossa, in conjunction with the revival of Roman law (which enshrined the imperial office above the law and implied a unified society under a single head), imposed upon mere kings at least a theoretical subjection to the emperor and gave rise to a large literature in defense of the independent nature of kingship. As it turned out, the implacable hostility of the papacy and the eventual fragmentation of the empire in Italy and in Germany made this a threat of no substance. The emperors of Germany were seen for what they were, and with the support of biblical references the idea that a king could have no temporal superior was vigorously sustained. In fact, the defenders of kingship were themselves able to use Roman law. On the grounds that "the king is emperor in his own kingdom," they applied maxims of Roman law respecting imperial authority to the king himself, at least within his kingdom. The most famous of these was that "what pleases the prince has the force of law," which in France contributed much to the elevation of the king above the law and beyond the reach of popular restriction.

What promised to be a limitation upon kingship, then, was used to promote kingship. The same was true of feudalism, for despite the practical checks imposed by the existence of large feudal principalities and by the contractual nature of the king's relations with his vassals, the kings of France did not hesitate to demand the loyalty and support due them as feudal lords. True, this was not always honored, but at least the idea of fealty to the crown as a legitimate basis for sovereignty was kept alive. The great feudatories acknowledged themselves as the king's men, his vassals; and while for a long time this placed little or no restriction on the exercise of their political ambitions, it secured the king's position at the top of the feudal hierarchy and gave him a legal basis for the ultimate subjection of his opponents when he was strong enough. In other words, although it might have been the product of political decentralization and collapse, feudalism could be used as a force, an organizing principle, whereby the great princes could establish relatively effective government within their states and the king could ultimately refashion a real monarchy throughout the kingdom at large.

This feudal supremacy grew in conjunction with theocratic ideas. As weak as he may have been, the king was the Lord's anointed.

Monarchy, an institution of biblical origin which in its imperfect way reflected the divine order of things, was consistently upheld by the bishops. The church saw in the royal person the elect of God and, on a more practical level, the defender of churches and churchmen and the giver of peace and order in an unruly world. In a day before the church at large was centralized under Rome, and when bishops who were themselves feudatories as well as spiritual leaders had rights, powers, and property to protect within the feudal arrangement, the crown promised to be the one lay power prepared to assist them. In return the church gave to the monarchy not only a strength to be derived from its teaching about the divine origin and authority of kings but also much material support by placing lands, wealth, and men at the king's disposal.

The success of the kings of France, however, rested finally on material strength. The domain of the early Capetians, from which they derived their substance, had been small and continually disrupted by uncontrollable vassals. There had been few significant additions to the domain before the accession of Philip II (1180–1223), although by this time it was better policed and managed and within it the lords who were direct vassals of the king had been brought to heel. With his mastery of the domain relatively complete and with the revenues and support of royal churches and abbeys, the king possessed sufficient resources to stabilize his relations with the feudal principalities of France. There was not, indeed there could not be, a conscious policy of the suppression of feudal lordships; but it was now possible to ensure the loyalty of the great princes and to guarantee their military and financial support when needed—in other words, to demand and to receive the feudal aids and the court service a lord had a right to expect from his vassals.

From Philip's time on, however, a significant series of additions to the royal domain destroyed the balance between king and princes, making the crown the greatest power by far and contributing much toward the eventual emergence of an absolute monarchy.

Most of these additions were made at the expense of the Angevin dynasty, which had emerged by the twelfth century as a great feudal power and a threat to the crown. By 1150 Geoffrey of Anjou had not only succeeded in establishing his control over Maine and Touraine but had also invaded and taken Normandy while England was caught up in civil war. He left this large collection of fiefs to his son Henry who, by marrying Eleanor of Aquitaine, acquired the extensive duchies of Guienne and Gascony, the counties of Poitiers, Saintes, and Bordeaux, and suzerainty over a host of important lordships and viscounties in central and southern France. The concentration of such vast holdings in the hands of a single vassal posed a serious threat to the French crown. It was an Angevin empire, stretching from the English channel to the Pyrenees, from the Atlantic to the Rhone valley. To make matters worse, in 1154 Henry also became king of England, acquiring a base of power independent of the French crown. Henceforth the kings of France did everything in their power to hamper all attempts to create a single state of these many lordships. At every opportunity they exploited the one weapon at their command—their legal rights of suzerainty—demanding homage from the kings of England for their continental holdings; intervening in their relations with their vassals; insisting upon restitution for any infringement of the complex rules of feudalism, all of which were interpreted strictly for the benefit of the French crown; encouraging and supporting feudal revolts against the English kings; and carrying on direct war against them when nothing else would do. By 1204 Philip II had swept the English out of Normandy, Maine, Anjou, and Touraine; his successors extended their control over Poitiers and much of central France; Toulouse was defended against further encroachments; and by the middle of the thirteenth century the kings of England found themselves forced to acknowledge huge losses and to hold what remained to them, Guienne and Gascony, on the basis of strict recognition of the kings of France as their liege lords. Not all the lands thus wrested from the English remained in the hands of the French crown. Some were granted in the form of fiefs to loyal supporters and members of the royal family. But many of them did. Philip II held on to large and wealthy Normandy. The French kings of the thirteenth and fourteenth centuries enjoyed material possessions the size of which made them irresistible. There was no abandonment of feudal form, however; the fiefs remaining outside the royal domain were treated in strict accordance with acceptable feudal practice, but in any conflict between the respective rights of lord and vassal the rights of the lord, the king, had no effective opposition. The steady growth of royal influence throughout France could no longer be withstood, and the feudal functions of the royal office were used to disguise the steady creation of a royal absolutism.

KINGSHIP IN GERMANY

In contrast to France, Germany promised at the outset a strong and stable monarchy but finished in disintegration. The development of duchies, which in the tenth century threatened to break up Germany into independent states, was successfully checked by the Saxon kings, whose revival of Charlemagne's imperial title accompanied the establishment of their hegemony over northern Italy. The Saxon kings of Germany were by no means feudal lords; indeed, feudalism made little progress in Germany before the twelfth century. Rather, the Saxon kings built upon the foundations of traditional Germanic kingship, strengthened by the principle of heredity of the crown at the expense of old ideas of election and by the support of the church in Germany over which they came to exercise almost complete control. The internal pacification of Germany and the relative stability of the eleventh century contributed to the beginnings of economic growth, the colonization of the eastern lands, the reclamation of land and the extension of the civilizing influence of the monasteries, thus helping to break down older regionalism to the profit of the monarchy.

The Salian kings of the eleventh century developed, in response to their many problems, what amounted to a program of royal centralization. They mobilized new rising classes in society and adapted the machinery of the primitive personal government of the Saxon kings to new circumstances. Earlier the kings had relied upon members of the royal family to administer crown lands, in the hope that family ties would ensure loyalty to the crown. Now the episcopacy was converted into an official class by Henry II (1002–1024), its members trained at the royal court, appointed to church office, and used to administer royal estates. Conrad II (1024–1039) deliberately sought support among the lesser nobility against the greater aristocracy; and Henry III (1039–1056) turned to the servile classes whose loyalty and obedience promised a reliable body of royal administrators. This last marked the beginning of a new class of *ministeriales* peculiar to Germany. Like vassals, they received land and honors; but they lacked the personal freedom and the social status of the traditional free classes. They were more obedient, therefore, and less dangerous to trust with the exercise of power. First employed by the church in the administration of ecclesiastical property, the *ministeriales* quickly took on increased importance when the crown turned to them to administer royal lands. Under Henry IV (1056–1106) they came to occupy positions of trust as intimate counselors of the king and began to break into the ranks of the aristocracy, all of which aroused a good deal of resentment. During the eleventh century, too, the lands of the royal abbeys were brought under the same management as the royal estates, marking the gradual recovery by the crown of lands and revenues earlier distributed to the church. There was also a strong attempt to consolidate the royal possessions into more contiguous, less scattered holdings through exchange, purchase, and feudal forfeiture; furthermore a concrete plan was developed to establish a permanent capital and a central royal domain in Saxony to provide the necessary material and military base for the growth of a strong monarchy.

While all of this was promising, the crown did not in the long run succeed in developing a united Germany. The ambitions of the Salian monarchs met with increasing opposition. It was not feudal opposition since, outside of Lorraine, Germany knew little of feudalism. In Germany, unlike France, the dukes had not succeeded in establishing feudal control over their territories, and counts and lesser nobles maintained a large degree of independence and fought free of all feudal subjection. In fact there survived an extensive class of free men who escaped the bonds of vassalage, owned their lands outright as allods without obligation to others, cherished their traditions of liberty and inherent personal rights, and were prepared to defend these against all threats. These lesser aristocrats slowly completed control over their peasants and evaded obligations to any superior by protestations of subordination to the monarch alone, which meant little enough since the king had no means of controlling them. They benefited from improved economic conditions, from the acquisition (through reclamation) of lands unburdened by any superior lordship, and from the founding of monasteries, which proved to be a sound form of economic investment. In maintaining control of these foundations, the revenues of which were an important part of their estates, the lesser aristocrats broke the royal monopoly over the German ecclesiastical establishment. They hotly resented the rising class of low-born *ministeriales,* and they resented too any attempt by the king to make common cause with the rising class of burghers in the new towns which they tried to subject to themselves. By the late eleventh century they were ready to throw in their lot with the papacy against the king, who by this time posed serious threats to their continued independence.

The growth of the papacy as a political institution will be considered later, but some of the effects upon Germany are pertinent here. The eleventh century papal program of reform, which hinged upon the free election of churchmen to their offices, threatened the king's control of the church. It opened the door in Germany to the growth of local influence and particularist interests, all of which were too likely to be directed against the crown, and promised to destroy the basis of German kingship as it had been constructed in the previous century. Theocratic kingship in the eyes of the church implied a limitation imposed by the "suitability" of the person of the king. The heredity principle, however, did not allow for intervention to determine the ruler's fitness to rule. The papacy therefore helped to revive the old idea, hitherto formal and symbolic, of imperial election. This placed in the hands of the German aristocracy, the electors, a powerful weapon against the crown. The papacy and the German aristocracy really had little in common. The former sought a monarchy responsive to papal leadership, not one bereft of power; the latter hoped to destroy the authority of the monarch, who threatened their particular interests. But they came together as a matter of expediency, throwing Germany into anarchy and incidentally destroying the basis for German authority in northern Italy. The civil war which lasted throughout much of Henry IV's long and troubled reign was so serious that there could be no hope of holding on to distant Italy; in Germany itself the war ultimately resulted in the recognition of the aristocratic nature of the German constitution.

After the pope's deposition of Henry in 1080, the aristocracy took advantage of the king's troubles to exercise governmental powers in their own lands on the grounds that there was no king. They reduced large elements of the free peasantry to dependence and entrenched themselves in new fortifications which limited severely the ability of the king ever to reimpose effective rule. The need for troops in this time of anarchy led also to the spread of feudalism. The *ministeriales* threw off their old servile status, converted their tenures into fiefs, built castles, and emerged as a class of free knights in the service of the princes. All the signs of feudal disintegration were present. There was even a growing differentiation within the aristocracy itself, with the emergence of a few great princes who forced lesser nobles into feudal dependence upon them.

What the new feudal aristocracy gained, the crown lost. The aristocracy successfully welded together into a single body of political authority their various rights, fiefs, lands, powers, and privileges, no matter how diverse their origins—whether exercised at one time on behalf of the crown or of some church, inherited, or merely usurped. It was impossible to check the exercise of their powers by trying to invoke old and by now forgotten custom. The aristocracy attached the various rights to their family castles which they held free of all obligations, thus implying that all their rights were part of a free heritage unlimited by any other authority. From the castle centers a rigorous administration of their estates was possible, which, when combined with the rights of government, allowed for a "territorialization" of power, the unlimited extension within a given territory of all the various rights of the lord.

These territories eventually became independent principalities. In the twelfth century the Hohenstaufen kings had no hope of turning back the clock. Faced with a development which made impossible the continued growth of the crown along the lines of the Saxons and Salians, the Hohenstaufen, especially Frederick Barbarossa (1152–1190), were forced to tailor the monarchy to fit the new conditions. Indeed, the Hohenstaufen estates, within which Frederick extended his authority to provide a secure basis for his rule, show the same pattern of territorialization as do other principalities. The old, close relationship with the German bishops was now broken; after some fifty years of independence Italian possessions would be difficult to re-win; the aristocracy in Germany was feudalized; the material basis of the crown had been shattered and could be rebuilt only with difficulty; and the papacy was now a force to be reckoned with, adamantly opposed to the reestablishment of a monarchy free from papal supervision. Frederick had, of course, some things to build upon: a universal desire for order, a general reaction in Germany against papal intervention, the Hohenstaufen estates as a material basis, and the very institutions of feudalism itself, which might be used, as they were in France and England, on behalf of the crown.

Frederick also drew upon the precepts of Roman law, now undergoing a scholarly revival in Italy, to defend the unlimited authority of the imperial office while continuing to foster older views of theocratic monarchy to check the pretensions of the papacy. To the papal suggestion that he held his kingdom as a *beneficium* conferred by the pope, he replied that he held it from God alone. But while publicists debated the theories of kingship, Frederick pragmatically sought to bend conditions to his needs. In Germany he did not struggle against feudal developments; rather he used them. He bound the greater princes to the crown as vassals whose loyalty was assured by granting them within their territories privileges of local government and the right to subordinate local lords. Thus he transformed Germany into a feudal kingdom within which his overlordship was certainly more than nominal.

Events, unfortunately, did not allow him and his successors to use feudal forms, as the kings of France used them, to develop royal authority. The crown was unable to absorb escheated or forfeited fiefs into the royal domain, as Philip II of France did, and it was constantly opposed in the founding of new towns and markets, both of which might have helped to secure a broader base for the German monarchy. This forced Frederick and his successors to seek such a base in Italy, which aroused the undying opposition of the papacy, the kingdom of Sicily, and the north Italian towns which feared for their new-won freedoms. By 1250 the dream of an Italian-based empire had been shattered. Further, the principle of election which had been revived in Germany was not allowed to die; both the papacy, which demanded the right to approve imperial elections (with increasingly less effect as time went by), and the electoral princes, whose independence was served by controlling the elections, combined to ensure that any attempt to recreate a hereditary German kingship would fail.

KINGSHIP IN ENGLAND

Although feudalism was contractual in nature, in England there were strong limitations upon any tendency toward political decentralization. William of Normandy's conquest of England in 1066 had brought in its wake not only continental feudalism but also the idea of the king's universal lordship based upon his rights of conquest. Feudal custom, a newcomer to the land, was therefore conditioned by the king's superior lordship. It was also conditioned by an earlier law of violence which continued in force and further strengthened the royal hand: war between subjects of the king was illegal as disruptive of the king's peace. The Conqueror also benefited from the traditional fealty of Englishmen to his Anglo-Saxon predecessors, which he now demanded and which was demanded in turn by his successors. The feudal right of private warfare, therefore, was strongly curtailed while the scope of royal jurisdiction was enlarged; feudal justice, having little recourse to private arms, became the special prerogative of the king's court. In the process the scope of royal jurisdiction was enlarged. But feudal ideas of the new regime were strong, and they complemented even if they did not displace the idea of fealty to the crown. For example, feudal defiance and rebellion against the king, which appears as a denial of fealty, continued to be excused and accepted as legal warfare, and was not viewed as treason until the fourteenth century.

The early government of England after the conquest was essentially aristocratic; that is to say, there were always some barons with the king, witnessing his acts, advising and assisting him. In the king's court as in other feudal regimes, there was some specialization of function, reflected in the titles of chancellor, steward, butler, constable. But because the royal fisc was large and carefully exploited, there emerged in time a staff of clerks in the royal household skilled in the administration of revenues and the exploitation of royal rights, the beginnings of an administrative bureaucracy. The preoccupation of the Norman kings of England with the royal demesne was especially marked in the reign of Henry I (1100–1135), who enriched the crown by shrewd management and by the employment of socially insignificant men rather than of magnates. This represented something of a distortion of traditional English kingship and of the role of a feudal lord, as well as a departure from the mode of government of his father William. Close cooperation with the baronage declined. Henry extracted revenues mercilessly, sold justice unblushingly, and steadily withdrew the administration of royal interests from the hands of the magnates into those of servants more immediately dependent upon the royal pleasure. The crown acquired the air of a particular interest, a private domain, causing a strain on traditional government which would not bear it long. At Henry's death the crown was momentarily weakened by a dispute over the succession between Stephen of Blois and Henry's daughter Mathilda. The dispute created the opportunity for a feudal reaction that sought to reestablish the strictly contractual basis of the crown's relations with the baronage. Stephen and Mathilda outbid one another for baronial support by granting away more than their predecessors had ever allowed to the magnates, especially control over local administration and local justice. Civil war, begun in 1138, continued off and on for fifteen years; royal government as developed by Henry was paralyzed; and Stephen, who eventually received the submission of the magnates, did so only with serious reservations on their part. For example one of them would only make homage to the king on condition that the king keep him intact in his feudal possessions and keep his promises to him. Church dignitaries took the occasion to extract promises from the king to preserve the "liberties" of the church, which had the effect of loosening royal control. Stephen's reign was therefore marked by a reversion to a contractual government between king and lords, a reaction against the narrow and personal exploitation of royal rights by Henry I.

By the middle of the twelfth century, however, theorizing about kingship was becoming increasingly popular, reflecting a growing awareness of a new force, nameless, although palpable, to be sensed in the royal office. John of Salisbury (d. 1178) was perhaps the outstanding medieval writer on political theory before the thirteenth century. He was born in England, studied in France, served in Rome, and pursued an ecclesiastical career in the service of the archbishop of Canterbury. His *Policraticus*, a treatise on the ideal ruler, is far from being an endorsement of absolute monarchy. The difference between a tyrant and a prince, he says, is that the latter follows the law; and if Roman law seems to release the prince from the bonds of law, this ought to be understood not as allowing him to perform injustice but rather as indicating that he should act not from fear of punishment but from love of justice. Despite such limitations, however, the figure of the prince and his clear superiority loom large in John's work:

> . . . the responsibility for the whole community falls on the prince. Whence deservedly is the power of all subjects gathered together in him, that he may be strong enough to seek out and perform what is needful for the welfare of each and all, and that the condition of the human commonwealth may be best disposed, when all are members of one another. In this, indeed, we follow nature, the best guide of life, which has located all the senses together in the head of man, that microcosm or little world, and has subjected all the members to it so that all may be rightly moved so long as they follow the decision of the wise head. . . . Therefore, as the usual definition has it, a prince is a public power and a certain image of the divine majesty on earth. . . . all power is from the Lord God, and has been with Him always, and is from eternity. Therefore, what a prince can do is derived from God in such a way that the power is never withdrawn from God, but He exercises it through a subordinate hand, making all things teach His mercy or His justice. Therefore, 'he who resists the power, resists the ordination of God' [Romans 13:2]. . . . when the ruler becomes cruel to His subjects it is not his own power that acts, but rather the dispensation of God, Who at His own good pleasure punishes or chastens His subjects. . . . Who speaks of the will of the prince in public affairs, since in these affairs it is not licit for him to will anything except what law or equity persuades or the consideration of the common utility requires? For in these affairs his will ought to have the force of judgment; and most rightly in such matters does his pleasure have the force of law, since his decision is not discordant from the intention of equity.[1]

Despite the safeguards of responsibility to God, kingship as a divine attribute and the royal will as law are the first steps toward a new concept, that of the state as having a power and a will of its own, as reflected in the description of the prince as a "public power." When John later goes on to say that the prince "bears the

[1] Ewart Lewis, *Medieval Political Ideas,* Vol. I (New York, Alfred A. Knopf, 1954), pp. 170–72. Copyright 1954. Reprinted by permission of Alfred A. Knopf.

public person" he is giving expression to the idea that the crown is the embodiment of the community itself.

Under the impetus of these ideas, now rapidly becoming more current, the vagueness of feudalism could be manipulated for the benefit of the crown. In England, Henry II (1154-1189) ruled a feudal state in which what we should now call his "sovereignty" became a cherished object of realization and in which the sovereign rights of the king were enforced in such a way as to draw the community closer to an exacting obedience to his will.

The practical problems facing Henry II on his accession—lawlessness, crime, the task of reestablishing order after the long civil disturbances of Stephen's reign—led him to take steps the need for which no one disputed; but he acted independently, giving greater scope to the effectiveness of the royal will, functioning more as a theocratic king than a feudal overlord. The extension of royal courts at the expense of feudal magnates created, especially in cases involving land, immediate access to a court operating under a procedure uniform throughout the kingdom. This removed delays, avoided the threat of force inherent in the customary trial by battle, and limited the effect of the local lord's prejudice or self-interest. There was also a wide extension of royal jurisdiction in criminal cases, whereby local communities were required to present those suspected of criminal acts to the itinerant justices of the king for trial.

The growth of the king's law as a visible force in the land was also marked by the development of central courts (the King's Bench to safeguard the rights of the crown and the Common Bench for those of private parties). Altogether it was a welcome extension of the king's authority over his subjects. Although at many points this extension of royal authority limited the independent activity of feudatories, it was generally accepted as directed at the common utility of the realm. Further, the king's will permeated government. It was exercised by a host of the most important officials of local government, the sheriffs, who manned the royal castles, had custody of escheated and forfeited fiefs, and were charged with the various collectorships at ports and markets—all constantly responsive to the royal command.

The barons were assured of real security in their tenures, thanks to the improvement of royal justice, but they were also increasingly at the mercy of the crown's interpretation of their obligations. That no one have his possessions disturbed without reasonable process at law nor his lands withheld without due cause—all to be shown before a neutral court of the king—provided welcome security. The partial loss of local jurisdiction thus entailed was a cheap price to pay. But Henry's justice was often sold for what it might fetch. To sue out writs of land action could be extremely costly, especially to the great. And in criminal law an arbitrariness of penalties remained.

While Henry II accepted the implications of feudalism, his reign nevertheless saw a narrowing of its liberties. His demands for feudal aids and especially his use of his rights of wardship and marriage and his exaction of relief were not well defined; in fact he took what he could, often creating individual hardship and laying the ground for a concerted reaction in subsequent years.

Despite a tendency (all too clear in retrospect) to destroy the feudal rights of the barons by a too meticulous exaction of his own, Henry II seems to have convinced the barons, and undoubtedly himself, that he was not using the vagueness of their customary obligations as an excuse to increase them immeasurably. Like a good lord, he seemed to "live of his own"; that is to say, he depended in the main upon the private resources of the crown rather than upon feudal exactions, except in cases of emergency. But large expenditures in subsequent years, especially the heavy campaigns on the continent, created a strain, and the precedents of Henry's reign would later tempt his son John into the development of what amounted to unlimited taxation.

When it came, feudal opposition was not blind reaction nor was it indifferent to what it considered good law and order. The barons saw the kingdom as a great "honor," a feudal domain in which the law could be changed only by the common consent of the lord's vassals and contributions to the lord could not be changed arbitrarily. But in fact royal government had become increasingly bureaucratic—royal officers, not vassals, gave judgment, handled finances, advised the king, and assisted him in military and administrative matters. An early reaction in Richard's reign, a prelude to the great uprising against King John in 1215, shows the barons acting not as rebellious individuals but in concert with a clear constitutional idea. The barons were not unreceptive to the institutions of royal government as they had been evolved but rather sought to share in them as the king's natural advisers and counselors.

Under John there was a continued extension, indeed distortion, of the royal power: hostages were taken to keep vassals on their good behavior; special charters of fealty were demanded in which the vassal agreed in advance to renounce lands and rights without legal recourse if suspected of opposition to the crown; and fines were levied so huge that the mere threat of their collection (which might strip a vassal of all his possessions) could hold him in line. The barons were caught without any defense, deprived of the legal security of Henry's reign, and trapped by the crown's claims which though technically legal promised the destruction of their own rights. Their reaction when it came, in 1215, was purely feudal and was justified as a legal defiance of their lord. It was directed toward subjecting royal government to "custom"—that is, to the law, vague as it was, governing feudal relations. In *Magna Carta* the king was required to promise that no free man be imprisoned, outlawed, or lose his tenure "except through the lawful judgment of his peers and the law of the land." Although the barons could not attack a king who held his office by the grace of God, they could bring him back into the feudal sphere by demanding the regular application of the common law as it then stood, and by defining and therefore limiting the extent of their obligations to him.

While *Magna Carta* was essentially a peace treaty between a lord and his defiant vassals in which only a small part of England participated, it was of critical importance for the future. The creation of the king's law as a common law and the increasing application of theocratic ideas of kingship had threatened tyranny in England. The question of whether justice was to be considered a royal gift, to be extended or withheld at the king's pleasure, or a right in itself, to be enjoyed by all independent of the personal will of the king, was definitively settled. There was no quarrel with the royal will itself provided it could be made to work within some set of acceptable rules. It was to be impersonal, not personal, impartial, not one-sided. Henceforth the struggles between the magnates and the king never threatened the destruction of a royal government which operated within the law, but only sought to resolve the question of its control.

REPRESENTATIVE GOVERNMENT

The contest, however, did not remain strictly between king and magnates. When in *Magna Carta* the barons spoke of the "community of the realm" they may have had in mind none but themselves; but as the term came to connote more than the barons alone, it made of their gains something far greater than a mere reassertion of baronial privileges. The emergence of a new social class of townsmen, whose numbers and wealth continued to multiply, forced modifications in the traditional forms of feudal government and led to a wider participation in political life not only in England but all over the continent. That participation took the form of representative institutions.

Representation is a legal fiction whereby one man takes on the person of another for the conduct of certain affairs. Its growth and acceptance were related to the increased legal interest in corporations and in the pervading influence of Roman law. Where older feudal and Germanic law insisted that all persons involved in a legal case had to be present, the very existence in the Middle Ages of so many corporate bodies—monastic chapters, cathedral chapters, towns, gilds, social and religious societies, universities, village communities, and so forth—made such a practice immensely inconvenient. It was much easier to treat the corporation in question as though it were a person, but this in turn required some means of personifying the corporation. During the late twelfth century, therefore, a large literature developed, not only on corporations themselves, but also on their personification—their representation by what were called "proctors." To be a true representative, the proctor needed "full power," *plena potestas* (the formula had been taken from Roman law) to conclude the business of the corporation he represented without referring back to it for further instructions.

The idea of representation recommended itself in an age dominated by corporate forms and obsessed with litigation, but its uses went far beyond legal cases. For example, the proctor of a community could act as its ambassador, and with "full power" granted to him could complete treaties or other agreements much faster than was otherwise possible.

It was in the area of government that representation made its greatest contribution. In times of emergency a king had the right to look beyond his normal feudal resources for the assistance necessary to perform his functions, but he had to rule according to law and justice and to protect the rights of his people. To the extent, therefore, that they were affected by his business of war and peace, taxation and legislation, they had a right to be heard. To deal with each person was out of the question. By summoning proctors from the corporate groups of his kingdom affected by his decisions, however, the king could, if the proctors had full powers delegated to them by those they represented, legally demand and receive the aid he required. The proctor performed a dual function for he had to ensure that the rights of those he represented were not abridged—that, in fact, the emergency for which an aid was demanded was real—before he gave his consent. This consent was not an expression of the sovereign will of the people, however, but rather a procedural consent which could not be withheld provided that the rights of those giving it were not abridged. It was the same as a proctor's consent at the outset to whatever decisions a court of law might make provided the customary forms and procedures of justice were observed.[1]

Nevertheless, the reader may see in representation one of the roots of modern democratic forms of government. As the feudal assemblies of the king began to include representatives of towns who, in the course of time, were able to influence government by placing conditions upon their consent to taxation, the concepts of public right and state sovereignty gradually superseded the private rights of feudalism. Representation, however, also strengthened absolutist modes of thought. True, in the Middle Ages the principle was a strong one that the prince was a lawgiver only in virtue of being chosen by and representative of his people—a reflection of the popular institutions of Germanic law. But the principle was easily warped, once conditions were favorable, by ideas derived from Roman law. Roman lawyers had developed a theory of ultimate popular sovereignty, locating the source of imperial authority in a transference to the emperor of the people's rights. As solicitous as the theory was of the people, it in fact led to the practical accept-

---

[1] Gaines Post, *Studies in Medieval Legal Thought* (Princeton, 1964), ch. II and III.

ance of the imperial will as law and of the imperial person as above the law. In 1158 the archbishop of Milan said to the emperor Frederick Barbarossa: "Know that the whole of the people's right to make laws has been granted to you," a statement which accommodated both Roman law and German tradition; but then he went on to conclude that the king's will was therefore law.[1] As we have noted, John of Salisbury spoke of the prince as bearing "the public person"—in other words, he "represented" that corporation which we might call the state. This is perilously close to identifying the state with the ruler. "What the ruler of a State does," says St. Thomas Aquinas in the thirteenth century, "the State itself is said to do."[2] In the course of time the ruler, representative of his people as bearing their corporate person, becomes the state. The saying attributed to Louis XIV in the seventeenth century, *l'état, c'est moi*, has its source in the notion of representation.

For the moment, however, we are interested in representation as it reflected the political recognition of new classes. The interests of merchants and townsmen generally coincided with those of rulers who sought to establish internal peace and order. There were sound reasons for rulers to consult with persons whose status would not normally entitle them to such consultation. The growing obligations of monarchy, the greater demand for ordered government and for the attainment through the king of the "common good," imposed obligations the extent of which could not be supported from the private resources of the ruler. Kings were increasingly forced to look beyond their customary revenues to finance the growing business of government. The doctrine of emergency—that pressing necessity affected not only the king but the entire kingdom, to be met by the resources of all—meant that in the name of the "common good" the king could go beyond the voluntary aids he might expect from vassals to demand the financial and military assistance of all his subjects. This reflected a dawning conception of a public right and a state sovereignty which would supersede in time the private rights inherent in feudalism.

It was a commonplace of the feudal world that an extraordinary grant of money to one's lord, for some unusual or particularly haz-

---

[1] *Monumenta Germaniae historica, Scriptores*, XX, 446.

[2] *Summa theologiae*, I, qu. 75, art. 4, ad 1.

ardous undertaking, required the prior consent of those who made it. In the face of recurrent financial crises, western rulers were forced to turn to the town as well as the church for help; in the event, it was not surprising to find representatives of towns present at the councils of kings. At first in Spain, later in England, Germany, Italy, France, and Bohemia there developed out of earlier feudal assemblies institutions partly representative in nature, called corts, cortes, parliament, diet, landtag, or estates-general; whatever their local variations in attendance, internal structure, or authority, these assemblies gave to new classes of people a political forum which had not hitherto existed and a place among the more traditional ruling classes. The first record we have of such an assembly comes from Burgos in 1189 under Alfonso IX of Castile; but the development was soon general, reflecting a widespread need on the part of rulers to seek the assistance of communities whose economic and political importance was obviously on the rise.

Of all such representative institutions in the Middle Ages, only the parliament of England has an unbroken development. In the Spanish countries of Aragon and Castile, the popular assemblies flourished and enjoyed considerable independence and authority in the Middle Ages, but the continued centralization of royal government and the evolution of royal absolutism gradually undermined them. The estates-general of France, brought to life by Philip IV to provide the broadest possible base for his attack on Pope Boniface VIII and continued as a convenient institution for raising taxes, did for a brief time in the fourteenth century threaten to limit the crown and aristocracy and to create for itself a central position in the constitutional development of France. But the older regional assemblies allowed the king frequently to bypass the estates-general, to receive taxes region by region; when in 1438 the estates-general allowed the establishment of a standing army and granted the king the permanent collection of the *taille* without having to refer back to the estates, the way was clear for the continued development of royal absolutism in France.

In England, where royal traditions, political forces, and theocratic ideals threatened a similar development, parliament in the long run made it impossible.

As elsewhere, the core of the English parliament was the small council of the king, comprising his officials, judges, and financial administrators, enlarged on occasion by summoning lay and ecclesiastical lords for some particular deliberation of great moment. This greater assembly was analogous to the lord's feudal court, which vassals had the duty to attend. They looked with suspicion on the tendency of the king to surround himself with a permanent corps of government specialists, and saw in parliament an instrument by which they, the "natural" advisers of the king, could exercise influence over his government.

In the thirteenth century the king also began to summon to these assemblies representative knights from the shires and representative burgesses from the towns. Where the lords attended in their capacity as individual tenants and vassals of the king, those knights and burgesses who came were elected in their localities to represent others. Although their appearance was irregular and sporadic at first, it became customary in the first half of the fourteenth century. What had been a baronial assembly was now becoming a national assembly, reflecting the kingship rather than merely the lordship of the ruler.

Although the purpose of these great assemblies was usually to approve taxes, they provided for many persons a means of petitioning the king to correct some abuse or reverse some injustice. Parliament was after all the king's court, where the king's justice might be invoked. It was precisely out of the act of petitioning that the legislative role of parliament grew. Those who sought the royal redress of some grievance did so by petition; these were collected, examined by officers appointed by the king, and perhaps formally approved or denied at the close of parliament. By the fourteenth century the knights and burgesses were collaborating by petitioning the king as a unit, thus gaining a better chance of approval. The petition became in fact the first stage in the enactment of legislation, for if the petition was accepted by the king it became law and was promulgated by the king in the form of a statute. It was in the fourteenth century also that the king was brought to agree that no basic law of the land could be changed without the approval of parliament. This together with the concession that the king would levy no taxes without the consent of parliament gave to the latter important bargaining powers with which to negotiate yet greater powers in the future.

A peculiar feature of parliament was the formation of a House of Commons separate from the lords. Such separate groupings were not in themselves unusual: in the Aragonese cortes there were four groups, the *ricos hombres* or great magnates, the *caballeros* or lesser nobility, the clergy, and the townsmen. But in England the knights of the shire, who had preceded the townsmen in attendance at parliament and who as landed proprietors had much more in common with the greater aristocracy than with the townsmen, nevertheless gradually came together with the townsmen to petition the crown. By the fourteenth century the two groups of representatives were sitting together in one house while the lords sat in another. This marked an important political coalescence of rural and urban interests and wealth, frequently reinforced socially by intermarriage. While not nearly so important as the lords, the commons grew in power because the long wars on the continent, creating a constant demand for money, led them to be courted by the government. Parliament was summoned with increasing frequency, which allowed the development of customary privileges and rights for its members and gave to it as a body a permanent and growing place in the government of England. Through its power over taxes it could and often did specify what the taxes could be used for, bargain for and obtain desired legislation, interfere with and influence the selection of royal counselors and officials. By the fifteenth century the House of Commons had the power to initiate all money bills, enjoyed relative freedom of debate, sought the king's response to all its petitions before granting taxation, and began to regulate how its own members should be elected.

VII
LAW

CUSTOMARY LAW

I N THE MIDDLE AGES, IDEAS ABOUT LAW DIFFERED widely from those held today. There being no conception of sovereignty, there could be no thought that law represented the command of a lawgiver. Among the Germans who settled in the empire, law was custom, occasionally written but usually held in the memory. Custom derived its sanction not from enactment by a ruler or some legislative body but only from age. Only old law was good law. When a community made new law, it indulged in the fiction that it was only revealing what was inherent in old custom. The law was revealed, declared, "found"—but not made.

Characteristically, law was a personal possession, a summation of the rights of an individual which were his and were not to be denied him, no matter where he might be. Roman law had been territorial in application. In some parts of the empire after the German migrations, the territorial principle was maintained, notably in Anglo-Saxon England, and in Visigothic Spain where there was a considerable fusion of Roman and Visigothic legal ideas. Elsewhere,

136

however, German tribes lived by their various customs, while Roman law persisted among those elements of the population descended from Roman citizens. It did so, however, as a personal customary code, the written sources of which were slowly forgotten. Whether Roman or German, a man was entitled to his own personal law.

In the popular mind law was a whole, not divided in the manner followed by legal scholars into natural law and positive law, divine law and man-made law. There was no part of it prior to or superior to another part; nor was there any part of it subordinate to some other greater principle such as the state or the prince. Where the state is an end in itself, as it is today, law may be viewed as the will of the state, subordinate to the ends of the state, and sanctioned by the coercive power of the state; but in the Middle Ages law, the embodiment of justice, was an end in itself. Law was primary, the state, whatever its form, secondary. "The state is only an instrument for putting the law into effect; its very being is derived from the law, which is superior to it. . . . The state exists for the law and through the law, not the law through the state."[1]

In such a view the relationship of the ruler to the law was clear. Law, the right of individuals, belonged to the community of which those individuals were a part. It was not the ruler's law. His function was to preserve it; but he was also subject to it. A king of the Visigoths, Recceswinth (649–672), was simply voicing a commonplace when he acknowledged that both king and people were bound by the law: "Therefore gladly fulfilling the divine commands, we provide moderate laws for ourselves and our subjects which [we] together with all kings who succeed us, and the entire general population of our realm are enjoined to obey, so that no person of whatsoever rank may put himself beyond the custody of the laws."[2]

Today law is enacted. Before enactment it is not law, and by a

---

[1] Fritz Kern, *Kingship and Law in the Middle Ages* (Oxford, 1948), pp. 153–54.

[2] Cited by Floyd Seyward Lear, "The Public Law of the Visigothic Code," *Speculum*, Vol. XXVI (1951), p. 3.

subsequent enactment it may again cease to be law. Having a temporal existence, law is usually easy to find. But in an age when law is timeless, an immemorial custom, how does a man know what is or is not law? Since the law was the possession of the community, it was assumed that it could be found in the conscience of the community—in practice that it resided in the hearts of the best men of the community, the *sapientes* or *boni homines* who were frequently summoned to declare the custom of the community. There was written law, of course—not systematic law codes but written records of the rights of individuals preserved in royal or ecclesiastical charters and collections of legal rules. Many of the tribal rules of the Germans were written down after their entry into the Roman Empire: Anglo-Saxon, Burgundian, Lombard, Visigothic, and Frankish customs were codified in imitation of Roman practice. But although they show some Roman influence, they all reflect the same features, a body of custom pertaining to the maintenance of private rights, concerned hardly at all with what we might call public law.

The notion that law was custom and that custom was old—that old law overrode new law, that good law was timeless and unchanging—might well have had a stultifying effect on the ability of a community to meet new conditions. In practice, however, especially because law was so inadequately recorded and subject to the hazards of memory, change was inevitable. Where old law— old custom—was ambiguous or obscure in the face of new conditions, new law was in fact created. The absence of legal training and a professional class of law keepers meant that jurisprudence was more likely to reflect contemporary needs than a precise application of a perfectly apprehended legal lore.

German law was taken up for the most part with establishing compensations for injury or damage to persons or property. There was little idea of crime in the sense of a public offense; the offenses were against individuals and were matters for private settlement between the parties concerned. Even the procedure was private. In the code of the Salian Franks, which was probably put in writing in Clovis' day, the plaintiff rather than some public authority summoned the defendant: "When anyone summons another to court, he shall go with witnesses to the house of that person, and if he is not present the summoner shall serve notice on his wife or his family that he is legally summoned."[1] The minute stipulation of fines for various kinds of wounds and other injuries, so characteristic of these codes, had as its purpose the limitation of the private blood feud between families in the interest of the general peace of the community.

While it might be possible to determine from an assembly of knowledgeable members of the community what were the rights of the concerned parties according to local custom, there was great uncertainty in determining guilt or innocence and in establishing the validity of evidence. The means adopted to determine guilt or innocence grew out of old pagan practices, their authenticity confirmed by their acceptance by the church. Unlike Roman law where the plaintiff had to establish his charge, in areas of Germanic customary law the defendant frequently had to clear himself from accusation. Compurgation was the most widespread practice. The accused had to find a body of oath-helpers, compurgators, who would swear to his credibility. The solemnity of the oaths, the threat of divine retribution for bearing false witness, the difficulty that the notoriously guilty might have in getting others to perjure themselves on his behalf, gave some assurance that the truth would out.

Where compurgators could not be found, the credibility of the accused was established in other ways, all designed to reveal the judgment of God. Old pagan practices of casting lots or of holding judicial combats were generally discouraged by the church, in the latter case with no success whatever. But the ordeal, presided over by a churchman, became the preferred means of testing guilt or innocence, or of establishing the credibility of someone suspected of perjury. There were many kinds of ordeals. Hincmar of Reims in the ninth century described the cold water ordeal as follows:

Now the one to be examined is bound by a rope and cast into the water. And it is evident that he is bound for two reasons; to wit, that he may not be able to practice any fraud in connection with the judgment, and that he may be

---

[1] O. J. Thatcher and E. H. McNeal, A Source Book for Medieval History (New York, 1905), p. 16.

drawn out at the right time if the water should receive him as innocent [i.e., if he should sink] so that he does not drown. In this ordeal of cold water whoever, after the invocation of God who is the Truth, seeks to hide the truth by a lie, cannot be submerged in the waters, for the pure nature of the water recognizes as impure and therefore rejects as inconsistent with itself such human nature as has once been regenerated by the waters of baptism and is again infected by falsehood.[1]

There were other kinds of ordeals, all sanctified by the church with masses, communions, benedictions, special prayers, and adjurations to the defendant to tell the truth. In the ordeal of hot water the priest blessed a cauldron of water, which was then boiled; a stone was put in it, and the accused had to reach in and get it out, after which his hand was bound up for three days. If, after the wrapping was removed, his hand showed signs of healing, his innocence was established; if not, then his guilt. The ordeal of hot iron required the accused to pick up a piece of red hot iron, take two steps, drop it, and then hasten to the altar to have his hand bound for three days before examination. Sometimes the accused was required to walk barefoot on hot metal plowshares or through a large fire, as Peter the Hermit did while on the First Crusade to verify his story that he had found the lance that had pierced the side of Christ during the crucifixion.

The ordeal was usually the last resort of a court unable to establish the credibility of accused or witness in highly suspicious cases. In the twelfth century the growth of legal studies and the development of a more systematic approach to the rules of evidence led to the condemnation of the ordeal as irrational and ineffective, while churchmen increasingly tended to look upon it as sacrilegious. In the Fourth Lateran Council (1215), Pope Innocent III forbade any priest's participating in an ordeal, thus depriving such tests of that divine sanction without which they could hardly be said to reveal God's judgment. The decision came just a year too late for a certain William Trenchebof in England, who was accused before the king's

---

[1] Adapted from University of Pennsylvania, *Translations and Reprints*, Vol. VI, no. 4, p. 11.

justices "for having handed to Inger of Faldingthorpe the knife with which Inger slew Wido Foliot. His story not being believed, let him purge himself by [the ordeal of] water. He has failed, and is hanged."[1] It was one of the rare cases of a failure in the ordeal. William should not have held his breath.

Unlike the ordeal, which rapidly disappeared once it was abandoned by the church, trial by combat remained an ineradicable judicial process despite all the condemnations of a church opposed to violence. Trial by combat, in which the contesting parties fought it out or chose champions to fight on their behalf, was merely the formalization of the earlier blood feud. As a form of judicial settlement it was no more rational than the ordeal, but among those whose way of life was ordered by warfare, whose possessions and social rank were ultimately dependent on military prowess, and whose highest ideals were those of bravery, courage, and pride in arms, trial by combat was a logical method of judicial settlement. It was condemned not only by the church but eventually also by rulers who saw in it a threat to order or an affront to reason. It persisted, however, throughout the Middle Ages, its ultimate demise the slow work of limitations imposed from time to time by royal authority and the development of fairer methods for defending people's rights.

THE COURTS

In the Merovingian state there had been judicial subdivisions of relatively small compass called "hundreds" (a term of Germanic origin) in which a count, acting on behalf of the king, summoned to his court all the freemen of the district from among whom jurors would be selected. Here the law was pronounced and the findings made by the jurors themselves, acting on behalf of the community; the count merely presided and effected the sentences. Under Charlemagne two courts at different levels were substituted in order to

---

[1] F. W. Maitland, *Select Pleas of the Crown*, Selden Society Publications, Vol. I (London, 1888), p. 75.

relieve local inhabitants from too frequent summonses. The count continued to hold court in the hundred only three times a year for major cases, where all the inhabitants were still required to attend; but the far more numerous minor cases were dealt with in more frequent courts to which jurors from the community were alone required to attend.

Thus the king met his obligations to defend the law not so much by legislating as by providing the means whereby the community itself could determine the law, and by making available the force to effect the community's decisions. The right of holding court was a royal right. The disintegration of the Carolingian state was reflected in the dispersion of this right; now every man strong enough wanted to be a judge for the income as well as the power that came with jurisdiction. Not only those who had been delegated some judicial authority by the crown (counts and their assistants, *missi dominici,* and immunists who acted as judges within their own territories on behalf of the king) but many who had had no legal right to hold court soon established their jurisdiction over as many persons as possible. Whoever controlled a group of lowly dependents or received rents and services from some rural tenants now claimed a legal jurisdiction over them as well. That many of these dependents were unfree, or were in the process of becoming so, led to their complete submission. Only where the individual maintained his freedom did he succeed in being heard by an assembly of free men—his peers. Popular courts continued to exist, functioning under the presidency of a magnate as they had before under a royal representative. The popular courts still required the attendance of all members of the community, but they tended to exclude both an unfree peasantry, which had to submit to the manorial court of the lord, and a growing nobility, which refused to demean itself by attendance.

In some areas, notably northern France, the old popular hundred courts virtually disappeared, their place taken by the baronial court for knightly persons and the seigneurial court for the peasantry. But in broad areas of Europe, especially of incomplete feudalization where allodial land was extensive, the ancient courts of the hundred and the county continued to flourish. Even in England where they not infrequently fell into the hands of the baronage, they remained significant institutions of local government as of local justice until the royal courts took their place.

FEUDAL LAW

The court of the feudal baron only rarely absorbed the functions of the older tribunals, but rather grew up alongside them in response to the appearance of an aristocracy with its own customary law, the law of the fief and of military service. The basis for the legal relationship between lord and vassal was supplied by the old notion that law was the possession of the community and that no ruler, no matter what his authority, could change it without consulting its members. As feudal customs of tenure, inheritance, aids, military service, wardship, marriage, and so forth, developed, they came to be thought of as any body of custom, as individual rights which were timeless and unchanging. They could therefore be "declared" or "found" only by the community whose law it was, in this case the vassals. Thus the Germanic notion of customary law was easily assimilated to the institution of feudalism.

The central feature was the lord's court, to which all vassals owed suit and where they sought a defense of their rights. Despite the fact that the court belonged to the lord, it was not he but the members of the court, his vassals, who were to render judgment.

The idea that where there is no justice there is no authority was firmly entrenched in feudalism. Should the vassal, as was common enough, fail to receive a just hearing in his lord's court, he could claim that the lord's authority no longer existed; he could, in other words, defy his lord and break the feudal tie. A more frequent and successful measure, from the thirteenth century on, was to appeal to his overlord, his lord's lord. In France and England this was most often the king, always anxious to interfere in the feudal relations of his greater vassals and, by drawing their disputes to his own court, to broaden his jurisdiction at their expense. The feudal court, therefore, while presided over by a lord, was a court of customary law which bound the lord as it did all others and where judgment was to be given by all those whose duty it was to attend.

As unwritten custom, often expressed in general terms and open to all kinds of application, feudal law had a vagueness and imprecision that led to much litigation, defiance, appeals, and warfare. As feudalism grew more complex and the relations between the members of the nobility more confused, even the question of which feudal court had competence often could not be settled. Under the influence of the growing knowledge of Roman civil law in the twelfth century, the imprecisions of feudal law began to give way before the discussions of lawyers who undertook to codify and to explain the law of the feudal court. In the process there was continued emphasis on the old idea of the superiority of law over persons of whatever rank. In the feudal court both the vassal and the lord could obtain judgment if either thought that his rights had been abridged by the other. But where the lord was also the king, there were elements at work which were not in themselves feudal. The king was the inheritor on the one hand of ideas which saw his office as divine and his elevation to it as God's work, and on the other of a tradition that he was the guardian of justice for all his people, not merely his immediate vassals—that his was public law.

ROYAL LAW

The idea of public law, while dormant during the Middle Ages, was not dead. Some of the Germanic codes, notably the Visigothic, defined certain offenses as being against the public interest. Charlemagne, while leaving untouched the various customs of his subjects, did not hesitate to issue orders of empire-wide application, amounting to legislation on behalf of what he conceived to be the public interest. Many kings, notably in Anglo-Saxon England, had been collectors, codifiers, and promulgators of customary codes; and while traditional attitudes—of the king as subject to law and the compilation of law as old custom—were never absent, the role of the king in preserving the law did not exclude the act of selection and emendation on behalf of the community.

In the face of traditional views of the law, however, the notion of public law was rudimentary. The concept of public law grew in conjunction with two ideas: the first was the growth of the idea of the state—a corporate body with interests apart from the several interests of individuals and with rights which, at least in times of emergency, took precedence over the rights of individuals. One factor which contributed to the growth of the idea of the state and public law was the enlarged study of Roman law from the twelfth century on. According to Roman law, reinforced in the thirteenth century by ideas derived from Aristotle's *Politics*, the "common good" was the proper end of all government.

The second and more immediate influence, however, was the extension of royal authority in response to traditional ideas of the king's role as the guardian of justice. Through much of the twelfth century, royal justice remained mostly a matter of protecting the king's personal rights. Questions of criminal or civil law, if they did not touch the person of the king, remained questions of local justice to be dealt with in seigneurial courts or in the popular courts of the hundred or county. Even where, as in England, the county court remained amenable to royal direction, it was usually dominated by the interests of local lords. Local justice remained for the most part popular or feudal, not royal.

But the monarchy was more than a private institution or a feudal office. It had a latent popular base. Not only sub-vassals but indeed all of the king's subjects could appeal to him when they felt they had suffered an injustice and he could do something about it. The traditional role of the king as the defender of the law required his intervention; and the exercise of an authority that had as its only justification the maintenance of right, when carried on in the interest of more and more people, turned royal courts into public courts and royal law into public law. Many treatises dealt with the question of the misuse of this authority, but in terms that made clear that the authority could not be questioned so long as it conformed with what was right and just.

The practical and political advantages to be gained from the maintenance of internal peace within a kingdom, to say nothing of the proceeds from fines and confiscations, may explain the readiness of a ruler to extend his immediate jurisdiction. In doing so, however, either by encouraging appeals to his court by those who claimed to have been injured or wronged, or by requiring the local popular courts to report crimes and to produce the offenders before his justices, he was responding to the demands of his office made explicit in his coronation oath. Bracton's treatise in the thirteenth century on the laws of England laid down what had long been commonplace, that the king when crowned should swear that all his Christian subjects should enjoy peace during his reign and that he would put down all rapacity and iniquity no matter what the rank of the perpetrator, "that all men may through his justice enjoy peace undisturbed."[1]

---

[1] R. W. Carlyle and A. J. Carlyle, *A History of Medieval Political Theory in the West,* Vol. III (Edinburgh and London, 1928), pp. 35–36, n. 1.

In England the process led to the development of a common law, that is, the gradual replacement of the varieties of customary and feudal laws by the machinery of royal justice, made available to more and more of the kingdom. Criminal justice slowly became the same everywhere; in civil cases, if one could pay the price (an important limitation) one could obtain from the royal court a writ to initiate a case before the king's justices or, where it was already in the hands of a privately controlled court, to have it removed to a court of the king. Common writs, increasingly common juridical procedures, common courts under the king's judges, in time forged a common law which obliterated the local customs of provincial England and the private jurisdictions of an earlier feudalism.

ROMAN LAW

Roman law continued to exist in large parts of the west after the empire within which it had been such a great unifying force had ceased to exist. This was especially the case in Italy where Roman civilization, despite the decay of Roman political power, continued to exert a strong hold. Roman law owed something to the legislation of the rulers of the late empire but far more to custom and to the commentaries of professional jurists. Roman law had been codified from time to time during the late imperial period of Roman history, and it was the code of Theodosius (438) which long continued in force in the Italian peninsula, side by side with the law of the Lombards which it had penetrated and modified. A later codification by the emperor Justinian not only brought the Theodosian code up to date but also did for the body of precedents in the works of professional jurists what Theodosius had done for the statutes of emperors. Some twelve books of imperial statutes appeared in 529, and a revised edition appeared in 534; fifty books, the *Digest*, condensed from the writings of the professional jurists of the second and third centuries, appeared in 532; and the next year the *Institutes*, a compilation of the principles of Roman law for the use of law students, was published. Together with some of the later legislation of Justinian himself and his immediate successors, called *Novels*, these comprised the *corpus iuris civilis*, the body of civil law.

In some parts of the western empire, Roman law had been effectively obliterated by the settlement of large numbers of Germans. In others where conqueror and conquered remained relatively aloof, Roman law continued in force as the personal law of the Roman as opposed to that of the barbarian neighbor. For the most part it ceased to exist as a written code or as a subject of formal study; but there did persist as many of its principles and procedures as could be useful to a more localized and simplified society, transmitted by judges and notaries who taught their successors the elements of their trade. In Italy, there also persisted some first-hand formal knowledge of Justinian's code, or at least of parts of it, evidence of which can be found in compendia of extracts made by ecclesiastics and monks whose interest was undoubtedly sustained by the fact that the church had since late antiquity been thought of as subject to Roman law.

By the eleventh century, Roman law had emerged as a subject of study independent of the curriculum of schools of grammar. At Bologna its study soon came to represent a return to a legal science unknown since the third century. The methods of the glossators, who subjected the Justinian corpus to a careful scrutiny, elucidated the legal principles lying behind particular enactments, developed techniques to reconcile apparent contradictions, and provided scholars with a scientific discipline of wide application and a body of legal principles which, though derived from antiquity, could be adapted to contemporary needs.

Roman law had a wide effect in Europe. The influence of Roman law studies in the twelfth and thirteenth centuries added to or modified older views of kingship, contributed classical notions of the political state, the *res publica*, as a fictive person, and justified government in the common good or common welfare, all of which assisted in producing the idea of the state, the public law, and the king as fount of that law. By the thirteenth century kings, emperors, and popes were manipulating the terminology of legal scholars to claim an authority to legislate and to judge far broader in scope than could have been imagined in an earlier day; kingship began to reveal an element of absolutism which was perhaps always latent but had been held in check by the popular elements of a Germanic tradition and the limitations imposed by feudalism. Even in England, where the institutions of the common law and the development of English legal education limited its influence, Roman law had considerable effect in the twelfth and thirteenth centuries, in discussions of the abstract nature of justice and the role of the ruler in its establishment.

Elsewhere than in England the impact of Roman law was far more profound, for often it met with customs and institutions already reflecting early Roman origins. In Spain, where regional laws had grown out of Visigothic and Roman customs, the popularity of the new law was very great and influenced the promulgation of codes. The most notable of these, the *Siete Partidas* of Alfonso X of Castile in the thirteenth century, virtually became a common law for the kingdom, replacing the multifarious local customs which had preceded it. The legal unity that resulted, of course, made a large contribution to the political unity that later followed, as well as to the authority of the king.

In the Middle Ages Roman law had persisted in the form of custom throughout southern France, and the new law quickly gained a validity there either alongside or in some cases in place of prevalent custom. In the north, where feudal law was firmly entrenched, the legislative activity of French kings in their *ordonnances* exhibited the strong influence of Roman law, and the discussion of sovereignty by feudal lawyers was a measure of the penetration of Roman legal concepts:

Truly the king is sovereign over all and has of right the general care of all his kingdom. He can therefore make whatever laws he wishes for the common good, and whatever he orders must be obeyed. There is no one beneath him so great that he cannot be hailed into the king's court for default of the law or false judgment and for any matter affecting the interests of the king. No one can make a new regulation with the force of law, or establish new markets, or new customs, other than the king of France, except in times of necessity. . . . But the king can do so when he pleases and when he sees that it is to the common good.[1]

Thus in France the role of the king in maintaining the common good implied a far greater prerogative than in England. There Bracton, no less familiar with the Roman law maxim that "what

---

[1] Philippe de Beaumanoir, *Coutumes de Beauvaisis*, 1043, A. Salmon, ed., Vol. II (Paris, 1900), pp. 24–25.

pleases the prince has the force of law" and that the prince was absolved from the law, nevertheless is careful to insist that the king can be thought of as the source of law only if he consults the magnates of his council. In Germany there was no successful resistance to the adoption of Roman law, which in its completeness, harmony, and unity exhibited an obvious superiority to the confusion of German tribal customs. Students from Germany poured into Bologna and other Italian university cities and returned home to advocate the adoption of a law whose systematic treatment of general legal principles was among its many obvious advantages. The reception of Roman law in Germany was hastened, no doubt, by the idea that the German empire was in some mysterious fashion a modern continuation of the Roman Empire of antiquity, and that therefore only the Roman law was worthy of the empire.

CANON LAW

The wide popularity of the study of Roman law owed much to the political debates of the eleventh and twelfth centuries about the respective authorities of *imperium* and *sacerdotium*, of prince and priest, emperor and pope. Roman law provided a good deal of ammunition then and later to all those who sought to base an independent secular power on old and venerable legal authority. For here was a code, the antiquity and authenticity of which were unquestioned, to which the church had been subjected and in which the emperor appeared as a supreme legislator, his law overriding all custom, his will unlimited by any other agency. In the twelfth century Frederick Barbarossa saw the advantage in encouraging the professors of Bologna in their study of Roman law; later, by the application of the neat formula that the king was an emperor within his own kingdom, the king of France could extract from Roman law whatever of its content and principles might contribute to royal absolutism.

But the study of Roman law was also encouraged by those whose views about secular government were quite different—by bishops and popes who saw in thorough legal training many advantages to the church itself. What few glimpses we have of the continuity of legal knowledge in Italy after the collapse of the empire in the west reveal the activities of churchmen. And the revival of formal legal education in Italy saw a large-scale participation of students whose careers lay not only in service to secular rulers but also in service to the church. The result was the development of a law of the church, canon law, by men who were thoroughly acquainted with the content and principles of Roman law and could apply them to a large body of new material. It was not so much the particular rules of a now long dead society which attracted them as the clearly defined and lucid legal concepts which they could put to use.

Although canon law as a legal discipline took its growth from the twelfth century, this is not to say that the church had hitherto had no law. Churchmen governed themselves and their affairs on the basis of rules derived from old and varied sources, including the Bible, the canons of early church councils, papal letters which could be cited in support of some precedent or some legal principle, elements of Roman law itself, local church customs and local church synods, and the writings of early church fathers. But the contrast between this disorganized body of material and the legal system of the Roman Empire was enormous. By the sixth century, Roman law, as it existed in the Justinian collection, was a perfected system while canon law was still in its infancy.

Much of the earlier law of the church in the west had been Greek in origin, derived for the most part from the canons of ecumenical councils held in the eastern empire. The needs of local bishops in the administration of their dioceses led, from the fifth century on, to compilations here and there of small collections as guides in the treatment of particular matters. Not until the eighth and ninth centuries did any collections of more than local interest appear. Like other churches in the west, the church in Rome had its own collections; and it was the customs of the church of Rome which began to gain a wide recognition in the west, mainly because of the authority of the emperor Charlemagne, who had obtained them from Pope Hadrian I in 774 and required their observance in all the churches of his empire. The confusion of codes and local customs continued, however, a reflection of the lack of cohesion and communication in the western church, until systematic collections were made by Burchard of Worms, early in the eleventh century, and Ivo of Chartres near the end of the century. Both produced large collections of church law, systematically organized and therefore of practical use to those who wished to consult them. Ivo of

Chartres made an additional contribution in the form of a prologue; here he laid down principles for the interpretation and harmonizing of conflicting legal texts, insisting that the texts ought not to be read out of context, and establishing a hierarchy of authority— pope, general council, local council—to assist the reader in sorting out apparent contradictions. While the works of neither Burchard nor Ivo gained universal recognition, they provided much material for a Bolognese law teacher of genius, Gratian, who produced around 1140 a yet more complete collection. The usefulness of Gratian's collection gave it a wide popularity and an authority never before achieved. Since Gratian was well trained in Roman law, his work in church law was markedly different from and superior to everything that had gone before. In it the texts are dated, placed in their historical setting, organized by topic, explained, and finally harmonized by the application of the scholastic method of citing authorities pro and con with a final solution supported by further legal evidence. All of this made Gratian's work so attractive to legal scholars as to put all other collections out of business and to achieve a place for the work as the basic textbook of canon law, first in Bologna and finally throughout the western church.

At the time of the appearance of Gratian's *Decretum*, as it was called, the papacy was entering into a period of great legislative activity as a result of its struggles with the German emperor and its enlarged role in European affairs. There quickly came into existence, therefore, a growing body of "decretals," papal letters on particular matters which raised points of law. It became increasingly necessary to organize collections of these to supplement the work of Gratian. In 1234 Pope Gregory IX finally published an official collection of such legislation up to his own pontificate, which he sent to the university of Bologna for the teachers there to lecture on. Thus the papacy took the inevitable step of legal codification. Gregory's *Decretals* did not supersede Gratian's *Decretum* but supplemented it. With those added by Boniface VIII in 1298, and after some further additions in the fourteenth century, the corpus of canon law remained unchanged down to its complete revision in 1917.

Canon law was the law of the church; that is, it dealt with the church hierarchy and its jurisdiction, legal procedure in ecclesiastical courts, the rights and duties of the clergy and of monastic communities. It also had much to say about those areas of life which today would be considered matters of civil or criminal law but in the Middle Ages were reserved to church courts—marriage and moral offenses. Canon law was more, however, than a set of rules for the internal life of the church. It inevitably had much to say, or at least to imply, about the relations that ought to obtain between the church and the secular world, and in the hands of canon lawyers it provided the material for the development of a full-scale theory of papal world monarchy.

The debt of canon law to Roman law was vast. Much of the procedure of Roman law was borrowed intact, as well as the entire technical apparatus of the civil-law commentators. Even more important, the development of a common law of the church provided a sound legal base for the evolution of the idea of the church as a unified corporation with the pope as its head. Christian society, if it was to be more than an abstract concept, needed a system of law which would at once bind it together and make it visible. This is what canon law did.

VIII
THE
CHURCH

EARLY ORGANIZATION

I N THE FIRST TWO CENTURIES OF ITS EXISTENCE,
the Christian church was scattered in small groups throughout
the Mediterranean, communicating with each other only intermittently and with great difficulty. Its organization was one of early
diversity followed by progressive standardization and the development of common forms. Its growth was facilitated by many things:
the lack of internal political barriers within the Roman Empire,
making travel and communication easier than it might have been;
the common language of a simplified Greek around the Mediterranean; and the dispersed communities of Jews within which the
earliest Christians first found a haven. Not the least important, however, was the inherent appeal of its message, a universal appeal at
a time when the horizons of the world had broadened. The affairs
of local communities had faded into insignificance within the world-
wide empire. Local religious cults associated with them had ceased

154

to have meaning. As local citizenship made way for the universality of empire, so the familiar local deities receded before the vision of a single God speaking to the universality of men.

The growth of Christianity was limited, however, by sporadic persecution, at the outset prompted by local ignorance and superstition, but later directed on a larger scale by the Roman state. Furthermore, Christianity had competitors in the many mystery cults which spread from the east throughout large parts of the empire. But its greatest obstacle came from within, from internal conflict in matters of faith and tradition. In the face of the outright persecution that threatened Christianity's very extinction, unity and harmony were all the more desperately needed. The result was a rapid development of the office of bishop, whose role of sustaining his flock against persecution grew increasingly important. The bishop came to be looked upon as the touchstone of orthodoxy at a time of uncertainty, the guardian of the true faith, the carrier of the correct traditions inherited from the apostles and held in common with the other bishops of distant Christian communities. By the time Christianity was legalized in the early fourth century and official persecution was transformed into official favor under Constantine the Great, the church had become an expanding society with a clearly defined and relatively uniform hierarchical organization. The primitive offices mentioned by St. Paul (". . . first apostles, secondly prophets, thirdly teachers, then miracles, then gifts of healing, helps, government, divers kinds of tongues") had now long since disappeared, with most of the functions assumed by the bishop assisted by priests, deacons, and others in lower church orders. The bishop ruled his community in patriarchal, indeed monarchical, fashion, and his rule became increasingly important in the west as the Roman state gradually ceased to function there and many elements of local government fell into his hands.

The basic unit of the church, therefore, was the bishop's *parochia,* which did not begin to be called by the more familiar word "diocese" until the seventh century. The *parochia's* center was a town or city, reflecting the urban nature of the church in its early centuries. It took a long time for Christianity to spread into the countryside. By the sixth century, however, rural dioceses were coming into existence, marking the steady progress of the struggle against paganism in rural areas. Where there was a bishop in the neighborhood, the rural district was gradually subdivided into parishes administered by members of the bishop's *familia,* his household staff, which comprised most of the clergy of the diocese. The *familia* were recruited as boys, trained in the bishop's household, educated at his hands, and, after moving up through the lower orders, ordained by him to the priesthood. The bishop's household, therefore, remained for long the most important—often the only— center of education and a continuing source of clergy for an expanding organization. As rural parishes became more thoroughly organized, their curates came to reside in them rather than with the bishop and to exercise some of the functions at one time performed only by him, for example, baptism and absolution after penance (although confirmation remained a sacrament to be administered by the bishop alone).

The territorial organization of the church owed much to that of the imperial administration which it replaced. The words *diœcesis* and *civitas,* from which we derive the words "diocese" and "city," had described territorial units of the empire, the latter being a subdivision of the former. Both were borrowed by the church, but used differently. The territory within which the bishop exercised his authority was more often than not the Roman *civitas.* For some time, however, his territory was called a *parochia,* and eventually, long after the original meaning of the term was forgotten, his diocese. The word *civitas* was then applied to that place where he had his church, which explains the medieval meaning of the word "city" as the residence of a bishop. In the course of time dioceses came to be grouped into "provinces," another term (*provincia*) borrowed from Roman imperial organization. In the province one bishop, usually because of the antiquity of his church, enjoyed a preeminence if not a legal authority over his neighbors. He was the "archbishop," or metropolitan. Not infrequently the shape and size of dioceses changed. Those ruined or devastated by wars were joined to others; those grown too large were divided; and in areas where Christianity penetrated for the first time and won converts, as in Germany, new missionary dioceses and provinces were established. Judging from contemporary practice such changes as these required the agreement of the bishop of Rome, the neighboring bishops, and the temporal prince.

THE OFFICE OF BISHOP

The bishop himself was chosen by the "election" of the clergy and people of his diocese. What had been, however, the usual practice in the early church became in time a juridical formula, rarely applied though not forgotten. The phrase "clergy and people" was vague enough to invite all kinds of theoretical definitions. One school of thought saw the clergy as the effective electors, the people to be called upon only to assent, to give formal approval, to a choice already made. Another saw a combination of the more important laity and the clergy acting together in the choice of the bishop, excluding others from effective participation. In attempting to distinguish among the clergy who should participate in the election, the more aristocratically minded claimed that the neighboring bishops ought to be the electors; a second group claimed that all the diocesan clergy in question should be concerned; but a third group, in the end the most successful, believed that the clergy of the church in which the bishop-elect would have his seat—the cathedral canons—should be the electors. The first to know of the vacancy and therefore the first to act, and the most immediately concerned about the choice, they could take concerted action as a corporate group to get their own candidate elected. By the tenth century even the papacy had come to recognize their electoral right. Likewise there grew a tendency to determine who among the laity should participate in the election; among these the bishop's immediate vassals and dependents claimed and frequently made good their right to take a part. In practice, however, while various groups might occasionally succeed in controlling episcopal elections, the authority of the temporal prince frequently blotted out the rights of others for many reasons.

Bishops became bishops only after consecration by other bishops, thus preserving an unbroken succession. Traditionally this rite of consecration came to be performed by the archbishop, who thus exercised some control over episcopal election. In the collapse of the Carolingian empire in the ninth century, some archbishops sought in the absence of strong princes to extend their authority, seeking to control the choice of bishops in their provinces without reference either to temporal authority or to the papacy. The archbishops were for a while able to profit from the feebleness of the monarch and the remoteness of the pope. But the development of the office of archbishop as a kind of local papacy had no canonical or historical justification, and it soon subsided under the onslaught of all the interested parties. The papacy encouraged the direct reliance on itself of bishops who were only too eager to escape the immediate control of archbishops. Also, the increasing influence of lay magnates over episcopal elections frequently forced the archbishop to accept the candidate of some king or count, to acquiesce in an appointment without being consulted, or even to tolerate the appointment of a bishop without performing his consecration. Although canon law insisted on the right of the metropolitan to consecrate the bishops of his province, he was on the whole quite incapable of checking the growing control of the bishops by lay powers. Consequently the office of archbishop remained one of prestige and dignity bereft of any juridical significance.

During this period, the Carolingian tradition that the king protected the church was not forgotten nor was the corollary that no election could be conducted without his permission. Indeed the king often presented a candidate himself, and he was difficult to refuse; in any event no bishop-elect could be consecrated without his consent. The dissolution of Carolingian authority which began in the ninth century dissipated this power over churches and episcopal elections. The successors of Louis the Pious claimed the right to control elections in the part of the empire over which they ruled, but as their own authority declined they exercised it only in limited areas. The usurpation of royal authority by a growing landed aristocracy often included the right to control the election of bishops. This was an important and cherished right, for it meant effective control of large estates and considerable wealth. In Germany, a resurgent empire in the late tenth century managed in time to check the attempts of the dukes to "mediatize" the bishoprics— to interpose themselves between the crown and the bishops. In fact much of the royal administration came to be based on the bishops who, as the king's appointees, were amenable to his direction. Wherever German domination spread, whether in Lorraine or in Italy, the tendency was always the same, to deprive local magnates of their control of the election of bishops, bringing the elections directly under the emperor.

In many parts of France the king was not strong enough to do the same. Many dukes and counts exercised control over bishoprics

—sometimes by force or by exerting pressure on the electors to have their own candidates elected, sometimes without challenge, their control of episcopal elections viewed merely as an exercise of rights with royal permission. By the end of the tenth century there was a fairly fixed division of control. The king held some—four archbishoprics (Reims, Sens, Tours, Bourges) and about twenty bishoprics out of a total of seventy-seven, a minority but, with very few exceptions, territorially compact. The rest fell under the domination of various magnates, some of whom held an imposing number, others only one or two.

Up to the eleventh century, the bishop's election appeared to be a public affair in which a large crowd gathered in the church to acclaim the candidate. In fact, the real election was usually over. If those in power had settled on a candidate, the public gathering and the acclamation were mere formalities.

Temporal control of the office of bishop was not as anomalous as it may appear to the modern observer. The endowment of churches by Carolingian monarchs and the employment of bishops as royal officials had brought about a close association of the episcopal office and the exercise of temporal authority. The bishop took on secular duties like the counts: his office was as much temporal as spiritual, involving judicial, fiscal, and even military duties. His rights of local government came from the "immunity," a royal concession which withdrew the bishop's land and people from the jurisdiction of regular royal officials whose place was taken by the bishop himself. In the Carolingian period most bishoprics had come to enjoy this right, a technique adopted to protect churches from the encroachments of powerful laymen without abdicating royal authority. With the subsequent weakening of the crown, however, the bishop was left as something of an independent ruler, in effect the count of his territory.

It was a short-lived independence if it was ever effective. Along with the general acceptance of the idea that the crown had authority over the church went the corollary that the crown had a duty to protect the church; authority and protection went hand in hand. When royal authority collapsed, the duty of "protection" usually slipped into the hands of others, and with it invariably went authority. Royal protection had often been exercised by a layman, called an "advocate," appointed by the king for that specific purpose. With the collapse of royal control, the advocate now had an opportunity to establish his personal control over the church in question. Great families frequently gathered several such advocacies into their hands, thus gaining control over several churches. Since protection implied lordship, episcopal independence had little chance of development within the area of the Carolingian empire; in Italy, however, after the decline of royal authority, the bishops enjoyed considerable independence in both spiritual and temporal matters from the late ninth century to the mid-eleventh. Elsewhere, however, a secular lord gave the bishopric to a clergyman for a life term, invested him with the symbols of his office—a temporal as well as a spiritual one—and then installed him in his cathedral. The bishop swore fealty and in many respects was looked upon as a vassal.

THE BISHOPRIC AS PROPERTY

The bishopric itself was akin to a benefice or fief, to be handed out to loyal supporters and taken back if they proved disloyal. The bishopric could and did receive gifts of land, and many came in time to comprise large estates. The possessions of the bishop constituted his "honor," on the analogy of the possessions of any great magnate—a collection of benefices compensating past services and making possible service in the future. Inevitably the bishop who administered such estates came to be incorporated into the feudal view of society. He received his diocese and church from a king or great prince, was considered as vassal as well as a great lord, had vassals in turn who might fulfill his military obligations among other things, and worked his estates with tenants and serfs supervised by his officials.

When a see became vacant, because of the incumbent's death or his deposition or transfer elsewhere, it returned to the prince, during which time its revenues became his; during the vacancy he exercised the right of patronage, the right of the bishop to appoint to lesser church offices within the diocese. As often as not offices were sold and the revenues of the bishopric used to reward vassals or to benefit the prince in other ways. No layman, however, sought to hold an episcopal see indefinitely, though they did in many cases hold abbeys and take the title of abbot for themselves. There were no lay bishops as there were lay abbots. It would have been too audacious for a layman to call himself a bishop without episcopal consecration. But the bishopric itself was often an item of commerce, to be disposed of by sale, gift, rent, as a form of dowry, or as an inheritance, the revenues of which might (like other parts of an estate), be divided among heirs. If a son were available, he could be made bishop, thus in fact inheriting the bishopric. When in 992 the count of Toulouse made over half the bishopric of Nîmes to his wife as a marriage gift, the extent to which proprietary interests in the church had become dominant can be readily appreciated; when a decade later the count of Carcassonne made over both his county and the bishopric of Carcassonne to his wife and his son, he obviously was thinking of the county and the bishopric as pretty much the same sort of thing. These were far from isolated cases. One who acquired a bishopric as a form of property, through sale, inheritance, or gift, did not necessarily become the bishop; rather he now possessed a proprietary right in the bishopric, which allowed him in effect to appoint the bishop. The church, which had played a considerable role in giving coherence to the west after the barbarian invasions, had been able to do so only in close conjunction with existing political authority; by the tenth century it had become the captive of lay interests.

CATHEDRAL CANONS

The bishop's *familia* included a body of priests charged with singing the divine office at appointed times day and night, thus carrying on the collective prayer that was thought to be especially efficacious. Before the ninth century there was no cathedral clergy as such—only clergy of the episcopal city—but from then on, the clergy of the cathedral began to play an active role as a group. Their duties included not only singing the divine offices but also collaborating with the bishop in administrative and even judicial matters. In the course of time, custom dictated that the bishop consult with them in many matters, especially the alienation of the goods of the church in which cathedral clergy themselves had considerable interest; eventually this custom was sanctioned by canon law. The importance of the cathedral clergy also increased during a vacancy; in the matter of electing a new bishop, they came in time to exercise more and more of a monopoly.

It took a long time, however, for the notion that these clergy formed a corporate body to emerge fully. Until the twelfth century they were still referred to as the clergy of the church, the cathedral clergy, and so on; it was only during the twelfth century that it grew common to refer to them collectively as a *capitulum,* a chapter, indicating the growing tendency to view them as a corporation rather than as a mere collection of individuals. This corporate character undoubtedly depended on, among other things, the by now long tradition that they live together according to a "rule" (*regulum:* hence the expression "regular" clergy). In the eighth century St. Chrodegang, bishop of Metz, imposed on his clergy the standards and discipline of the monastic life.

After I had been made bishop of Metz and had begun to attend to the duties of my pastoral office, I discovered that my clergy as well as the people were living in a most negligent manner. . . . Relying on divine aid and encouraged by my spiritually minded brethren, I thought it necessary to make a little rule for my clergy, by observing which they would be able to refrain from forbidden things, to put off their vices, and to cease from the evil practices which they have so long followed.[1]

Chrodegang's rule required that his clergy live in common, eat at a common table, sleep in a common dormitory, observe common hours of worship and other duties, obey the precept of silence, and so on. It was, in fact, the imposition of a semimonastic life. Later, Chrodegang's regulations were revised in conformity with some writings of St. Augustine including a letter he had written to a community of nuns in which he described the common life of the clergy of his cathedral in Hippo. This "rule" of St. Augustine, an adaptation of Chrodegang's first attempts, became widely adopted from the time of the Carolingian church reforms in the ninth century. By the Second Lateran Council (1139), the pope required that all regular canons adopt the Augustinian rule.

It was not always easy to enforce the common life. Some bishops had a long struggle, if they concerned themselves with morale and organization at all, to get their clergy to give up their prized independence for a communal existence under the discipline of a

---

[1] Thatcher and McNeal, *op. cit.,* p. 492.

common rule. Even then there was a tendency to a mildness in interpretation: canons were allowed to have their private houses in the cloisters, a practice current in the ninth century as a result of the acquisition of endowments. Each canon had a proprietary right in his house which he could transfer to another canon by sale, gift, or inheritance.

Though living in common, the canons did not at first hold common property. The cathedral had property and the bishop had property, two forms of property which were often confused; but the canons themselves had to rely upon the bishop for their upkeep out of the revenues of the church. Often, however, little or no provision for the canons was made, leading to their destitution and demoralization. Church synods in the ninth century sought therefore to regulate what incomes the canons ought to have. Usually these incomes were established by endowing the college of canons as a whole out of the estates of the cathedral. Hence arose the "prebend," a word generally applied to the food supplies of the canons, later to the landed sources of their income or to the income itself. In time the institution of prebends would contribute to the development of the corporate nature of the college of canons as a juridical person, since the college received the administration of the incomes in question as a body, thus forcing the members to act together. The rights of the college of canons were frequently confirmed in perpetuity by a papal bull or a royal grant; while not absolutely necessary, confirmation was nevertheless useful as an instrument of public law, confirming rights which might be questioned in the future. The possessions of the canons, as distinct from those of the cathedral church, were often increased by grants from the bishop and by the gifts of the faithful in return for specific services and prayers. The canons played a large role therefore in the system of land tenure, receiving rents and often acting as corporate lords of villages with customary rights of property and dominion.

The prebend and the canonry itself were inseparable. To be a canon gave one the right to a prebend, that is, to a share in the corporate income of the college; to be given a prebend was to be accepted in the body of canons. The control of the distribution of the prebends by the canons themselves meant in effect that they could exert control over the membership of their college. Often the bishop lost completely his right of collation, his right to appoint to canonries; sometimes he held on to only a limited right of confirmation. The canons themselves were no more immune to the perpetration of abuses than individual bishops, and the sale of canonries was not uncommon, usually disguised by having the candidate or someone on his behalf make an appropriate gift to the college. While this was acceptable when voluntary, there were other practices more reprehensible, amounting to the outright sale of church offices. The prebend was coming to be looked upon as analogous to a feudal holding, to take up which one was expected to pay the equivalent of a feudal "relief." The tendency also grew, as it did with feudal tenures, to look upon the prebend as a form of private property. This led to frequently successful attempts to pass the prebend on to a relative.

With the growth of papal influence over the church after the eleventh century, the office of canon gradually came to play a role of more than local significance. The great prestige of the papacy led many to seek papal confirmation of their possession of church offices, finding in such confirmation a stronger claim to the office than could be obtained elsewhere; of course the many claims and counterclaims led to litigation which often enough had to be settled in the papal court. This casual intervention of the papacy in the collation or granting of church benefices was gradually transformed into a right, the exercise of which ran afoul of the interests of others. Thus the canonry especially lent itself to a papacy which, in its growth, was pressed to find incomes for its increasing number of servants. Unlike the parish priest, the canon had no immediate parishional responsibilities; there were literally thousands of canonries in the churches of Europe, and they were on the whole relatively well endowed. There was at hand, therefore, a large pool of potential revenue which could be tapped without seriously upsetting the parishional functions of the church, and the papacy was quick to see in these offices a solution to an immediate problem.

Not only the papacy, however, looked to the canonries. So did secular rulers, just as pressed as the papacy to find sinecures for their officials. But especially in many cathedral and collegiate churches, local noble families exercised a virtual monopoly over the membership of the chapters, and in many cases looked upon them as private preserves. Papal interference was therefore hotly resented, since papal criteria of ecclesiastical fitness and appropriate education left out of account the aristocratic interests of local families, and papal appointment deprived local powers of an important kind of political patronage.

The result was a lively debate in the thirteenth and fourteenth centuries over the question of "papal provisions," in which the papacy was accused of hungering after the revenues of the church to the detriment of the spiritual welfare of Christians everywhere. The success in many European quarters in frustrating the exercise of papal provisions limited the number of offices available to papal candidates; it also made it impossible for the papacy to impose standard qualifications on and play any role in reforming large parts of the church.

THE PARISH

Parochia, a word which might apply to any territorial circumscription, was often used to describe the territory of a bishop. In time it came to be limited to a subdivision of the bishop's diocese, and by the eleventh century the parish was coming to correspond in territory to the rural village. It was a self-contained unit, directed by a priest whose monopoly of spiritual direction was protected against outsiders. The faithful were to attend their own parish church and no other; within the territory assigned to his church the parish priest need fear no competition. He remained, however, under the direct authority of the bishop of the diocese, and his church was responsible for an annual payment to the bishop which had grown out of an earlier custom of making annual gifts. It was also customary to provide the bishop with hospitality when he visited the parish and to provide transportation—a set of obligations similar to those of the vassal toward his lord. Newly appointed priests sometimes even paid the bishop a special tax like feudal relief.

Like the cathedral, but on a much smaller scale, the parish church had its own estates, comprising the original endowment of the founder. The founder of a church had to set aside an endowment providing it with sufficient revenue, usually amounting to at least the equivalent of a peasant's holding in the seigneury. In addition the parish church was often the recipient of gifts from the bishop, from monasteries, or even from laymen. These possessions provided revenues, as did the collection of the annual tithes and regular offerings. The tithe became obligatory from Carolingian days, payable by parishioners to the parish priest. The tithe was levied at first only on agricultural goods and later on other forms of revenue; it was divided into four equal parts which were distributed to the bishop, the poor, the needs of the priest and his assistants, and to the upkeep of the church. Offerings were also important, and some became fixed through custom, particularly gifts for certain ecclesiastical functions such as baptism, marriage, and burial, despite church legislation against levying charges for such services.

The parish church was considered, together with its possessions, an object of property. Theoretically the church belonged to the saint to whom it was consecrated and whose representative the priest was. But the powerful exercised real proprietary rights: every village church was in fact the private church of the lord who inherited the rights of the founder in the church's endowment and who viewed his rights in the church in the same way as his other property rights, to be sold, given, passed as an inheritance or a dowry, or even pawned. The great majority of such proprietors were laymen, and therefore it is no surprise to find that churches were often used as benefices to reward vassals. Not all churches, however, were in lay hands. Many had been founded by bishops, or were presumed to have been so founded, and others had been given to bishops. Many passed into the hands of monasteries as pious gifts. The parish church in the hands of a bishop or monastery was usually handled with more concern for the spiritual welfare of the parish, but essentially it lost none of its character as a species of property. There was the same confusion of private rights and public institutions, productive of the same practices of sale, exchange, and gift. The lord, whether lay or ecclesiastical, chose the curate, received an oath of fidelity, put the candidate in possession of the church usually in return for a payment (*introitus*), and continued in many cases to exercise a large control over the patrimony, especially the tithes.

MONASTERIES

Although the monastic rule of St. Benedict of Nursia (d. 543) gradually became the basis for all monasticism in the west, the ideal which inspired the movement had much earlier origins. Monasticism grew in Egypt and spread rather quickly in the eastern

Mediterranean. What started as a hermit movement in the Egyptian desert soon took on organizational features which, although themselves uninfluential in the west, gave birth to a large literature which did much to stimulate western admiration. In the west the idea of a life lived in common according to a rule gradually took hold in the second half of the fourth century, primarily as a principle for the organization of the bishop's household; but the example of the Egyptian fathers also inspired hermits, whose asceticism in turn attracted followers and imitators.

Benedict of Nursia, who had renounced the world at the age of fourteen, finally settled at Monte Cassino where, around 535, he drew up for his followers a rule of great importance in the history of monastic institutions. It laid considerable emphasis on internal order, the discipline and labor of the monks ("Idleness is the enemy of the soul"), and the preeminent role of the abbot, whom all the brethren were to obey without question: "Let no one in the monastery follow his own inclination, and let no one boldly presume to dispute with his abbot." The abbot was to seek the advice of the assembled brethren on all important matters, however, and in matters of lesser import at least that of the senior members; at all times he was to govern the house in accordance with the rule.[1] Throughout, Benedict envisaged a self-contained community dependent on no external authority, associated with no other community. The observance of his rule gradually spread throughout the west, aided considerably by Charlemagne's legislation requiring that it be adopted by all the monasteries within his empire. While there was no organizational unity in western monasticism, therefore, and each house remained a law to itself, the idea nevertheless took hold that there was a single monastic vocation which all monks followed no matter where they were or what variation of custom they observed.

There were in fact two kinds of monastery, that of monks living under the rule of St. Benedict and that of canons living under the rule of St. Augustine. Houses of regular canons and monasteries proper had much in common. In each the inmates lived a common life in the cloister, shared common meals, participated in common services at certain regulated hours, and owed obedience to the head of the house, whether abbot or prior.

---

[1] H. Bettenson, *Documents of the Christian Church* (London, 1947), p. 164.

Houses of regular canons and monasteries each had a "patrimony," that is, landed possessions and other sources of income accumulated over a period of time through gift or purchase. The patrimony comprised not only the church building itself and those buildings associated with it but also agricultural land together with a laboring peasant population, frequently whole villages. The community of monks or canons, therefore, often enjoyed quite a few of the public powers so freely distributed in the late Carolingian period, for example, the rights to coin, to authorize markets in return for annual fees, to summon the local militia, the right of *ban*, and so forth.

Despite many similarities, however, the life of the monk was often more austere than that of the canon. The canons might enjoy certain small personal luxuries, in many cases still lived in separate houses rather than in common, and in almost all cases enjoyed personal possessions which the monk had abandoned by his vow of poverty.

As with all churches, the proprietor of a monastery was in theory the saint to whom it was dedicated, represented on earth by the abbot and the monks who resided in it. In fact, however, the abbot who governed the house came to be looked upon as the effective proprietor for life. In his person were centered both the public rights and the responsibilities of the community, to which was assimilated all the monastic possessions. However, the monasteries could not resist the secularizing trend to which the church as a whole was succumbing. By the early Carolingian period monasteries, like so many other ecclesiastical establishments, had passed into the hands of prince or bishop. According to canon law the monastery fell under the jurisdiction of the bishop in whose diocese it was located, but the authority of the bishop was purely juridical. Now he sought to strengthen it by becoming the proprietor of the monastery as well. Many monasteries also came into the hands of the king, who looked upon them as a form of royal property and dealt with them as with other items of the royal fisc. If he bestowed one on an abbot elected by the monks, he did so only in return for an oath of fealty. Thus the monastery frequently took on the appearance of a benefice received in return for service. Frequently, however, the king bestowed the monastery on some ecclesiastic or layman whom he wished to reward, who then took the revenues of the monastery (though he was held responsible for the support of the monks) and sometimes even took the title of abbot for himself. Like other forms of benefices, therefore, monasteries became a kind of property, to be disposed of by will, sale, exchange, gift, inheritance, or as benefices to obtain the services of subordinates.

With the property right usually went the right to choose the abbot if not, indeed, to take the office for oneself. It was a right that might be renounced in favor of the monks themselves as Benedict had stipulated in his rule, thus providing for what was called "free election." Such a renunciation might be for a single occasion or in perpetuity. Even so, a peaceful and uncontested election was not always easy to come by, and an arbiter was frequently needed. This should have been, and sometimes was, the bishop of the diocese; usually, however, it was the secular prince. In other words, even when the right of choosing the abbot was left to the monks, a right of confirmation was usually retained.

Secular dominion such as this meant that in the main the monastic patrimony would be used for secular ends. Monastic lands were used as benefices to reward military followers, to build fortifications where the terrain was favorable, to obtain services from the abbot who was viewed as a vassal, who often had to provide hospitality for his lord and to keep retainers to fulfill his military obligations. Some monasteries were kept in a continuous uproar when a lay abbot insisted on living there with his circle of warriors, family, women, dogs, and horses.

The process of converting religious revenues to secular use frequently resulted in the complete impoverishment of the monks. One way to avoid this was to set aside some proportion of the monastic patrimony for their exclusive use. In collegiate and cathedral churches, as has been stated, these were divided into prebends constituting the property and its revenue assigned to a canon as his permanent portion. In the monastery, any subdivision of property contradicted the old notion of communal use, but it was the best safeguard that reformers, both secular and ecclesiastical, could devise, given the universal concept of property rights. There was a tendency, therefore, for monastic goods to be divided into two parts: one for the abbot's exclusive use, the other for the monks. It was a partial reform only, since the abbot's share was often still directed to secular ends.

All this led to a swift decay of monastic life and organization from

the ninth century on, after the reforming impulse under Charlemagne had died out. It must be noted, of course, that there was
much physical destruction of monasteries at the hands of Norman
and Saracen invaders, but even those houses that escaped plundering could not escape the effects of secularization. Monastic withdrawal, the life of contemplation and prayer, the maintenance of
a special society which might serve as a spiritual model to others,
were almost impossible. The moral breakdown of new members of
monasteries, in imitation of their elders, made the disorder complete.

MONASTIC REFORM

The more abuse, however, the more cry for reform. It was a
cry heard most frequently in local church synods, and its constant
reiteration was evidence of the powerlessness of churchmen to do
much on their own. Significant reform could be effected only with
the collaboration of secular lords willing to abandon some of their
rights, and this was slow in coming. By reform was meant a return
to a strict (or at least a stricter) observance of the Benedictine
rule and, especially, the free election of the abbot by the monks
without secular interference. The latter was a concession the laity
was not generally ready to make. But it was just such a concession
that Duke William of Aquitaine did make in 910 on behalf of a new
foundation, the monastery of Cluny, commending it to the protection of a papacy so distant as to leave the house virtually independent and renouncing for himself and his heirs all proprietary
rights. Others began to follow his lead, and the first abbot of Cluny
was soon requested by other secular lords to reform or to restore
houses which they possessed. This was followed, in many cases, by
the transference of the government of these houses to the abbot of
Cluny. The result was a new form of monastic organization, later
approved by Pope John XI in 931, whereby one abbot ruled over
several houses. In time there was something in the neighborhood of
2000 houses in various states of dependence on Cluny. It was a
large organization in which all the monks held the abbot of Cluny
as their superior, the old Benedictine tradition writ large; but it
was a tradition on which was grafted the more recent idea of
feudal dependence. Each of the houses was taken in by Cluny

according to the terms of a charter specifying its obligations, much as a vassal entered into the protection of a lord.

Throughout the tenth and eleventh centuries Cluny had a wide impact, its houses spreading from Burgundy and Aquitaine through northern France, England, and elsewhere. Cluny was fortunate in its early abbots, men of long life and outstanding reputation. Its influence was great, not only because of its growing number of dependent monasteries and the high repute of its abbots but especially because it represented an ideal of spiritual rejuvenation and coherence long before the church could develop any machinery for effecting widespread reform. In this sense it made a real contribution to the reforms of the church at large beginning in the second half of the eleventh century.

Cluny departed in no sense from the ideals of the rule of St. Benedict, but there was some difference in emphasis. The liturgical functions of the monk were enlarged, the efficacy of common prayer being so highly thought of that service in the choir came to dominate the days and nights of the monks almost to the exclusion of all other duties. Manual labor now had little place (since there was a tendency for monks to be ordained) and was left to the many serfs who tilled the lands that the new order accumulated. Even intellectual pursuits could find little encouragement under such a regime. However, the monastic retreat to the choir did not mean the abandonment of useful social functions. The order was renowned for its hospitality and charity to the old, the sick, the poor, and the pilgrim.

Cluny, if the best known, was by no means the only center of monastic reform. In the tenth century the activity of reformers in Lorraine, also intent on a return to the rule of St. Benedict, testified to the continuing strength of the monastic ideal. In some places, for example in the monastery at Gorze which had been in virtual ruins in the earlier part of the century, ascetic severity outstripped the requirements of the rule. Monasteries were often encouraged to reform by bishops who cooperated in the effort to reorganize the monasteries in their dioceses, especially those houses that fell directly under their control. Reform was also encouraged by some lay magnates. From Lorraine the movement spread into parts of Germany and came under the protection of the German kings Otto I and Otto II, who frequently granted the right of free election. Noticeable and important differences remained: monastic reforms in Lorraine, though spreading from one house to another, did not, as with Cluny, lead to the development of an order of affiliated houses under a single abbot; further, proprietary rights in these houses were not abandoned. Princes and bishops might be moved by either piety or considerations of policy to encourage the moral regeneration of monasteries, but they were not going to abandon what had come to be a juridical right of property. Monasteries were neither commended to the papacy nor, when they were held by bishops as proprietors, exempted from their immediate jurisdiction. These were fatal flaws, guaranteeing that such reform as might be achieved, important as it was, would not outlive its initiators.

While monastic reform in the tenth century brought some innovation in organization and in liturgical observance, there was no radical departure from Benedictine tradition. The eleventh century, however, witnessed the emergence of a new spirit that attempted to recapture the asceticism of the desert fathers. This was especially true in Italy where there was a marked tendency toward a severe eremitic life. The movement did not embrace large numbers, but in time it did produce a form of monastic organization somewhat different in spirit from the Benedictine tradition within which Cluny remained. It was not so much that the Benedictine rule was abandoned as that it was interpreted in as strict a sense as possible. The emphasis on withdrawal from the world was reinforced by the introduction of a new element, the *conversi*—lay brothers—to handle all matters relating to the material welfare of the community. Houses such as Vallombrosa or Camaldoli were not themselves large, but they were important in introducing a greater austerity in the monastic regime. This austerity soon became the ideal even beyond the confines of Italy. Bruno of Reims in 1084 founded the Carthusian order, in effect a community of hermits, the rigor of which remained undiluted throughout the Middle Ages. The new house of Citeaux, founded in the late eleventh century, was infused with this new spirit and evolved a form of organization which had a wide influence, quickly becoming an organization of associated houses which resembled Cluny only superficially.

The closest the Cistercians came to a constitution was a document entitled the *Carta caritatis* governing the relationship between all Cistercian houses. It was a body of rules which constantly grew, different parts of it marking different stages in the development of the order during the twelfth century. The development of an "order" avoided the isolationism of early Benedictinism, and reform could therefore be continuous rather than local and sporadic; but the heavy centralization of Cluny, based on the obligations of daughter houses to mother house, was also avoided. The opening paragraph of the charter is an obvious dig at the Cluniacs:

[The founders of the order] decided to call this decree the Charter of Love, because it refuses to impose any taxes and pursues only love and the interests of souls in divine and human affairs. As we know that we are all servants, however unprofitable, of the one true King, Lord and Master, we do not exact any earthly benefits or temporal contributions from the abbots and from our fellow monks whom the kindness of God has placed under the discipline of the Rule by means of us, the most wretched of men. Wishing to do good to them and to all sons of Holy Church, we have decided not to burden them or diminish their substance in any way, lest, in our desire to become rich by impoverishing them, we run into the evil of avarice. . . .[1]

It was laid down that each house keep the Benedictine rule uniformly, maintain common customs and liturgy, and avoid seeking privileges conflicting with the common institutions of the order. There was a system of visitation, whereby the abbot of Citeaux and the abbots of the chief houses of La Ferté, Pontigny, Clairvaux, and Morimond were to visit all the monasteries founded by their houses at least once a year; and Citeaux itself was to be visited annually by the abbots of the last four houses. The visitation served the purpose of general inspection, made available the advice of others, and provided a gentle stimulus for the maintenance of high standards.

Once a year a general chapter of all the abbots of the Cistercian houses was held; here changes or additions to the statutes of the order might be made and abbots found not diligent enough corrected "in a spirit of love" or, if sufficiently delinquent, suspended or deposed. The individual houses did not monopolize the election of their own abbots; if the house in question had founded daughter

---

[1] Brian Pullan, *Sources for the History of Medieval Europe from the mid-eighth to the mid-thirteenth century* (Oxford, 1966), p. 84. Copyright © 1966. Reprinted by permission of Basil Blackwell and Barnes & Noble, Inc.

houses, their abbots could participate in the election also. The abbot of Citeaux, therefore, was chosen not only by the monks of Citeaux itself but by the many abbots of the houses founded directly by Citeaux, including the four chief daughter houses mentioned above.

In general, then, while the isolation of early Benedictinism was avoided, so was the heavy centralization of Cluny. There were a number of built-in correctives for abuses; even the abbot of Citeaux himself was not free from surveillance, criticism, and ultimate deposition by the chapter general, if deserved. This was not a single monastery with many dependencies, but rather several monasteries in an association at once flexible and hierarchical. The Cisterican organization in turn strongly influenced a new order of canons founded by St. Norbert, the Premonstratensians. Norbert was a strong admirer of Citeaux, and his order borrowed much of the Cistercian organization—chapter generals, visitations, and the use of lay brethren. Even Cluny, in an effort to remain viable, borrowed some of these features.

What gave the new "orders," as opposed to the old independent Benedictine houses, their unity and cohesion was the exemption they enjoyed from outside control. Cluny had such exemption. The Cistercians effectively obtained it by getting their charter confirmed by the bishops of the dioceses in which their houses were situated. In due course the whole order was exempt, as were the Premonstratensians. In fact it would have been impossible for a widespread order to emerge without some such exemption from the jurisdiction of the local bishops. Monasticism was ceasing to be an institution of local independent houses, and was becoming one of orders of potentially universal scope. This is the reason that the papacy would come to play a significant role in monasticism's future, since the papacy was the one agency of the church that could speak with universal authority.

During the twelfth century a remarkable increase in all monastic orders occurred, but popularity had its dangers. By the end of the twelfth century laxity, compromise, the slackening of discipline, the relaxation of the rule, and the influence of secular ideas sapped the movement of its sense of direction at the very time when social change, especially town growth, created new demands which the existing church organization could meet only with increasing difficulty. There emerged a new type of lay fervor and piety, often anticlerical and sometimes heretical. These movements were usually urban in origin and strongly emphasized the ideal of poverty in reaction against a property-owning church and popular religious ideas rather than formal liturgy. The rift between popular religion of this sort and the visible church was patched over for some time by the new orders of Franciscans and Dominicans, founded early in the thirteenth century, with their emphasis on preaching and poverty. These mendicant orders acted as a focus for popular piety in a way that neither the existing monasteries nor the secular church could. Their great innovation, as far as institutional organization was concerned, was the establishment of a type of order in which the members, instead of retiring to the cloister, had work in the secular world as their primary mission. Mendicancy, despite some later relaxation, gave to these two orders, and others founded on their model, a unique character. Further, such an order was one family, not a collection of separate houses, and its organization neither allowed for autonomy nor demanded stability. As a result, the head of the order was powerful as no head of a monastic order had ever been, and because of the closeness of the Franciscans and Dominicans to Rome, the papacy had a greatly increased role as leader of movements affecting the rejuvenation of social morality. Confronted by the decay of traditional monasticism in the fourteenth and fifteenth centuries, the papacy could therefore take a hand in their reorganization, sweeping the independent houses into congregations with governmental features often borrowed from the successful arrangements of the mendicants.

IX
THE
PAPACY

THE BISHOP OF ROME

OF ALL THE BISHOPS, THERE WAS ONE WHO came to hold a special place for Christians in the west— the bishop of Rome. His prestige in the early church sprang not merely from his close association with the city that for so long had dominated the civilized world but also from the particular reverence Rome was held in by Christians as the place of martyrdom of the two most venerated apostles, Peter and Paul. The bishop of Rome, whose later monopoly of the title "pope" reflected the uniqueness with which his office was invested, kept alive the memories of Rome as the center of world rule; and after the general influx of Germans into the west, especially into Italy, he often acted at least nominally on behalf of an emperor now distant and ineffectual in far-off Constantinople.

More important than this secular image of Rome, however, was the spiritual position that the popes claimed in relation to other bishops. This was based upon a particular reading of Christ's words to the apostle Peter: "Thou art Peter, and upon this rock I will build my church; and the gates of hell shall not prevail against it. And I

178

will give unto thee the keys of the kingdom of heaven: and what-soever thou shalt bind on earth shall be bound in heaven: and whatsoever thou shalt loose on earth shall be loosed in heaven" (Matt. 16:18–19). This was looked upon as a commission to govern Christ's kingdom on earth, which Christ had given to Peter and which Peter had passed on in turn to his successors, the bishops of Rome. Although all bishops might claim to exercise spiritual powers which came to them directly through succession from the apostles, the pope claimed that one apostle, Peter, held a special position as the juridical superior of the other apostles, a position which the pope had inherited *vis-à-vis* the other bishops.

Such claims did not always go uncontested: "Every bishop . . . can no more be judged by another than he himself can judge another," maintained St. Cyprian of Carthage in A.D. 256 as a rebuke to the pope in a dispute over the propriety of rebaptizing those who had held heretical views. In the main, however, the papacy had its way. It enjoyed the support of imperial authority: the emperor Aurelian (270–275), in settling the question of a disputed bishopric, awarded it to that candidate who received the recognition of the bishop of Rome; and the emperor Theodosius (379–395) defined the orthodox as those who were in communion with Rome. Church councils also reinforced the steady growth of papal prestige and authority. At the Council of Sardica (343–344), the appellate jurisdiction of the Roman bishop was recognized:

. . . if any bishop has been accused, and the assembled bishops of that region have tried him and deposed him, and he appeals and flees to the blessed bishop of the Roman church and wishes to be heard, and the bishop of Rome considers it just that the case be reexamined, he may deem it worthy to write to the other bishops who are in the neighboring ecclesiastical province to look into the entire matter again with great care and to make a determination based upon the truth.[1]

Henceforth the claim to a superior ecclesiastical administration, based on Peter's superiority to the other apostles, would be the leitmotiv of papal history: "We bear the burdens of all who are

---

[1] H. Denzinger, *Enchiridion symbolorum*, 30th ed. (Freiburg, 1955), pp. 34–35.

weighed down; indeed, through us they are borne by the blessed apostle Peter who, we are assured, protects us in all those things pertaining to his ministry and watches over us, his heir."[1]

The significance of the Petrine claim was bound to grow as, on the one hand, the church grew and, on the other, imperial government in the west collapsed. These two factors demanded a reassessment of the relationship of the society of Christians to the political society of the empire. There could be no confusion of the two when the state persecuted the Christians before the fourth century; but as the machinery of the state came apart in the west, the only visible form of whatever it was that might be called "society" increasingly appeared to be the corporate union of Christian believers, the universal church. Once society was thought of in this way, certain logical conclusions were easily reached. There was no questioning the fact that society had an end, a purpose. Since the Christian view of the world was strongly permeated by the belief in salvation, society's purpose could only be the salvation of its members. Every society requires a government qualified to lead it to its designed end. The end being spiritual in nature, obviously the best governors were those expert in spiritual matters.

When such ideas came into conjunction with the Petrine theory, all the basic ingredients of a papal monarchy were at hand. Vigorous popes, such as Leo I in the fifth century, rarely missed an opportunity to express their authority, claiming that a patriarch of Constantinople enjoyed his office only through papal approval or declaring invalid the decisions of bishops in council that displeased them.

However, the actual supremacy of Rome over churches other than those in its immediate area was for long a pious theory. It was only with the pontificate of Gregory I at the end of the sixth century (590–604) that the theory began a slow, halting translation into fact. This translation occurred less through any dogmatic assertion of claims than by Gregory's statesmanlike exercise of a patriarchal jurisdiction in dealing with problems of poverty and hardship, especially of those people displaced by the Lombard incursions into Italy; his adoption of the monastic ideals which he so

---

[1] Pope Siricius (384–398), in Denzinger, *op. cit.*, p. 43.

THE PAPACY / 181

admired, such as submission to authority; and his extension of Christianity through missionaries to areas of Europe outside the confines of the old Roman Empire. All of this contributed much to the steady elevation of the papal office in the western church.

THE POPES AND SECULAR AUTHORITY

No matter how one looks at the persecution under the empire, at least the relations between church and state were clear. But once the church acquired a legal status and the emperors themselves became Christian, the relationship became clouded. Although the church fathers had generally recognized the divine character of the civil order of society, they insisted that the civil ruler, if a son of the church, was amenable to ecclesiastical jurisdiction. St. Ambrose, bishop of Milan (374–397), wrote to the emperor Valentinian that in matters of faith bishops are accustomed to judge emperors, not emperors bishops. The emperor, he said in one of his sermons, is within the church, not above it. These were no idle statements. On one occasion he excluded the emperor Theodosius from the church in Milan on the grounds that he feared to offer the sacrifice of the eucharist in the emperor's presence because of the emperor's responsibility for a massacre of Christians in Thessalonica. On another occasion, he reproved the emperor for ordering some Christians to rebuild a synagogue which they had destroyed, refusing to celebrate the eucharist until Theodosius had rescinded his order. These were clear assertions of the principle that the church might exercise important coercive powers even over the head of civil society and that in religious matters the civil ruler had no authority whatsoever.

On the other hand, the emperors saw themselves as theocratic monarchs, the anointed of God, chosen to lead Christian society to salvation. In this view there could be no acceptance of an independent role for the church; it existed only as an agency of the monarch in his divine work. Some bishops accepted this view and indeed welcomed the participation of the emperor in the determination of dogma and church discipline; nevertheless there was growing alarm over what was coming to be seen as unwarranted interference in spiritual affairs by one who was, after all, only a layman. Then, too, the facts of political disintegration in the west and the emergence of the Christian church there as the one remaining common bond tended to reinforce the view that society and Christendom were one and that the spiritual goal of such a society, salvation, could only be achieved under the direction of those best fitted in spiritual matters to exercise leadership—the bishops, and ultimately the pope. Secular government, in this view, retained an important place in assisting the spiritual head in his work, but it did not have an independent role.

The growing distaste for imperial interference had little practical effect as long as the Roman church remained in the embrace of the Roman Empire. In Constantinople, the imperial capital from the fourth century on, papal resistance to the imperial view was merely looked upon as treasonous. The opportunity for a clean break came, however, in the eighth century when the last remnants of imperial authority in Italy were extinguished by the steady encroachments of the Lombards, and the bishop of Rome was forced to turn for support to the king of the Franks. This was a significant break with Constantinople. It had been preceded by bitter quarrels over imperial taxation of Italy, which fell particularly hard on papal estates, and over doctrinal matters which had arisen from the iconoclastic controversy, a quarrel over the role of icons or images in Christian worship. The sharpness of the issue is reflected in the words of Pope Gregory II (715–731) to the emperor: "We derive our power and authority from the prince of the apostles, Peter, and we could, if we wished, pronounce judgment upon you"; and again: "Listen to us, emperor, cease behaving like a priest . . ., Dogmas are not the business of emperors, but of pontiffs, because we have the sense and the mind of Christ."[1] What Gregory thus began, one of his successors, Stephen III (752–757), completed, by consecrating Pepin, the usurper of the Merovingian throne, as king of the Franks. In one stroke he gained a protector against the Lombards in Italy and independence from the Byzantine emperor.

Henceforth the "caesaropapism" of the emperors—the exercise of supreme ecclesiastical as well as secular authority by the emperor—no longer acted as an obstacle to the claims of the papacy, at least not in the west. Undoubtedly the popes thought to find in

---

[1] Walter Ullmann, *The Growth of Papal Government in the Middle Ages* (London, 1955), p. 6.

the Franks a secular power which would accept the role provided by papal theory, that of assisting the church in the task of spiritual leadership of all Christians—a secular power, in other words, which would rule in accordance with Christian justice as defined by Rome. But they found, in fact, that they had exchanged one master for another. Charlemagne, Pepin's son and successor, always accorded to Rome a position of primacy within the church, but he never conceded to it any complete jurisdiction. He looked upon his own role as had the Byzantine emperors theirs. He did not hesitate to legislate as a matter of right in ecclesiastical affairs, as befitted a ruler who held his office directly from God and was responsible to God alone. In a letter to the pope, he clearly defined their respective functions as he saw them:

It is for us [meaning himself] with the aid of divine piety, to defend by force of arms the Holy Church of Christ everywhere from the attack of pagans and the devastation by infidels from without, and from within to fortify it with the knowledge of the catholic faith. It is for you, holy father, to aid our arms with hands upraised to God like Moses, that by your intercession the Christian people under God's leadership and grace may always conquer everywhere the enemies of his holy name, and the name of our lord Jesus Christ may shine throughout the whole world.[1]

But the collapse of the Carolingian empire in the ninth century allowed the continued development of papal formulas of supremacy. There was a steady insistence that the church of Rome was the principal church; its ruler was the vicar of St. Peter, the source of doctrine, the ultimate resort of penitents, the interpreter of ecclesiastical order, the fount of ecclesiastical law. Pope Nicholas I (858–867) maintained not only that Rome was the head of all Christian churches but that, as far as the earth was Christian, the pope was "prince over all the earth," acting as such on behalf of God. The ideal, though not to be realized for some time in the future, was obviously a church government centralized through a strict ordering of the church hierarchy. But such an ideal was bound to impinge upon secular government which controlled the local church

---

[1] Setton and Winkler, *Great Problems in European Civilization*, 2nd ed. (Englewood Cliffs, 1966), p. 155.

hierarchy. If in fact all of Christian society were ordered beneath the pope and the latter were possessed of a juridical authority inherited through Peter from Christ, then there could be little room for secular rulers except as protectors of the church, assistants in its work, and subject to its sanctions. This was a view which had a long history. Nicholas I clearly looked upon papal authority as twofold, or, to use the metaphor of the time, thought of the church as possessing two swords, material and spiritual; the spiritual sword was to be wielded by the church, the material on behalf of and under the guidance of the church. Thus, while secular authority remained important in the eyes of the church for the extirpation of heresy, the extension of Christianity in pagan lands, and the physical protection of churchmen and church property, it had no business sitting in judgment on the clergy, over whom it had no jurisdiction, nor in frustrating the decrees of the pope, behind which lay the ultimate authority of Christ himself.

Nicholas' claims derived some strength from a set of documents (though he himself seemed to feel no need to lean on them) which appeared in the ninth century purporting to be the work of the well-known Isidore, bishop of Seville, and therefore now called the Pseudo-Isidorian decretals. This was a set of papal letters and conciliar acts drawn from the pre-Constantinian epoch, some forged and some genuine, which among other things exalted the papal prerogatives. They originated in the Frankish kingdom, where archbishops threatened to establish a real and immediate authority over the bishops of their provinces and secular lords exercised an increasing control over the church, the evil results of which could be combatted only by establishing the right of the bishop to appeal directly to Rome. This the forged decretals did. By creating for the papacy a long history of unlimited authority, these forgeries were obviously designed to assist bishops to escape local domination.

The collection also included one of the most famous forgeries of history, the Donation of Constantine, the origins of which lie back in the eighth century. The Donation of Constantine was based on a long-accepted legend about the conversion and baptism of the emperor Constantine by Pope Sylvester (314–335) and purported to be a deed of gift from the emperor to the pope:

Inasmuch as our power is earthly, we have decreed that it shall venerate and honor his [the pope's] most holy Roman Church and that the sacred see of the blessed Peter shall be gloriously exalted above our empire and earthly throne. We attribute to him the power and glorious dignity and strength and honor of the Empire. . . . And the pontiff [of Rome] shall be the highest and chief of all the priests in the whole world. . . . To the holy apostles [and to their successors, the pope] we grant and by this present convey our imperial Lateran palace. . . . We convey all provinces, palaces and districts of the city of Rome and Italy and of the regions of the West . . . as a permanent possession to the Holy Roman Church.[1]

The Donation thus conferred a historical legitimacy upon the pope's government of the city of Rome and a vague dominion over the western empire.

Papal government of Rome and its surrounding area was an established fact. The bishop of Rome had been acting as governor and judge, as well as spiritual leader, long before the Donation; and both Pepin and Charlemagne had confirmed his rule over a territory which extended from Rome to Ravenna and included a large portion of central Italy. That the papacy was able, under the most trying conditions, to provide effective leadership in Italy is shown by the role of some of the popes, notably Leo IV (847–855) and John X (914–928) in combatting the Saracen invaders of the peninsula. It was under Leo that the walls of the Vatican were raised against recurrences of the Saracen raid of 846, and John X led the army that defeated the Saracens at the battle of the Garigliano River. Papal political leadership, while it had its ups and downs, was a recognizable force, and papal government was certainly as legitimate as any other in the west, needing no Donation of Constantine to support it. But the vague and grandiose language of the Donation permitted a yet wider interpretation of papal political authority than merely as a provincial government within the framework of the Carolingian empire. Taken together with the ideal of a unified Christendom and a pope who was "prince over all the earth," both the Donation and the larger collection of Pseudo-Isidore contributed much to the theory of papal world monarchy.

While such ideas had a large though distant future, they counted for little during the late Carolingian period. The possession of churches, monasteries, and all forms of ecclesiastical property by

---

[1] Bettenson, *op. cit.*, pp. 137–142.

a secular landed aristocracy meant that in fact there was no unified church other than in the abstract realm of faith. Even where bishops managed to remain relatively independent of secular control, as they did especially in Italy, this represented no victory for church unity. Bishops were just as jealous of their independence and authority as other aristocrats. As for the papacy itself, lay control was a fate that not even it could escape. While Carolingian authority remained effective in Italy, the popes had been limited in their independence even though they had a protector to fall back on. Consequently, the progressive collapse of Carolingian authority during and after the ninth century, far from contributing to papal independence, in fact made it impossible. As an office of considerable wealth and no little political power in Italy, the papacy was coveted and fought over by rival factions in Rome from the late ninth century to the early eleventh. With some exceptions, the caliber of the men who occupied the see was dismally low, and the office ceased for a long time to exercise even a moral leadership in Europe, to say nothing of political influence. As has been shown, there were strong reform currents in the tenth century, especially within the world of monasticism, but the one office that might have given it universal scope and application was buried in local strife. During much of the tenth century, Rome was dominated by a certain Theophylact. First he, then his widow Theodora, her daughter Marozia, and Marozia's son Alberic successively through intrigue and assassination exercised a control which in effect reduced the office of bishop of Rome to pitiful insignificance. When Alberic's son took office for himself as John XII (955–964), the papacy reached its nadir.

GREGORIAN REFORM

Salvation of a sort was just over the horizon—in fact, just over the Alps. Its instruments were the kings of Germany, who established their hegemony in much of Germany, revived the imperial ideal of Charlemagne, and extended their influence and their possessions in the Italian peninsula.

From Henry II (1002–1024), the emperors carefully bound the church of Germany to the imperial office. Indeed, Henry's great benefactions to the church led to his later canonization; and while his successor Conrad was interested in the German church primarily as a basis of political power and a source of revenue, his successor in turn, Henry III, was deeply affected by the religious sentiment of his time. Henry III was on good terms with many of the monastic leaders, especially Cluniacs, and was a leading exponent of moral and ecclesiastical reform. These ideas for reform centered mainly on the questions of simony (the buying and selling of church offices) and lay investiture (the bestowal by a lay lord of the spiritual symbols of office on the recipient of a bishopric or abbey). Henry III abandoned these practices which had hitherto marked the relationship between king and church and which degraded the church. Nevertheless Henry III remained very conscious of the sacred duty of his office.

In Italy, where the Roman church was in such a sad state, that duty was clear. Summoning a synod in 1046, Henry deposed a bishop of Rome who had been accused of simony, set aside a couple of rival popes, and then saw to the election of a German reformer to the papacy. In all of this he observed legal forms as much as possible, but in fact it was the royal will that was being enforced in fulfillment of the traditional role of protector of the church. From this time on, the papacy began to attract to its service others zealous for reform. While these reformers did not immediately attack the fundamental arrangements of the church in society, they saw in the renewed importance that the emperor had given to the papacy a means for effecting reform on a broader scale than heretofore. To them it was unthinkable that the papacy be allowed to sink back into dependence on local families, and at the outset they continued the imperial policy of defending the Roman church from Rome itself. The scope of this policy was soon enlarged, however, into a defense of the church everywhere against any intrusion of lay authority, including that of the emperor himself.

Hitherto little exception had been taken to the traditional theocratic role of kings nor to the traditional institutions of the proprietary church provided that it was well regulated. Abuses there were in plenty, and they were always roundly condemned; but there had been no attack on a political order so hallowed by time as to be considered public law. It was an order, however, that the reforming papacy inaugurated by Henry III soon set aside as being contrary to God's will. In 1059 Nicholas II issued a decree on papal elections which proved to be an important preliminary to the establishment of a new "right order"; the decree aimed at freeing papal elections from outside control, a first step toward freeing all church appointments from lay control:

> . . . on the death of a bishop of this universal Roman church, the cardinal bishops, having first very thoroughly discussed the matter together, shall then summon the cardinal clergy to them, and then the rest of the clergy and people shall in the same way come to consent to the new election. . . . The churchmen shall lead in electing the pope, and the others shall follow. . . . If anybody is elected and even ordained and enthroned in violation of this our decree promulgated by decision of the Council, everyone shall hold and recognize him not as a pope but a devil, not an apostle but an apostate. . . .[1]

The decree reduced the role of the Roman people to the formality of acclaiming an already elected pope and elsewhere referred to the rights of the emperor in papal elections in such vague terms as to be virtually meaningless: "Due honor and reverence shall be preserved for our beloved Henry. . . ."

The Henry referred to here, the minor son of the now dead Henry III, was in no position to assert his traditional rights; by the time he was, he found himself embroiled in a bitter controversy with the papacy which, in the hands of Gregory VII (1073–1085), had placed itself at the head of a reform movement no longer interested merely in the correction of abuses but rather in a complete redefinition of the relations between the laity and the church.

One of Gregory's colleagues and one of the most vigorous reformers in the papal curia, Cardinal Humbert, had already produced a program that went far beyond reform of existing practices. Lay investiture undoubtedly gave rise to many abuses, not least of which was the continual temptation to hand out ecclesiastical offices in return for compensation. In attacking these abuses Humbert was led to attack the existing order, long established in Europe, whereby the ruler effectively controlled the church. He saw the king, therefore, not as the wielder of sacred authority but only as another layman with no valid role to play in episcopal or other ecclesiasti-

---

[1] Pullan, *op. cit.*, pp. 54–55.

cal elections. The spiritual estate was superior to the secular; the layman was inferior to, and ultimately subject to, the ecclesiastic.

When, therefore, Gregory VII inaugurated his pontificate by legislating against simony, clerical marriage, and the investiture of clergy by laymen, he may have been responding to imperative, widely held moral attitudes, but he was also expressing a view of the relationship of the church to the laity which was in fact revolutionary. How revolutionary may be seen by glancing through the *Dictatus papae* inserted in Gregory's register early in his reign, a list of bald propositions that were probably headings for a series of arguments which were not completed:

1. That the Roman Church was founded by God alone.
2. That the Roman Pontiff alone is rightly to be called universal.
3. That he alone can depose or reinstate bishops.
4. That his legate, even if of lower grade, takes precedence, in a council, of all bishops and may render a sentence of deposition against them.
5. That the Pope may depose the absent.
6. That, among other things, we also ought not to stay in the same house with those excommunicated by him.
7. That for him alone it is lawful to enact new laws according to the needs of the time, to assemble together new congregations, to make an abbey of a canonry; and, on the other hand, to divide a rich bishopric and unite the poor ones.
8. That he alone may use the imperial insignia.
9. That the Pope is the only one whose feet are to be kissed by all princes.
10. That his name alone is to be recited in churches.
11. That his title is unique in the world.
12. That he may depose Emperors.
13. That he may transfer bishops, if necessary, from one See to another.
14. That he has power to ordain a cleric of any church he may wish.
15. That he who has been ordained by him may rule over another church, but not be under the command of others; and that such a one may not receive a higher grade from any bishop.
16. That no synod may be called a general one without his order.
17. That no chapter or book may be regarded as canonical without his authority.
18. That no sentence of his may be retracted by any one; and that he, alone of all, can retract it.
19. That he himself may be judged by no one.

20. That no one shall dare to condemn a person who appeals to the Apostolic See.
21. That to this See the more important cases of every church should be submitted.
22. That the Roman Church has never erred, nor ever, by the witness of Scripture, shall err to all eternity.
23. That the Roman Pontiff, if canonically ordained, is undoubtedly sanctified by the merits of St. Peter; of this St. Ennodius, Bishop of Pavia, is witness, many Holy Fathers are agreeable and it is contained in the decrees of Pope Symmachus the Saint.
24. That, by his order and with his permission, subordinate persons may bring accusations.
25. That without convening a synod he can depose and reinstate bishops.
26. That he should not be considered as Catholic who is not in conformity with the Roman Church.
27. That the Pope may absolve subjects of unjust men from their fealty.[1]

The premise basic to much of the *Dictatus papae* is that Rome is identifiable with Christendom and that the bishop of Rome is the bishop of Christendom—that is to say, that whatever jurisdiction a bishop has locally in a diocese, the pope has universally throughout the Christian world. Thus it was possible to insist on the papal right to depose, reinstate, or transfer other bishops, an idea that had been anathema to the early church; thus, too, one could elevate Rome as a court of final resort where all appeals would be welcome and the judgment of any other authority reviewed and if necessary reversed, while the pope himself could be judged and his decisions reversed by no one. Although the *Dictatus papae* includes the first explicit claim that popes may depose emperors, it is not directly concerned with the relations between the papacy and secular authority but rather with the relations between the pope and the rest of the church. But the program it embodied struck at the roots of the existing order.

It was not a program that could be immediately fulfilled, but in ensuing decades there was a steady erosion of the hitherto unassail-

---

[1] S. Z. Ehler and J. B. Morrall, *Church and State Through the Centuries* (London, 1954), pp. 43–44. Copyright 1954. Reprinted by permission of Biblo & Tannen, Inc.

able prerogatives of the lay world in ecclesiastical affairs. The program became widely popular because it was directed, among other things, to stricter disciplining of the clergy and the application to it, apparently as a response to popular pressure, of ideals derived from monasticism. Thus many married priests suffered the indignity of having their marriages declared invalid, their wives described as concubines, and their children bastards, a high price to pay for the immorality and laxity of some of their brethren. Papal success depended on other things than popularity, not least of which was the maintenance, despite occasional setbacks, of the independence of the papacy from secular control, especially that of the German emperors. A series of regulations from the twelfth to the fourteenth centuries ensured that papal elections would remain relatively free from external political influence. The papal patrimony, both inside and outside Italy, also contributed much to the eminence of the popes, who ruled as independent princes over extensive territories with no political superiors, while gradually acquiring feudal and other rights and incomes abroad which extended their influence throughout the west. From the late eleventh century, when the crusade was launched by Pope Urban II, papal claims to a universal leadership of Christian society received visible form.

THE PAPAL COURT

In the eleventh century the papal government was still a highly personal thing; indeed the court of the popes never lost its patriarchal character throughout the Middle Ages, despite its growth and elaboration. The bishop of Rome was father of a *familia* of clerical assistants and servants bound to him by intense filial loyalty. Before the twelfth century no matter was too small to demand his personal attention. The intimacy of the papal household, however, was soon lost. The growing importance of the papacy increased the range of its activities from the time of Gregory VII, which in turn required more and more officials. The pope's concern with the lines of control to be established over the church brought in its wake many quarrels over the right relation between popes and secular rulers. There was an increasing subordination of the church to Rome. In the twelfth century papal legates played an important part in making more immediate the pope's authority in Germany,

France, Italy, and even Spain. A series of large and impressive ecclesiastical councils over which the pope presided and through which his authority was promulgated in great solemnity made a growing church unity visible. More and more, the laity as well as the clergy sought the pope's arbitration in matters under jurisdictional dispute or his confirmation of their rights or offices, which while often not strictly necessary, seemed to bestow on these rights a greater validity. The result was a swift and to some a distressing growth in the papal court of the business of ecclesiastical patronage—canonries, deaneries, parish churches, and the like, together with the revenues associated with such offices; the papacy gradually passed from arbitrating disputes over appointments to reserving more and more of these to itself at the expense of traditional patrons, laymen, bishops, or collegiate clergy. All of this transformed what had been a handful of papal helpers into a large and expensive bureaucracy.

By Gregory VII's day there had come into existence a body of special assistants to the pope which would play an important role in the central government of the church—the college of cardinals. The college of cardinals originated in 1059 when Pope Nicholas II gave to certain bishops and priests of Rome a special role to play in the election of popes. The electoral college he created was comprised of seven bishops from small dioceses near Rome who traditionally performed liturgical functions in the church of St. John Lateran in Rome and of twenty-eight priests of as many Roman churches (called *tituli*) who performed similar functions in the four great Roman basilicas of St. Lawrence, St. Peter, St. Paul Outside the Walls, and St. Mary Major. These bishops and priests were called "cardinals" from the Latin verb *incardinare*, used for clerics who performed liturgical and other functions in churches other than their own. Even before they were formed into an electoral body, some of them had begun to play an important role in papal affairs, for among their number could be found some ardent reformers recruited from outside Rome by Pope Leo IX. But it was the legislation of Nicholas II on papal elections that gave them importance as a body. At first, the cardinal bishops had a more important place in the election of a pope than the cardinal priests, but the distinction between them became a mere formality when they were joined by the deacons of the Roman church, traditionally seven in number but now increased to nineteen. Unlike the cardinal bishops and cardinal priests, the deacons were not associated with churches other than their own—they were not "incardinated"— yet they were also called cardinals, evidence that by the late eleventh century the word had lost its primitive meaning and now connoted participation in the supreme government of the church.

There can be no denial of the importance of the college of cardinals as a body and of many of its members as individuals. As a body it came in time to replace the Roman synod, at best a solemn but intermittent affair unsuited for the purposes of sustained government. The college acted as a permanent body of advisers, meeting regularly and frequently in consistory. There they discussed with the pope matters of both ecclesiastical and political importance. Furthermore, they shared in the judicial functions of the pope, relieving him of the necessity of direct participation in most of the cases to be heard in his court but reserving to him final approval of sentences. Increasingly there appeared in the papal correspondence, especially that dealing with major matters, a reference to the fact that the pope's decisions were made "on the advice of our brethren" (*de consilio fratrum nostrorum*), a reflection of the college's growing role in papal government.

As individuals the cardinals, whether bishop, priest, or deacon, were of higher dignity than any churchman other than the pope himself; and with their elevated rank went an increase in personal prestige and importance. Their support was particularly valuable when, as happened more than once, the papal office was in dispute between two claimants. Many cardinals served from time to time as papal legates in various parts of western Christendom, wielding on the spot the fullness of authority on behalf of the pope; and in Rome itself there were always some cardinals who exercised a considerable influence over papal policy. While there were often rivalries within the college between individuals or factions, the cardinals were always careful about their prerogatives, especially their incomes, and closed ranks in the face of any threat to their corporate privileges.

During the thirteenth and fourteenth centuries the cardinals gradually extended their privileges, power, and revenue. That they were likened to Christ's apostles did not completely obscure the relatively recent origins of the college, but at least it reflected contemporary notions of the college's importance, as did the repeated comparison of it with the Roman Senate. Even philology was pressed into service, and "cardinal" was soon derived from the word *cardo,* a hinge—the cardinals were the hinge upon which the church swung. As their status rose so did their income. In 1272 they got from Gregory X half the annual tribute paid to the papacy by the kingdom of Sicily; they gradually established their rights to a portion of the "common services," payments made to the papacy by churchmen who received church benefices from the Holy See; and in 1289 they received from Nicholas IV half the ordinary revenues of the Roman church. Thus, too, the college shrank in number, became aristocratic in composition, and not unnaturally reached out for a greater share in church government.

There is a revealing document, a "capitulation" of 1352, drawn up by the cardinals in the conclave which was held to elect a pope on the death of Clement VI. Before proceeding with the election, the cardinals drew up a set of provisions, sworn to by all the cardinals, to be upheld by whichever of them was elected. These provisions were for the restriction of the number of the college, an increase in their control over their own membership at the expense of the pope's traditional right of appointment, a limitation of the pope's authority to discipline or censure cardinals, and so on. By 1378, the cardinals had reached the stage of virtually deposing one pope, Urban VI, and electing another, Clement VII, thus bringing about a great schism in the western church which lasted for some forty years. They made up an oligarchic body indeed, and although canon lawyers were on the whole reluctant to grant them any constitutional prerogatives which might suggest any limitation on the absolute authority of the pope, in practice they exercised a large influence in all kinds of affairs.

The four great offices of papal administration were the Camera, which handled finances, the Chancery for correspondence, the Penitentiary for everything touching on matters of faith, and the Rota, the judicial tribunal. Each of these offices employed a more or less numerous staff of scribes, clerks, and notaries, virtually all of them in the ranks of the clergy; they were rewarded for their services from the incomes of the benefices in churches throughout Europe which had been granted to them by the pope, although lesser servants—couriers, for instance—were paid wages. In addition, the personal household of the pope, including not only his chaplains but the many household servants and the troops who guarded his person and residence, swelled the numbers of those who peopled the Roman curia, to say nothing of the households of the cardinals, who in a smaller way attracted to their services similar retinues. It has been estimated recently that the popes of the fourteenth century in Avignon themselves employed some 450 to 650 men, of whom most were in almost constant attendance at the papal court.

COUNCILS

As an institution of law and government the general council had a long history. Even before the first general or ecumenical council was held in Nicaea in 325, it had been the custom for neighboring bishops to come together in regional conferences or synods to discuss common problems and adopt common measures. Not only did such regional gatherings continue, but from the fourth through the ninth centuries there was a succession of great councils of universal scope held in the eastern part of the empire, some of which were also recognized by the church in Rome as ecumenical and authoritative. All had been summoned on the authority of the emperor in Constantinople; all had been occasioned by critical disputes over ecclesiastical doctrine. In the west, however, it was only after the Gregorian reform movement gathered way that the popes began to use councils of bishops and abbots, regional as well as general, as instruments of discipline and reform and as a means of making more visible and more effective their legislative powers. From 1123 to 1311 there were seven councils, to say nothing of many local synods held by the pope himself or at his prompting, each occasioned by the consequences of some great crisis and each providing the pope with a forum in which to promulgate laws respecting simony, lay investiture, clerical discipline, public morality, violence, crusading indulgences, heresy, usury, and so forth. The very existence of such councils depended upon the will of the pope, and their decrees or canons had authority only when he confirmed and promulgated them. Though summoned to consider certain particular problems, all had in common the fact that they were extraordinary assemblies rather than continuing agencies of government, in which and through which the pope, whose authority needed no conciliar confirmation, might nevertheless in more solemn and public fashion exercise that moral and spiritual leadership which was his supreme duty. The ecumenical council, therefore, while an ecclesiastical institution of respectable antiquity, had no constitutional standing.

The day was not far off, however, when many churchmen would agree that the council was in fact the supreme governor of the church, the pope merely its executive agent. This revolutionary idea was occasioned by one of the most serious crises to afflict the church in the Middle Ages. Pope Gregory XI (1370–1378), the seventh pope in succession to rule the church from Avignon, decided to return the papal court to Rome, despite an abortive attempt by his immediate predecessor, Urban V, and in the face of strong discouragement from an entourage almost totally French. He left Avignon in October 1376. His troubles in a turbulent Rome in the ensuing year persuaded him that he had made a mistake, but before he could complete his plans to return to Avignon he died in Rome in March 1378. Canon law about papal elections was clear: the cardinals had to enter into conclave at the place of the pope's death and were to conduct no other business until a new pope had been elected. The cardinals, most of whom were French, found themselves under immediate pressure from the Roman populace to elect a Roman, or at the very least an Italian. They were warned by a deputation of Roman officials: "If you don't, then first all we officials will be killed, and then certainly all of you." That the cardinals were strongly influenced—they were later to say coerced —into electing an Italian who was himself not even a cardinal is impossible to deny. But that their election of the new pope, Urban VI, was a legitimate one seems evident. They may have thought that they had made the best of a difficult situation, for Urban had for years been an official in the papal curia, a member of the "establishment" so to speak. However, Urban turned savagely on the college, rebuked its members for their way of life, embarrassed and degraded them in public, and threatened to deprive them of revenues and privileges. Soon they drifted off from Rome, one by one, and meeting again safely in Fondi, they declared Urban's election invalid, elected a French cardinal who took the name Clement VII, and moved back to Avignon.

There were now two popes, two colleges of cardinals (for Urban immediately created another), two papal courts claiming to be the center of Christendom. Any hope that Urban and Clement might reach some compromise proved vain; any hope that when one pope died his college of cardinals would recognize his rival and thus

heal the rift proved equally futile. Urban was succeeded by Boniface IX, Innocent VII, and Gregory XII; Clement by Benedict XIII.
The division seemed permanent. This was the crisis which, as one
solution after another was proposed and rejected, forced upon those
most disturbed by its consequences the realization that only an
ecumenical council could save the church.

In the face of tradition it was not easy to rationalize the revolutionary idea of the supremacy of the council. There was some
faint support to be found in the literature of canon law dealing
with the hypothetical case of a pope who might fall into heresy.
That a heretic could continue to preside over the church was unthinkable; but to try him as other heretics were tried could not be
allowed, for the law was clear that no one could judge a pope. To
some commentators the general council suggested itself as a convenient means out of this impasse. They found it possible to con-
ceive of the council's performing a function on behalf of the church
at large when the pope was incapacitated owing to heresy. The
council might thus be thought of not merely as a public assembly
of ecclesiastics but as a body representative of the corporation of
all Christians. Canon lawyers had had much to say about corporations—usually cathedral colleges—and their rights during those
times when they had no head, no bishop. In the present circumstances, when the church appeared to be headless, it appeared
self-evident that the church as a corporate body could take to itself
the authority needed to defend the integrity of the church. That a
general council "of the universal church, representative of it and
acting on its behalf can and ought to be held," either because
"there is no pope, or because there is doubt as to who is pope,"
was the thesis of Jean Gerson (1362–1429), chancellor of the University of Paris, one of many who undertook to define the new constitutional role of the council. Members of the two colleges of
cardinals finally took the lead in summoning a general council to
meet at Pisa in 1409 without the consent of either of the two popes.
The result was greater chaos. At Pisa both Benedict XIII and
Gregory XII were deposed and Alexander V elected; but since
neither Benedict nor Gregory recognized the council's acts, the
church now had three claimants to the papal throne instead of
two. Another and greater council, at Constance in 1414, finally
settled the problem by obtaining the withdrawal of two of the
claimants, ignoring the claims of the third which were later

abandoned, and electing Martin V, who received the recognition of the whole church. But in the process the council carved out for itself a large constitutional position which was enacted into law. It claimed that it held its authority direct from Christ, that all persons, even popes, had to obey its decrees, and that it was henceforth to meet on a regular basis.

The absolute authority of the papacy seemed at an end. In the interval between deposing the various claimants in 1414 and the election of Martin in 1417, the council became in fact the center of church government, while attempting at the same time to perform the extraordinary functions of a council in matters of general reform, discipline, heresy, and the like. In neither sphere was it very successful. It was not organized to handle day-to-day business, hitherto the function of the papal curia, and in too many minds reform began and ended with the limitation of the papal right to grant church benefices, which had threatened local interests.

The next council, which opened at Pavia in 1423, was a complete failure. Martin V transferred it to Siena for political reasons. Many of those in attendance, suspicious of his intentions, negotiated assurances of safe-conduct and immunity from the officials of the town, and the assembly which gathered there in July 1423 had the aspect of a meeting of rival parties rather than of a general council. The internal organization was modeled on that of the council of Constance, which in turn had been suggested by the organization by nations of the arts faculty of the University of Paris. At Constance, in order to offset the influence of the great number of Italian bishops, the Germans, English, and French proposed that all votes be taken by nation rather than by head, which was adopted. To the four nations a fifth was added with the arrival of members from the Spanish kingdoms. Both at Constance and now at Siena, this kind of organization tended to give to all deliberations a partisan quality reflecting national interests rather than those of the church at large. Some even wanted to go further and to impose national representation on the college of cardinals. The failure of Martin V to attend the council and its gradual desertion by most of its members brought it to a close in February 1424, its only effective decision being to hold the next council at Basle.

The council at Basle lasted from 1431 to 1449; it had to face the hostility of Pope Eugenius IV, who was distrustful of its views and sought its subjection, but in its early years it enjoyed such widespread support that the pope for the time was powerless. At Basle the council virtually incorporated itself, demanding oaths from all its members to uphold its supremacy. The by now traditional organization by nations could not be adopted because the conciliar party could rely for certain on only two of them, the French and the Germans; within the nations, also, the influence of bishops who supported the papacy might be too strong. So internally the council was organized into four commissions, to handle matters of faith, peace, reform, and general affairs, composed of an equal number from each nation and an equal number of persons of all rank. The presence of large numbers of university graduates could then offset the influence of the hierarchy.

Basle had a lengthy career before its final collapse. It took on all the attributes of a sovereign body, developed a chancery, referred to its envoys as legates, received and handled supplications for ecclesiastical benefices, and established a Rota to deal with legal appeals from ecclesiastical courts and a Penitentiary for all spiritual matters. But it steadily lost the support of the cardinals and most of the senior members of the hierarchy, while national interests came to dominate its deliberations; national autonomy, a growing phenomenon in the fourteenth century, drew much support from a conciliarism which undermined the universal authority of the papacy and allowed states to intervene incessantly in ecclesiastical affairs. Further, the council lost credit by failing to meet the general expectations of those who sought widespread church reform. In the question of reunion with the orthodox church of Byzantium, a recurrent project of long standing, the inability of the council to get the recognition of the Greek envoys and Pope Eugenius' success in having the discussions carried on under his supervision in Italy allowed him to score a telling blow. In 1437 he called for the transfer of the council to Ferrara, thus completing a split between the recalcitrant majority and a minority which obeyed and henceforth acted, at Ferrara and later at Florence, as a small but obedient assembly. The majority which remained behind took the final step of deposing Eugenius and electing Felix V, only to find that the conciliar theories upon which they had based their decisions were no longer of moment in European politics. Europe was not ready to face another schism, and European states continued to recognize Eugenius. The principles of conciliarism, already opposed by many, were now completely discredited. Not long after, Pope Pius II could refer to any appeal from his authority to that of a council, as though the latter were superior, as a "detestable corruption" exhibiting a "spirit of rebellion," a "pestilential stench," and a threat to the Christian flock to whose shepherd, the bishop of Rome, Christ had given the injunction "Feed my sheep."

After some forty years the council had failed to achieve a constitutional place in the church.

X
EDUCATION

CHRISTIAN AND PAGAN

WITH THE SETTLEMENT OF LARGE NUMBERS of Germans in the western empire, there came a marked decline in education. How far we should go in attributing this decline to the newcomers is hard to say. Certainly Roman education was for the most part an urban matter; most Germans settled in rural districts, thus limiting severely whatever role the Roman schools might have played in their cultural assimilation. Then, too, Roman education was based on a literature and language and reflected attitudes and assumptions foreign and for the most part meaningless to the Germans. But while the Germans were indifferent, they were not usually hostile to the traditional education of Roman citizens. Other factors contributed to the decline of this education: its dependence on the cultural legacy of a pagan past which grew increasingly irrelevant as time went on and the collapse of state support.

The tension between Christian belief and pagan education had presented no problem in the early years of Christianity when the church's membership was drawn from the underworld of the submerged and the servile, comprising, as one hostile critic put it, "illiterates from the dregs of the populace and credulous women with the instability natural to their sex."[1] Its members could not afford, and for that matter did not need, the literary and rhetorical training which made up the curriculum of Roman schools. Christians joyfully waited for the imminent end of the world, when the meek and lowly would enter upon their inheritance; it was natural enough to scorn the vain and superficial arts of pagan Rome.

But the world stubbornly showed little sign of coming to its end, and meanwhile the church began to draw into its ranks many who were well educated, themselves the products of pagan schools. Consequently there soon appeared a certain ambivalence in the attitude of churchmen toward the things of this world, especially pagan learning. To be sure, such learning as the traditional education had to offer had its dangers, but there could be little complaint against rhetoric as such, which might be excellent discipline for the Christian as for the pagan. There was, however, real danger lurking in the literature upon which the study of rhetoric was based. Without exception it was a pagan literature, filled with allusions to polytheism, often offensive to the faith of Christians, not all of it edifying, a good deal of it open to the accusations of immorality and downright indecency, and in its philosophical implications frequently subversive of Christian doctrine. The call to a simple piety, untrammeled by pagan philosophy, was made most eloquently by the great church father Tertullian (c. 160–c. 230), himself a product of the schools of his day, a lawyer and a master of Latin prose. "What has Athens to do with Jerusalem?" he asked. "What concord is there between the Academy and the Church? Away with all attempts to produce a mottled Christianity of Stoic, Platonic, and dialectic composition. . . . With our faith we desire no further belief." In another third century source we read: "Avoid completely heathen books! For what have you to do with strange words or laws or false prophecies, which are a ready source of error for unsteady minds?"

Almost all those who opposed Greek and Latin literature and philosophy did so on the grounds of their immorality and frivolity, their error and lack of truth. But there were now many who came to the defense of the classics, not perhaps as we might today on the

---

[1] Minucius Felix, *Octavius*, VIII, 4.

grounds of their beauty or their artistic "truth" but because of their utility as an intellectual and moral preparation for the study of Holy Scripture. St. Clement of Alexandria (fl. A.D. 200) considered that since God was the author of all truth, what truth might be found in pagan literature must have had a divine origin. St. Jerome, a brilliant scholar of the fourth century, though constantly troubled in his conscience by his admiration for the classics, especially Cicero, still boldly defended secular literature by likening it to the captive maiden in Deuteronomy (21:11–13) who might properly be taken to wife after her head had been shaved and her nails pared—thus secular learning might be embraced after all error, idolatry, and lust had been shaved off and cut away. St. Augustine, greatest of the Latin fathers, admired the best in pagan literature, and even while refuting pagan philosophy where it contradicted Christian theology, conceded that the philosophers of old had often held opinions approaching to the one true religion.

Nevertheless, Christians remained troubled by the pleasure to be derived from classical literature, the sheer beauty of which often enticed the recent convert into apostasy. This suspicion of beauty lingered throughout the Middle Ages. Ovid might contain a little gold, but it was buried in a dung heap. Virgil was a beautiful vase, filled with poisonous snakes. There were many to regret their reading of the classics in their youth, as though feeling remorse for some immoral and shameful escapade. To delight in literature when young only to reject it at a more mature age was not uncommon. Pope Gregory I (590–604) is a case in point. He was a product of Roman schools, educated, as Paul the Deacon tells us, in the liberal disciplines, second to none in Rome in *grammatica, rhetorica, dialectica.* He followed an administrative career, advancing until he became praetor of Rome; but on the death of his father he abandoned his civil offices, founded half a dozen monasteries in Sicily and another in his father's house in Rome, which he then entered as a monk. Later, as pope, he had occasion to chastise the bishop of Vienne: "It has come to our attention, the thought of which fills one with shame, that you have been teaching *grammatica"*—a serious fault, Gregory went on, since one does not hear the praises of Christ and those of Jove from the same lips. Gregory even prided himself on his stylistic defects and barbarisms, thinking it unfitting that the words of God be subject to the grammatical rules of Donatus, the author of a standard textbook of grammar. Still, it was

Gregory who, during his pontificate, took a momentous step in the history of western culture; in 596 he dispatched a mission to the Anglo-Saxons in England, headed by Augustine, a monk of the monastery he had founded in Rome. The mission had as its purpose the conversion of the English; it could hardly be foreseen that the new converts would quickly absorb large elements of western learning, preserve them, and retransmit them to the continent in later centuries.

In the fourth and fifth centuries there had been no scheme of purely Christian education with which to replace the traditional schools; the elderly might regret their reading of the classics, but if the young were to be taught at all they had to go to schools which still pursued the old curriculum. There were attempts to replace the offensive pagan authors by creating a more acceptable literature using classical forms as vehicles for Christian learning. Thus Juvencus, a Spanish ecclesiastic of the early fourth century, narrated the gospels in hexameters; another author used Virgil as his model to tell the story of the creation and fall; but these and other such imitations had little chance of replacing the real thing. More important in the long run were works of Christian authors on religious or ecclesiastical themes which, while they played no immediate role in formal schooling, provided the basis for religious instruction and doctrine when education became the prerogative of churchmen after the sixth century. The works of St. Augustine, for example, did not replace the classics of ancient Rome, but they fashioned a Christian view of the world within which the classics would in time be absorbed. And the works of Pope Gregory I enjoyed great popularity in the Middle Ages, especially his *Pastoral Rule* on the duties of the priesthood, which acquired authoritative status throughout the church and became for the secular clergy what Benedict's rule was for the monk.

SECULAR SCHOOLS

During the late empire a liberal education was not only a badge of social rank, it was a sure avenue toward imperial service. Some of the great servants of state were those who achieved their position through the literary skill that commanded so much admiration at the time. During the Roman imperial period the state had gradually undertaken the support of higher education without, however, curtailing the activity of private teachers. There was increasing legislation in the third and fourth centuries revealing the concern of the government for the position of public teachers and the welfare of education in general. In some of the larger centers state schools were established; the smaller municipalities ran their own, but even here the imperial government often exercised control over appointments and determined minimum salaries of teachers. By the fifth century, while elementary education still remained in private hands, higher education was for the most part controlled by the state.

Although there were schools of law and of what passed for philosophy, it was on grammar and rhetoric that the energies of most teachers and students were expended. There was much emphasis on good reading aloud, grammatical and metrical analysis, and the ornaments of literary style. A good grammar teacher went much further than this, however, elaborating on the subject matter of the literature being read, so that grammar actually served as a vehicle for the communication of a large amount of information about a wide range of subjects. The teacher needed a broad if not very deep knowledge of such things as etymology, history, mythology, law, mathematics, natural history, music, and astronomy, and, if he were a Christian, of biblical and church lore. All too often, however, there was a temptation to take the easier way, to concentrate on form and phrase, figures of speech and literary ornamentation, with less and less concern for content. More often than not grammar became mere drill, rote learning, a preparation for the increasingly popular study of rhetoric.

The discipline of rhetoric, becoming divorced from the public life and legal oratory characteristic of an earlier day but now increasingly moribund, often produced pompous banalities which passed for brilliance, cast in the form of panegyrics or public declamations. It exercised a peculiar fascination over those who followed literary fashion, with unhappy effects on grammar in the large sense, as a means of acquiring a genuine liberal education. Training in the use of words in order to influence others may have been a useful form of education, but when devoted to achieving pleasurable effects on an audience, often on trivial or even absurd themes, its purpose became too narrow. The west of the fifth century soon abandoned what had become mechanical and sterile.

Because the professors had enjoyed state support, with guaranteed salaries to go with a high social status, the collapse of Roman administration in the west posed a serious threat to them and their schools. In Italy, where Theodoric the Ostrogoth attempted to maintain Roman traditions, public support of education continued in the sixth century, and many of the educated clergy of the church in Italy, to say nothing of the aristocratic laity, learned their letters in schools which operated on the old models. St. Benedict of Nursia, founder of Monte Cassino, was educated in Rome in the "liberal arts," which he later rejected in order not to lose his immortal soul. There were well-known schools of rhetoric in Milan and Ravenna. Many of the public schools were still pagan and secular in nature; but Theodoric's great minister Cassiodorus (d. 575) began to encourage schools similar in form but primarily Christian in spirit. In doing so he took the first step toward the eventual establishment of a church monopoly of education, though such may not have been his intention. He had a great interest in education and sought to supply the facilities for the study of Christian literature in the thorough way that had long been applied to pagan literature. After retiring from public life to spend his last years in the monastery at Vivarium which he had founded, he continued to pursue intellectual interests, assisted by a number of pupils; and the monastery, which he endowed with his library, became for some time a center of literary activity and a model for monasteries of the future. In a work which became a handbook for monastic schools, he drew up an ideal curriculum for his monks based on the old Roman division of the seven liberal arts, divided into groups of three and four, the *trivium* and the *quadrivium*. The former encompassed grammar, rhetoric, and logic, the latter arithmetic, astronomy, geometry, and music. This had been a traditional Roman division of learning, most recently taken up and expanded by Boethius (d. 525). It was this tradition upon which Cassiodorus drew, justifying, as so many of his predecessors had done, the study of secular literature as a means to a spiritual end, a fuller and richer comprehension of divine truth. His efforts were important in two ways, therefore: first, as Theodoric's minister, in attracting scholars into public service, continuing aid to the public schools, and encouraging similar schools inspired by Christian principles; and later, as a monk, in giving to monasticism a literary and intellectual function which lay the ground for the monastic schools of the future.

CHURCH SCHOOLS

In Rome by the end of the sixth century the pagan schools had withered away; the *schola cantorum* founded by Pope Gregory I taught not only music but also letters, and here many of the future popes of the seventh and eighth centuries would be trained. Education was by now almost solely serving the interests of the church.

This was generally the case not only in Rome but in other episcopal centers. Increasingly the careers which demanded literacy became fewer. Those who entered on a career in the church, which did demand literacy, were taken into episcopal households, often at an early age, where they received instruction in letters and in sacred knowledge from the bishop himself or from some teacher in his service. Parishes too began to provide the elements of an education in response to the same needs. The church schools were essentially professional in purpose, although they frequently educated members of the laity, young men who later abandoned the ecclesiastical career for which they had been destined in their youth. In the parts of Italy subject to the Lombards, although the Lombard kings apparently maintained something of an active palace school in Pavia, public schools in general disappeared. Their place, however, was slowly filled by the church schools, since the church was the only institution capable of and with a reason for maintaining at least a limited system of instruction. Elsewhere than in Italy there is some evidence of the continuing, though declining, influence of the secular schools in the sixth century, but in the main those who wrote did so on religious and theological themes. In Spain, theological disputes left little energy for the cultivation of the art of the rhetor; and even the knowledge of Greek, now rare, was exploited merely to translate sayings of Egyptian abbots. Churchmen put what learning they had to the task of combating heresy and rustic paganism. There were still a few, like the bishop of Vienne who annoyed Pope Gregory, whose admiration for the literature of the pagan past continued to find expression. But their numbers seem to have declined rapidly through general indifference to the culture of the past, while what education was to be found within the church grew increasingly more professional.

Monasticism made the largest contribution to the maintenance of education. Cassiodorus had not been alone in encouraging study within the monastery; even though St. Benedict, himself educated in the traditional Roman schools, had not prescribed an education for his followers, he had required that a portion of each day be set aside for religious reading, which certainly presupposed some minimum of education. Other monastic rules—in Gaul, for example, where Benedict's influence would not be felt until much later— made similar demands. That learning found something of a haven in the monastery was of enormous significance for the future. Irish and English monasteries were particularly important in this regard; for while learning entered on a rapid decline on the continent after the sixth century, the formation of libraries in monasteries such as Wearmouth and Jarrow (whither their founder, Benedict Biscop, brought back books each time he returned from one of his six visits to Rome) guaranteed the preservation and transmission of significant elements of learning. Biscop's collection included some classical as well as ecclesiastical works, and their spread through borrowing and copying is attested by the famous library at York which was composed of transcriptions of manuscripts which he had earlier collected.

How we measure the decline of learning and education after the sixth century depends on what we consider important. While some civic centers and monasteries in Italy produced an occasional scholar, there is evidence of widespread illiteracy. Certainly there were fewer scholars of note and fewer notable centers of learning; in Gaul especially, where the schools of law and rhetoric had shown remarkable tenacity, there was swift decay under the Merovingians, and both the Greek language and firsthand knowledge of the literature of ancient Rome faded fast. In the monasteries, education amounted for the most part to training in reading the Latin scriptures and in singing the offices. On the other hand, the Englishman Bede (c. 673–735), whose education was wholly received in the monastery, acquired a rich learning, and while he may not have been typical, he is an example of what could be learned in the cloister and reminds us that we must temper our notion of intellectual decline.

However, Bede also demonstrates what had long been a characteristic of learning—the tendency to collect as well as one might with limited resources the knowledge of the past, to order it, to simplify it in the process, and to pass it on. In other words, we shall look in vain for originality after the sixth century. What was deemed worthy of preservation was frequently determined by its value in a Christian society, although Christianity itself could hardly be blamed for the lack of originality that was generally characteristic of secular learning since antiquity. Long before Bede there had been attempts at comprehensive compilations of knowledge. Cassiodorus, as we have seen, made a collection on the liberal arts, with much borrowing from earlier treatments and little originality. The most important encylcopaedia, however, was compiled by Isidore of Seville (570–636). It came to serve as a major source of knowledge for future generations, a kind of textbook of the Middle Ages. It was a work of some twenty books of the most diverse information, much of it fantastic, the model of many a later work, but not to be replaced as a standard authority until the thirteenth century.

Bede himself compiled an encyclopaedia, although he is best known now for his *History of the English Church and People*. He also wrote many separate commentaries on biblical books. His little textbooks designed for students of Latin reveal his study of the grammatical treatises of late Rome, and his work on chronology contributed to the present system of dating events before or after the birth of Christ rather than from the creation of the world. While, therefore, educational decline was rapid elsewhere, in the north of England Bede played an important part in preserving a culture which in the course of time would be called upon to help renew education on the continent. One of his students, Egbert, as archbishop of York, established there an episcopal school of considerable repute; Egbert's pupil, Alcuin, master of the school of York, was later responsible for the renewal of education in the Carolingian empire as Charlemagne's chief minister.

CHARLEMAGNE AND EDUCATION

Alcuin had long been preceded on the continent by Irish and English missionaries whose monastic foundations and whose influence initially kept alive a tenuous tradition of learning. But the general literacy of the west had declined to the point where Christianity itself was threatened, a matter of no little concern to those churchmen and secular political leaders who took seriously their role of leadership in a Christian community. It is evident from Charlemagne's foundation of a palace school, his employment and encouragement of the best scholars to be found, including Alcuin and others, and his educational legislation that he viewed a properly educated clergy and a basic religious education for the laity as the cornerstone of his kingdom. His concern over the low state of learning is apparent from the letter, written in language strongly reminiscent of the Anglo-Saxon tradition represented by Alcuin, which he sent to Abbot Baugulf and his brethren in the monastery of Fulda. The letter was later widely circulated among other abbots and bishops:

Be it known, therefore, . . . that we . . . have thought it useful that the bishoprics and monasteries entrusted by Christ's favor to our charge show zeal in teaching not only the requirements of the regular life and the intercourse of holy religion, but also reading and writing, to those who by the grace of God are capable of learning, each according to his capacity. Just as the monastic rule gives order and grace to honorable conduct, so too perseverance in teaching and learning gives order and grace to one's sentences, so that those who strive to please God by right living do not neglect to please him by right speaking. . . .

Often in recent years, when letters were sent to us from various monasteries telling us how eagerly the brethren there prayed for us, we noticed in most of the letters upright sentiments and uncouth language; what pious devotion faithfully prompted in their hearts their uneducated tongues could not put into words without stumbling. Consequently we began to fear that as skill in writing was worse than it should be, so wisdom to understand the sacred scriptures might be even worse than it should be. We all know quite well that although verbal errors are dangerous, errors of understanding are much more dangerous.

Therefore we exhort you not only *not* to neglect the study of letters but also, with humble mind, pleasing to God, to strive to learn so that you may succeed in penetrating the mysteries of divine scripture the more easily and correctly. Since, however, images, tropes and other similar figures of speech are to be found in the sacred pages, it is undoubted that anyone reading such things will understand their spiritual sense all the more quickly if first he has been fully instructed in the mastery of letters.[1]

Obviously the state of learning was low even in the church, but Charles had no other agency on which he could place the burden of establishing and maintaining educational standards. The purpose of this renewed education was religious, the proper understanding of Holy Scripture, but since this required a mastery of grammar a sound Latin education was necessary. Charles wanted an educated clergy to act as teachers, and called for schools for children to be founded in the monasteries and episcopal churches for teaching the Psalms, the *computus,* grammar, and singing. It was a limited program, with rather minimal examinations to ensure that priests had some familiarity with the creed, the penitential, and the gospels, and were able to write. These modest requirements are themselves a measure of the decline in learning by Charlemagne's day.

Charles' legislation had considerable effect. Church synods repeated his various instructions and encouraged the creation of episcopal and parish schools. There is evidence also that monastic schools opened their doors to the children of the laity. The palace school at Aachen served as a model and also trained many ecclesiastics of the next generation. There Alcuin, from 782 until his retirement to Tours in 796, was the prime mover in establishing standards of spelling and handwriting and in fashioning a curriculum out of the seven liberal arts in which, in view of the religious ends of this education, he stressed grammar and rhetoric. His own works show little or no originality. Cast in dialogue form, they draw heavily on earlier sources and present instruction of a very elementary nature. But there can be no underestimating the importance of his work and that of his contemporaries under the aegis of Charlemagne in establishing educational standards, providing educational and theological treatises, correcting corrupt texts, and encouraging the teaching of the young. The total effect of Charles' reforms was astonishing, although unfortunately not long lasting. Especially where royal encouragement met with episcopal enthusiasm, there

---

[1] Luitpold Wallach, "Charlemagne's *De litteris colendis* and Alcuin," *Speculum,* Vol. XXVI (1951), pp. 288–305.

was a marked increase in the education of boys, which contributed much to the future of the clerical vocation. Monastic schools, while they did not neglect education in singing, copying music, and such practical subjects, often went further; devoted as they were to the religious life, some of them became important centers of theology, the one discipline of "higher learning" before the twelfth century.

The slender and scattered evidence of education and learning in the ninth and tenth centuries, the frequent reiteration of injunctions to establish schools, and the obvious difficulties of finding adequate teachers, all testify, however, to the short-lived nature of educational reform after Charles' death. Many bishops resisted the role thrust upon them of educating the laity. They would have preferred only the responsibility of training future clergy. Hostility to the classics, upon which a good deal of traditional instruction was still based, undoubtedly played some part in this resistance. Those who supported secular learning did so for the now classic reason that it was a means to an end, a necessary preliminary to religious knowledge. Sporadic attempts to put the royal legislation on education into effect continued to be made, therefore. Some monastic schools continued to provide instruction for boys other than oblates, who were in the process of joining the monastery; at St. Gall, as at a few other houses, the two groups were taught in separate schools. But the evidence for the continuation of schools in the ninth and tenth centuries is thin, and it is all too clear that the Carolingian program, while it established a pattern of church schools for the future, was not sustained. If Charles had had any idea of initiating universal elementary education, it came nowhere near being realized.

Among the many legacies left by the Carolingian reforms in education and learning was the firm marriage between school and church, and a curriculum almost solely literary. Further, there was the fact that education was a public matter, a matter to be legislated about, whether by church authorities, secular rulers, or town councils. Although increasingly ignored, Carolingian legislation remained as a basis for the future, to be built upon by the papacy in later centuries. Finally, through its emphasis on the establishment and maintenance of good texts, the Carolingian reform stimulated the growth of monastic *scriptoria* and the development of important libraries, which in some places would serve as centers of learning and sources of knowledge in the future. In the main, however, education before the twelfth century remained a rearguard action, its object the preservation rather than the acquisition of knowledge, its locale a few cathedral and monastic schools.

THE REVIVAL OF THE TWELFTH CENTURY

By the twelfth century the monasteries, by their nature ill-suited to teaching outsiders on a large scale, had for the most part declined as centers of culture; the cathedral schools, which became much more important in the course of the century, were small and not very numerous. Even as late as 1215, Pope Innocent III repeated legislation to the effect that all cathedrals ought to employ a schoolmaster, evidence that the ideal of a widespread educational system within the church remained far from realization. Still, the growth of intellectual activity in the twelfth century had a profound effect on such schools as there were and led to the growth of many more. It also created out of some of them a new educational institution, the university.

In northern France especially, the revival of learning found expression in and took the form of a revival of the discipline of dialectic, and its most exciting by-product was the attempt to submit the mysteries of Christian faith to rational explanation. This led to frequent controversies between exponents of conflicting attitudes, giving to the schools in which they taught a wide notoriety. Dialectic, as an exercise of reason, threatened to subordinate divine authority to rational analysis; and the debates about the respective roles of reason and authority in the discernment of truth, as about the question of universals, that is, the degree of reality to be attributed to abstractions, engaged the minds and energies of scholars everywhere, brought masses of students to hear the lectures of those who were engaged in philosophical and theological controversies, and produced quarrels and scholarly vendettas which on more than one occasion led to accusations of heresy and demands for retraction.

The revival in intellectual activity brought in its wake new educational material. The old *trivium* and the virtually neglected *quadrivium* were given more substance by the acquisition and absorption of the "new logic" of Aristotle (the *Prior* and *Posterior*

INTELLECTUAL CENTERS

▲ Monastic centers of learning, eighth to twelfth centuries.

○ Intellectual centers and universities, twelfth and thirteenth centuries.

Analytics, the *Topics,* and the *Elenchi,* which after about 1128 took their place beside the *Categories* and *Organon,* the "old logic") and by the new mathematics and science including the works of Euclid and the *Almagest* of Ptolemy. These works became available through translations from the Arabic and were accompanied by Arabic works on algebra and trigonometry. Aristotle's treatises on physics and meteorology also received Latin translations, as did a large corpus of Greek and Arabic works on medicine. The effects of the new learning were felt everywhere: there was a rapid development of logic as the central core of all learning and a growing sophistication in the three main areas of advanced study—theology, medicine, and law. The stimulus to already established schools, especially cathedral schools, was immeasurable. Chartres and Orleans, Reims and Laon, Beauvais and Soissons, and many others gained fame as centers of classical learning and the new dialectic; but it was Paris which quickly outshone all these and became the home of the first university in northern Europe. The effects were also felt in England, especially at Canterbury, where the scholar-bishop Theobald (1138–1161) gathered about him a coterie of literary and legal scholars and his successor Thomas Becket did much the same. In Spain were to be found some of the most important centers for the translation and interpretation of Greek and Arabic works. But in Germany, where bishops were caught up in imperial politics, cathedral schools were not notable, and German students, as eager as others to gain access to the new learning, flocked to France; one wrote back to a fellow student who had elected to stay behind and attend the lectures of one Heribert at Hildesheim that Heribert was "a man who not only did not study in Beauvais himself but also, in an insolent and mean way, prevented others from doing so. He should never have dared let himself be hired as an instructor."[1] If one had not studied in France, one's qualifications to teach were highly questionable. In Italy, too, the higher clergy was too immersed in imperial or local politics, and education tended to develop in the hands of private teachers, often laymen, who kept alive the traditions of the notary and the scribe. The services of these private teachers became of increasing

---

[1] Helene Wieruszowski, *The Medieval University* (Princeton, N.J., 1966), p. 121.

importance in those communities where the growth of the merchant class placed a premium on literacy and a knowledge of the legal formulas of contracts, loans, and other financial and commercial documents.

UNIVERSITIES

It was in Italy that the first real university developed—to be precise, in the city of Bologna which already had a large reputation for its schools. There the *ars dictaminis,* the discipline of the notary, kept alive the literary traditions for which Bologna had been noted and served also as a bridge to the study of Roman and Canon law for which the city was well on the way to becoming famous. In Bologna there were many schools: there were the schools of letters run by the church and by the municipality, there were schools of law run by laymen, and there were schools of canon law in the monasteries.

Roman law had never died out in Italy; popular legal institutions in the west reflected in their procedures the law of the empire codified by the emperor Theodosius II in 438. The later more scientific codification by the emperor Justinian (527–565) never had an impact on the west, except in those few areas under immediate Byzantine jurisdiction, but copies were sent to Rome and there is some indication that a tenuous knowledge of Justinian's legislation persisted in the west. Certainly law as a subject for study maintained a modest place in the curriculum of Italian schools, imbedded in the *trivium* under the rubrics of grammar and rhetoric. The revival of learning and education in the twelfth century marked a rapid development of legal studies in Italian towns: Pavia, Milan, and Verona were centers of the study of Lombard Law; Rome, Ravenna, and especially Bologna, of Roman law. Even in the schools of Lombard law, Roman law was studied as a kind of universal code which might be used to supplement and elucidate the local law of a particular people.

The great revival of Roman law is associated with a teacher, Irnerius, who taught at Bologna between the years 1100 and 1130; he was certainly not the first to teach law there, but his fame as a teacher was such that later generations attributed the rediscovery of the Justinian corpus of law to him. What distinguished Bologna this early was the prominence given to the *Digest*, the largest and most important section of Justinian's collection, and the rapid development of legal studies as a separate course rather than as part of the arts curriculum. There was a sharp distinction between law students and all other students, the former tending to be older, in many cases already family men or men in holy orders launched on an ecclesiastical career—in effect a body of professionally oriented persons much more independent than ordinary students.

The growing fame of the law schools of Bologna attracted increasing numbers of students from elsewhere; and it was these foreign students who helped to give shape and direction to the development of the university. Being foreigners, they were subject to many disabilities, both legal and financial; but being numerous and older than other students they had it within their power to take measures to protect themselves. Under the influence of contemporary gild movements, the students came together in corporations by national origin, which by the middle of the thirteenth century had amalgamated into two large gilds, the Italians and the Ultramontanes (from beyond the Alps), distinct but closely allied to one another. The word "university" (*universitas*) was a generic term used to describe gilds and collectivities of all sorts; its application to gilds of students and professors would shape its modern meaning as an institution of higher learning.

The student gild or university was strictly an organization of foreigners, that is, non-Bolognese. Its original purpose was to defend the interests of its members against rapacious townsmen and teachers, to adopt rules of membership, to seek freedom from taxation and the jurisdiction of local courts, to regulate room rents, book prices, and the quality and quantity of instruction. In the process it evolved internal officers and a corpus of legislation which provided the basis for an entirely novel educational institution. It excluded the teachers, most of whom were townsmen, and attempted to reduce them to the role of employees. By the threat of boycotting the professors, the gild of students was able to compel the professors to take an oath of obedience to the rector of the gild and to comply with the statutes of the gild, which in some cases proved to be severe limitations: the professor could get a day off only after receiving permission both from his own students and from the rector and counselors of the gild (two days if he wanted to get married); if he proposed to leave town, he had to make a deposit of sufficient size to ensure his return; at any time that he failed to attract five or more students to his class, he was fined; he had to begin his lectures promptly on time and stop lecturing within one minute after the bell—should he wander on, the students themselves were required to get up and walk out. If during his lecture he skipped over something or put off some difficulty until the end of the lecture, he was fined; and the legal text that he was lecturing on was so arranged that he had to cover specified portions by specified dates. The collection of fines from delinquent professors was made easier by requiring a deposit from them at the beginning of the academic year.

The university in Bologna, therefore, was a self-governing gild of law students. There was also a university, or gild, of doctors (teachers), smaller and less powerful. They were naturally opposed to the formation of a gild by the students and to the students' election of a rector and their promulgation of statutes. They denied to the students the character of a profession, insisting on the fact that they were merely disciples being introduced to a profession and therefore not yet in possession of a claim to the privileges of incorporation. The argument may have satisfied law professors; it had no effect on the growth of student power, based squarely as it was on the threats of boycott against individual professors and of removal from the city against the townsmen.

At the outset the teachers depended on the fees of the students for their income and had to negotiate with them individually or in groups, which explains how the students quickly gained the upper hand. From the point of view of the teacher, it could never have been a very satisfactory arrangement. The eminent jurist Odofredus (d. 1265) ended a course of lectures to one class with these plaintive words: "I tell you that next year I intend to give my ordinary (morning) lectures as required by the regulations, just as I always have; but I'm not going to give extraordinary lectures, since students are not good payers. They want to learn; they don't want to pay."[1] Soon, however, the raiding of the professoriate by neighboring towns, a practice familiar to the administrators of modern universities, made it necessary to meet the competition by

[1] Hastings Rashdall, *The Universities of Europe in the Middle Ages*, Vol. I (London, 1936), 209, n. 1.

the creation of endowed chairs with guaranteed incomes. The fact that the city took on responsibility for the salaries of the professors proved to be the first step in the gradual acquisition by the city government of ultimate control over the university. Elsewhere in Italy, at universities which were founded on the model of Bologna, city authorities established boards of governors which by the sixteenth or seventeenth century managed to destroy the autonomy of the students.

The rector of the student university was elected biennially, had to be a cleric of some five years standing in the law course, and at least twenty-four years of age. His jurisdiction drew its sanction from the general statutes of the university, and he had little discretion in their application. While he had a large jurisdiction over the members of the university, that is the students, it did not include criminal jurisdiction until the fifteenth century when it was conceded to him, provided that both parties in a dispute were members of the university. The rector also exercised considerable jurisdiction over others who were not members of the student body, especially tradesmen connected with the production of books and those whose business it was to rent lodgings to students. The fact that the rector was a cleric ensured that those students who were in holy orders would not be tried by a layman, which was forbidden by canon law. On the other hand the university of doctors had both criminal and civil jurisdiction, but its effectiveness was seriously limited by the large claims of the students, and any sentence they ventured to pronounce depended on the cooperation of town authorities for enforcement.

The rector governed with the aid of a number of counselors, and together they formed an executive body which convoked the university and proposed legislation. The rector's office, of only two years' duration, had little chance of developing into an autocracy; there was little in the way of emoluments, and the holder was often required to expend large sums commensurate with the dignity of his position. By the sixteenth century the acceptance of election had to be made compulsory, and precautions were taken to ensure that the rector did not leave town before his term expired.

The graduate at Bologna entered into a society of scholars which, owing to the intervention and encouragement of the papacy, had wide recognition. The law schools of Bologna had originally been run by a professional gild which accepted or rejected candidates for membership without reference to any outside authority. But the growing interest of the papacy in education, especially in the legal education of Bologna where so many of the popes and cardinals had themselves received their early training, brought many modifications. Pope Honorius III in 1219 insisted that the doctorate, itself a license to teach, was not to be bestowed without the consent of the archdeacon of Bologna. Graduation thus ceased to be a simple acceptance into the teacher's gild by the teachers themselves but rather the conferral of a status in the academic world at large; when in 1292 Pope Nicholas IV gave such graduates a right to teach anywhere, graduation became in fact an initiation into an international fraternity.

There are many points of comparison and some of complete contrast between the schools at Bologna and the development of the university in Paris which occurred around the same time, that is in the late twelfth and early thirteenth century. To be sure, there was legal instruction in the schools of Paris, but on nothing like the scale and with none of the wide repute associated with Bologna. Further, in 1219 Honorius forbade the teaching of civil law in Paris in order that the energies of the scholars there would not be diverted from that discipline which was making Paris in its way as famous as Bologna, namely theology.

In Paris earlier in the twelfth century there had been the cathedral school, the school of the collegiate church of Ste. Geneviève, and the school of the church of canons regular of St. Victor's. The last two had external schools for students who were not oblates of the house. It was the fame of the teachers of these schools, notably Peter Abelard (d. 1142) which attracted large numbers of students to Paris; but by the end of the century it was the cathedral school alone which had benefited from the great influx, and it was from this school alone that the university would develop. From the outset, then, the university in Paris was connected with a single school, and that one the school of the local bishop, rather than a host of schools in the hands of private teachers.

Each bishop had the responsibility of founding and maintaining a school in connection with his cathedral. Either he or some member of the cathedral chapter took on the responsibility of teaching the students. If no one within the chapter was suitable, however, a qualified outsider might be hired. From the eleventh century on, there was a tendency to connect the duty of teaching to the office of the chancellor of the cathedral, whose ordinary functions of keeping records demanded a certain modicum of learning. Where the cathedral school grew in size, however, the chancellor was likely to hire others to assist him in the task of teaching, often assigning them responsibility for teaching grammar while retaining for himself instruction in theology.

In the twelfth century the rapid spread of education led to an increase in the number of potential schoolmasters eager to make their living by teaching, either in a cathedral school or by setting up shop on their own with the chancellor's license to teach as a kind of recommendation. In some instances cathedral chancellors were only too eager to sell such licenses; but the Third Lateran Council of 1179 not only forbade the sale of licenses but went on to enact that licenses had to be granted to any who were properly qualified. With free licenses readily available, the number of teachers swelled considerably, especially where, as in Paris, the increasing number of students created a large demand. The chancellor retained the right to judge the fitness of a prospective master, but soon enough the body of masters themselves disputed that right, seeking to control entry into their own group, their gild. Their numbers became so enlarged that they spilled out of the cathedral grounds; they enjoyed in common the privilege of clerical status, being subject to ecclesiastical rather than lay jurisdiction; by about 1170 they already formed some kind of vague society; and by the early thirteenth century they had taken on the attributes of a corporation. That Innocent III recognized that they could be represented at the papal curia by a "proctor" indicates that their corporate nature was well on the way to general acceptance.

Unlike Bologna, however, Paris saw the development of a gild of teachers, not students. This was undoubtedly hastened by their struggle with the chancellor, whose monopoly in granting licenses denied to them complete control over their own membership. They could not deprive him of his right, but they could and did refuse to accept into their gild anyone who did not meet their own criteria; in effect, the candidate had to meet the requirements of both the chancellor and the gild before his full acceptance. As a result, the "inception," which was in origin something of an informal initiation into the local brotherhood of teachers, soon developed into a solemn ritual of acceptance into the gild of masters. Finally the masters, with the support of the papacy, forced the chancellor to grant the license only to those presented by the gild or university, thus gaining complete control over who could or could not teach at Paris.

Within the university of masters an internal development of some significance for the future occurred during the first decades of the thirteenth century. Possibly in imitation of Bologna, more likely as a consequence of similar social conditions, members of the university tended to form groups roughly reflecting the areas of their origin. At Paris these "nations" were four in number, France (that is, the area around Paris), Normandy, Picardy, and England (the last including the Germans). Each of these nations was headed by a proctor, whose term of office was very brief—at first a month or six weeks, later in the thirteenth century three months. Not until this development was well along did there finally emerge an officer, the rector, as the visible representative of the combined nations.

This development of nations with their proctors and rector was characteristic of the masters of arts, those who taught grammar and logic, the main emphasis increasingly on the latter. It did not affect the masters of canon law and theology; but by the middle of the thirteenth century the rector of the arts faculty, in view of the fact that he was the head of by far the largest faculty in the university and therefore the focus of much of the struggle for freedom from the supervision of the chancellor of the cathedral, emerged as the effective head of the university at large. Perhaps because the chancellor himself continued to act as head of the theology faculty, long preventing that faculty from developing a head of its own to contend with the arts rector for leadership of the whole, theology, the queen of the sciences, holding pride of place in the academic hierarchy, found itself subordinated to the rector of an inferior faculty.

There were other universities in the process of development at this time, often modeled on or at least influenced by the arrangements adopted at Bologna or Paris. At Orleans, which grew in importance as a law school after civil law was banned at Paris, there was an organization of student nations, although the gild of masters, remaining subject to the *scholasticus* of Orleans, the equivalent of the chancellor in Paris, managed to limit their independence. Toulouse, founded to combat heresy in southern France, was firmly in the hands of its masters, especially the Dominican order. Vicenza and Padua in northern Italy came into being as the result of migra-

tions of students from Bologna; there, as at later Italian foundations, the model of Bologna was followed, with the establishment of
student universities divided into nations with a heavy emphasis on
legal studies. Because they were associated with and encouraged
by the municipalities themselves, the professors were paid by
the town authorities. At Oxford the growth of the university was
preceded by schools of some considerable reputation, but there is
no satisfactory explanation for the development of a university
there rather than in any one of several other towns. Certainly, there
was no cathedral school from which, as in Paris, one might grow.
But soon, on the Paris model, masters and students were placed
under the jurisdiction of the chancellor of the cathedral church of
Lincoln, although, unlike Paris, there was no rivalry between chancellor and masters. On the contrary, the chancellor soon became the
elected head of the gild of masters and in effect the head of the
university.

While new universities continued to be founded on the medieval
model, especially in Germany, the world of the intellect already
threatened to pass them by. A large renewal of interest in the classics, which received considerable stimulus from the literary work
and fame of Francesco Petrarca (1304–1374), revealed a civilization
the dimensions of which seemed immeasurable. Petrarch and his
literary successors warmed to the Ciceronian ideal of *humanitas,* the
development of every facet of the human spirit, and sought its realization in the study and imitation of classical literature. The hunt for
manuscripts of the works of ancient authors, the refinement of Latin
style, and the rapid acquisition of Greek opened up the study of
the societies of Greece and Rome—their history, geography, politics, religion, and mythology. The "humanists" who threw themselves into this kind of literary and historical activity did so for the
most part outside the confines of the universities, which they
scorned for their arid logic-chopping and uncouth Latin. They often
formed their own societies or academies where they could meet, exchange ideas, and stimulate one another. Their ideal of intellectual
universality had its limitations: for example, they had little interest
in the kind of scientific speculation and observation that would produce a Galileo in the sixteenth century. But the ideal of a well-
rounded individual was a potent one, and the growing influence of
the humanists on education gave to the term "liberal arts" a connotation that clings to it still.

XI

THE
EARLY
MODERN
STATE

THE HUMANISTS' PREOCCUPATION WITH ANTIQ-
uity—their propensity for finding models for their own
society in the ancient world—colored their view of the
thousand years that had intervened. These became the
"middle" ages, a long stretch of barbarism, ignorance, and bad
Latin, now to be superseded by a rebirth, a "renaissance," of the
forms and ideals of classical antiquity. Thus the humanists helped
to create a historical period, the medieval, which historians have
found convenient to retain for want of anything better. The sum-
ming up of such a vast span of time in a single term imposed on it
a seeming uniformity, however, that long obscured much of its
development and creativity. Words such as "medieval" and "feudal"
have been and remain sufficient to damn whatever they are applied
to. But despite humanist enthusiasm, the world of the fifteenth and
sixteenth centuries was not a product of antiquity. Its economic
forms and political loyalties, its varieties of speech and habits of
mind, its views of man and his universe were molded during those
very Middle Ages it was so fashionable to disparage. Further, this
was a European world in a cultural as well as a geographical sense,
a conception which had not the remotest connection with antiquity.

The idea of a European community took a long time to grow. It was made possible by the loss of North Africa to an alien Moslem world, by the subsequent failure of the crusades to hold the eastern Mediterranean, and by the deepening division between Latin catholicism and Greek orthodoxy. From the fifteenth century on it was strengthened by the Turkish threat, which enhanced the sense of common cultural values in the west. Primarily, however, the idea of European community was the product of the long history of the western church whose place it would soon take as an integrating notion. The words "Europe" and "Christendom" became virtually synonymous. The humanist Aeneas Sylvius Piccolomini, the later Pope Pius II (1458–1464), not only described Europe as the heart of Christendom but used the adjectives "European" and "Christian" interchangeably. "Europe," up to this time a geographical term, would henceforth carry some, if not all, of the burden hitherto borne by the word "Christendom."

If the universal church ceased to be universal and therefore incapable of serving as an integrating force in the west, it was because the authority of the papacy, the one institution that could express that universality, finally had to give way before the development of autonomous political states. This development was one of the most striking features of European history after the thirteenth century. The idea of the state as a self-sufficient society was compounded of many elements, some of which have already been considered. By the end of the thirteenth century there was an increasing tendency throughout western society to look to secular governments rather than the church for direction and protection. These governments— whether of kingdoms, great ecclesiastical and secular principalities, or independent city-states—enjoyed a growing monopoly of political power over those dependent upon them, measured by their increased activities in the matters of taxation and legislation. As their effectiveness grew, so did the respect and loyalty they were able to command.

Because of the influence of corporate theory in the Middle Ages, it was increasingly easy to think of the aggregate of persons in a given political community as a single body. Some writers took a leaf from the church's book and called this community a mystical body—*corpus mysticum*—by which they probably meant no more than the lawyer's "fictional person." No matter what the abstraction (in time *status*, "state," would be preferred), it was soon given life

by a sense of national identity, a tendency to emphasize the similarities within a group and the differences between it and others. In
some quarters there was even discernible a sense of patriotism, of
loyalty to the "fatherland," the *patria*. This was evident earliest in
France. In the literature of the *chansons de geste*, the epic poems
of heroic deeds which so delighted the noble classes, France was
often referred to as "holy soil"; to fall in battle in its defense was
as ennobling and sanctifying as dying for the faith on a crusade.
This assimilation of crusading idealism to the defense of the kingdom gave to the incipient national spirit of the time an emotional
flavor hitherto unknown, and contributed much to the idea of the
inviolability of the state and its rulers. "He who wages war against
the king works against the whole church, Catholic doctrine, holi-
ness, justice, and the Holy Land." For the unknown preacher who
declaimed thus, as for an increasing number of others, the preservation of all the highest ideals was bound up with the safety of the
crown.

   As a principle of political organization, the state grew at the expense of the universal church. Lay education—the education of
men for careers outside the church—increased with the multiplica-
tion of lay officials employed by secular governments, marking the
end of the church's control of the educated class. The long conflict
between papacy and empire inaugurated by Gregory VII and
Henry IV allowed lesser governments relative freedom to develop
independently and gave rise to a large political literature which
helped to erode papal claims to political universality. By the fourteenth century the ideal of a single Christian society was being
replaced by, or at least had to make room for, the ideal of a strictly
human society with temporal ends. The "common good," borrowed
from Aristotle, was elaborated as the ultimate sanction of government. And by the fifteenth century the papal schism and the conciliar
movement revealed the growing autonomy of secular governments
and the inability of the church to maintain itself as a unifying
principle. National representation and the defense of national interests turned the council of Constance and its successors, which
might have symbolized the unity of Christendom, into arenas for
international negotiation. The popes finally avoided the threat to
their primacy which the councils posed by making tacit arrangements or formal agreements (concordats) with secular governments

to allow them a share in the nomination of church officers and the taxation of the clergy in their territories. By recognizing and dealing with individual states, the popes were successful in destroying conciliarism, and they regained in theory an untrammeled plenitude of power. In fact, however, they paid a heavy price. The concordat implied negotiation between two equal parties. The language of papal decretals might still be colored by the medieval concept of Christendom as a unitary society; in practice the concept was dead.

This entire development was accompanied—indeed hastened— by a growing barrage of criticism leveled against the church as a propertied institution. Throughout the Middle Ages the corrupting influence of wealth had been a favorite theme of moralists. The elevation of poverty as an ideal state (an idea to which monasticism had contributed) culminated in the life of St. Francis of Assisi and the mendicant movement that he inspired. Within the Franciscan order, which grew with incredible rapidity in the thirteenth century, a serious division soon developed between those who felt that as a large institution the order must modify its founder's rigid precepts about absolute poverty and those who demanded their strict observance. The latter's claim that Christ and his apostles owned nothing had obvious implications for Christ's vicar, and was soon condemned by the papacy as a heresy. But to compare the presumed poverty of Christ with the obvious wealth of the church was a telling blow. The contrast appealed especially to those who viewed the church not so much as a universal society with broad moral and governmental responsibilities requiring material means for fulfillment but as an organization limited to spiritual functions. There was no condemnation of the church's role in what we should now call social services. Indeed, the later Middle Ages witnessed an increase in local endowments of colleges, hospitals, and schools administered by churchmen. But critics of the fourteenth and fifteenth centuries rang all the changes on the theme of papal wealth and papal taxation. As the ideal of the church as a universal political community declined, so did the recognition of its need for political power and revenues to administer such a community. Thus, apologists for the secular state could make common cause with reformers and moralists who inveighed against the corrupting influence of the wealth of the church.

While the emergence of the modern state had profound effects on the church, it also hastened the demise of feudalism as a political and military institution. The limited effectiveness of feudal levies forced the increasing use of mercenary soldiers. Although in the twelfth and thirteenth centuries mercenaries were only occasional adjuncts to the feudal host, their importance in warfare steadily increased. The extended range of diplomatic activities of many European rulers demanded the deployment of forces over greater distances and longer periods of time than allowed by the restrictions of feudal usage. It became increasingly common for those who owed their lord military service to make a payment instead, the money being used to hire professionals the nature of whose service was not limited by feudal custom. There was a similar development in the nonfeudal city-states of northern Italy, where by the fourteenth century the citizen armies gradually disappeared to be replaced by bands of mercenaries whose leaders, the *condottieri*, hired out to this town or that depending on how much they were offered.

The professionalization of military service gave to those rulers with large potential revenues a distinct superiority over their smaller neighbors. It also meant the steady erosion of the political independence of the nobility within these territories. The extension of royal law, the influence of Roman Law, the tendency to identify the person of the ruler with the state he governed as bearing the "public person" gave to the ruler an inviolability which gradually deprived feudal resistance to his authority of all legitimacy. But if feudalism as a military and political institution declined in the later Middle Ages, it left deep marks on the social structure of Europe. The nobility, whose ranks became ever more jealously guarded, enjoyed legal advantages, monopolies of ecclesiastical and military positions of prestige and command, political patronage, and extensive local influence over tenants and petty neighbors. The peasantry, for the most part no longer bound by the legal restrictions of serfdom, remained committed to a host of vexatious obligations inherited from the past. Indeed in Germany, where throughout the Middle Ages there had been a long tradition of a free and relatively independent peasantry, the landed aristocracy became increasingly successful in imposing hitherto unknown burdens reminiscent of the serfdom of the west.

Finally, the growth of the state was aided by the development of the new moneyed classes of the towns, whose members sought the advantages found in the kind of ordered society that strong government can provide. Their wealth, in the form of loans and taxes, helped to finance royal enterprises; in time the moneyed classes gained influence in the councils of government, especially in financial matters; and as servants of the new lay state, they did much to enhance its prestige and extend its authority.

SUGGESTIONS FOR FURTHER READING

The following have been selected mainly with an eye to their accessibility to students. With the exception of a few substantial works, marked with an asterisk, they are all available in paperback editions. Some of these are recent reprints or translations of works written some years ago, and in these cases the date of first appearance is noted in parentheses.

GENERAL

Brentano, Robert. *The Early Middle Ages*. New York: Free Press of Glencoe, 1964.

Cheyney, Edward P. *The Dawn of a New Era*. New York: Harper & Row, 1962 (1936).

Lewis, Archibald R. *Emerging Medieval Europe, A.D. 400–1000*. New York: Knopf, 1967.

Lyon, Bryce D. *The High Middle Ages*. New York: Free Press of Glencoe, 1964.

Southern, R. W. *The Making of the Middle Ages*. New Haven: Yale University Press, 1961 (1953).

Thrupp, Sylvia L. *Early Medieval Society*. New York: Appleton-Century-Crofts, 1967.

ECONOMIC

Adelson, Howard. *Medieval Commerce*. Princeton, N.J.: Van Nostrand, 1962.

Bennett, H. S. *Life on the English Manor.* Cambridge University Press, 1960 (1937).

The Cambridge Economic History, Vols. I-III. Edited by J. H. Clapham et al. Cambridge University Press, 1942–1963; Vol. I, 2nd ed. 1966.

*Duby, Georges. *Rural Economy and Country Life in the Medieval West*. Translated by Cynthia Postan. Columbia, S.C.: University of South Carolina Press, 1968 (1962).

Latouche, Robert. *The Birth of Western Economy*. London: Methuen, 1967 (1956).

Lopez, Robert S. and Irving W. Raymond. *Medieval Trade in the Mediterranean World*. New York: Norton (1955).

Mundy, John H., and Peter Riesenberg. *The Medieval Town*. Princeton, N.J.: Van Nostrand, 1958.

Pirenne, Henri. *Economic and Social History of Medieval Europe*. New York: Harcourt, Brace & World (1933).

White, Lynn, Jr. *Medieval Technology and Social Change*. London: Oxford University Press, 1962.

POLITICAL AND LEGAL

Barraclough, G. *Origins of Modern Germany*. New York: Capricorn Press, 1963 (1946).

Bloch, Marc. *Feudal Society*. 2 vols. Chicago: University of Chicago Press, 1964 (1940).

*Carlyle, R. W., and A. J. Carlyle. *A History of Medieval Political Theory in the West*. 6 vols. Edinburgh and London: Blackwood, 1903–1936.

Fawtier, Robert. *The Capetian Kings of France*. London: Macmillan, 1962 (1941).

Fichtenau, H. *The Carolingian Empire*. New York: Harper & Row, 1964 (1949).

Jolliffe, J. E. A. *The Constitutional History of Medieval England*. 4th ed. New York: Norton, 1961.

Morrall, John B. *Political Thought in Medieval Times.* New York: Harper & Row, 1962 (1958).

Strayer, Joseph. *Feudalism.* Princeton, N.J.: Van Nostrand, 1965.

*Ullmann, Walter. *Principles of Government and Politics in the Middle Ages.* London: Methuen, 1961.

ECCLESIASTICAL AND EDUCATIONAL

*Deansley, M. *History of the Medieval Church.* 10th ed. London: Methuen, 1959.

Haskins, Charles Homer. *The Renaissance of the 12th Century.* New York: Meridian Books, 1951 (1927).

Knowles, David. *The Evolution of Medieval Thought.* New York: Random House, 1962.

Mollat, G. *The Popes at Avignon.* New York: Harper & Row, 1965 (1949).

*Rashdall, Hastings. *The Universities of Europe in the Middle Ages.* New ed. 3 vols. London: Oxford University Press, 1936.

Tierney, Brian. *The Crisis of Church and State, 1050–1300.* Englewood Cliffs, N.J.: Prentice-Hall, 1964.

*Ullmann, Walter. *The Growth of Papal Government in the Middle Ages.* 2nd ed., corrected. London: Methuen, 1965.

Wieruszowski, Helene. *The Medieval University.* Princeton, N.J.: Van Nostrand, 1966.

INDEX

Aachen, 212
Abelard, Peter, 221
Adriatic Sea, 53
Advocate, 104, 105–6, 159–60
Advowson, 27
Aegean Sea, 12, 54
Africa, North, 4, 5, 12, 32, 53, 54, 227
Agincourt, battle of (1415), 26
Aids, feudal, 98, 127, 131, 143
Alans, 3
Alaric, king of the Visigoths (d. 410), 3
Alberic, 186
Albigensian crusade, 20
Alcuin, 210, 211, 212
Alexander III, pope (1159–1181), 58
Alexander V, antipope (1409–1410), 197
Alfonso IX, king of Castile (1188–1230), 132
Alfonso X, king of Castile (1252–1284), 148
Alfred, king of Wessex (871–899), 24

Allodial land, 43, 94, 99, 106, 110, 119, 142
Alps, 12, 74, 99, 186
Alsace, 10
Amalfi, 53
Amaury de Montfort, 20
Ambrose, St., bishop of Milan (374–397), 181
Anagni, 22
Anatolia, 31
Angles, 23
Anglo-Saxons, 23–4, 40, 138, 144, 205
Anjou, county of, 20, 25, 117
   counts of, 18
Anselm, archbishop of Canterbury (1093–1109), 27
Aquinas, St. Thomas (c. 1225–1274), 56–7, 131
Aquitaine, duchy of, 19, 21, 25, 26, 32, 117, 171
Arabia, 11
Arabs, 11, 12, 30
Aragon, kingdom of, 21, 30, 132, 133
Arianism, 8

Aristotle, 55, 57, 144, 214, 216, 228
Arnulf, duke of Carinthia, German emperor (887–899), 11
Ars dictaminis, 217
Arte della Lana, 76
Asia Minor, 31, 66
Asturias, 30
Attila, king of the Huns (d. 453), 4
Augustine, St., of Canterbury, 205
Augustine, St., of Hippo, 162, 167, 204, 205
Aurelian, Roman emperor (270–275), 179
Avignon, 23, 195, 196

Balkans, 3, 5, 31, 32, 76
Baltic Sea, 52
Ban, 45
Banalities, 45
Banking, 61
Bar-sur-Aube, 64
Bari, 53
Basle, council of, 198–99
Basques, 30
Baugulf, abbot of Fulda, 211
Bavaria, 9
Beauvais, 216
Becket, Thomas, archbishop of Canterbury (1162–1170), 27, 216
Bede, 209–10
Belgium, 4, 10
Benedict VIII, pope (1012–1024), 14
Benedict IX, pope (1032–1044), 14
Benedict XIII, antipope (1394–1423), 197
Benedict of Nursia, St. (d. 543), 166, 167, 169, 171, 205, 207, 209
Benedict Biscop, 209
Beneficium, 93, 122
Berbers, 12
Biscop, Benedict, *see* Benedict Biscop
Bishop, office of, 155, 157–61, 168, 189–90
Black Death, 49
Blanche of Castile, 20
Boethius, 207
Bohemia, 30, 132

Bologna, 147, 149, 151, 217–21, 222, 223, 224
Boniface VIII, pope (1294–1303), 22, 23, 132, 151
Boniface IX, pope (1389–1404), 197
Bordeaux, 117
Bourges, 159
Bracton, 145, 148–49
Brandenburg, 28
Britain, 10, 23–4
Brittany, duchy of, 20
Bruno of Reims, 172
Building, 77–8
Burchard of Worms, 150, 151
Burgos, 132
Burgundians, 4, 8, 138
Burgundy, 171
Byzantine Empire, 5, 11, 14, 15, 31, 32, 53, 54, 66, 182, 183, 217

Calais, 26
Camaldoli, monastery of, 172
Camera, papal, 194
Canon law, 55, 149–52
Canons, cathedral, 157, 161–65, 167–68, 174
Canterbury, 27, 216
Canute, king of England (1016–1035), 24
Capetian dynasty of France, 18–23, 103, 114–18
Capitulation of 1352, 194
Carcassonne, 161
Cardinals, 188, 192–95, 196, 197, 198, 199
Carolingian dynasty and empire, 9–12, 18, 19, 53, 54, 90, 91, 92, 94, 102–6, 114, 157, 158, 159, 160, 183, 185, 186, 210
Carthage, 11
Cassiodorus, 207, 208, 210
Castile, 30, 32, 132, 148
Catalonia, 30
Champagne, counts of, 64
Champagne fairs, 64, 65, 74
Chancery, papal, 194
Chansons de geste, 228
Charlemagne, *see* Charles the Great

Charles, duke of Anjou, king of Sicily (1265–1285), 18
Charles the Bald, king of the West Franks (840–877), 10, 95, 105
Charles the Fat, king of the Franks (deposed 887), 10, 11
Charles the Great (Charlemagne), king of the Franks (768–814), 9, 10, 18, 28, 41, 90, 102, 103, 104, 105, 106, 109, 144, 150, 167, 170, 183, 185, 186, 210–14
Charles VI, king of France (1380–1422), 26
Charles Martel, mayor of the palace (714–741), 9, 12
Chartres, 216
Chartreuse, monastery of, 172
Chrodegang, St., 162
Cicero, 204, 224
Citeaux, monastery of, 172–74
Civitas, 156
Clairvaux, monastery of, 173
Clement II, pope (1046–1047), 14
Clement V, pope (1305–1314), 23
Clement VI, pope (1342–1352), 194
Clement VII, antipope (1378–1394), 194, 196, 197
Clement, St., of Alexandria, 204
Clermont, 31
Cloth industry, 74–6
Clovis, king of the Franks (d. 511), 8, 138
Cluny, monastery of, 170–73, 174, 187
Commenda, 62
Commendation, 42, 43, 87, 88
Common good, 131, 144, 147, 148, 228
Common law, 43, 128, 144–47
Commons, House of, 133–34
Commutation, 4, 8, 49, 79
Compostela, 31, 32
Compurgation, 139
Condottieri, 230
Conrad I, king of Germany (911–918), 12, 13
Conrad II, king of Germany, emperor (1024–1039), 14, 95, 118, 187
Constance, Council of, 197–98, 228

Constance of Sicily, 16, 17
Constantine the Great, Roman emperor (312–337), 155, 184–85
Constantine, Donation of, 184–85
Constantinople, 2, 4, 11, 32, 54, 66, 178, 180, 182, 195
Conversi, 172
Cordoba, 30
Councils, church, 150, 179, 192, 195–200, 228–29
Count, Carolingian, 102–3
Courts, feudal, 111, 142, 143–44, 145
  hundred, 141–42, 145
  manorial, 142
  papal, 187, 188, 191–95, 198
  royal, 126, 145
Credit, 60–1
Crusades, 31–2, 54, 98, 140, 228
Cyprian, St., of Carthage, 179

Dacia, 3
Danube River, 3, 30, 31
Decretals, 151
Decretals, pseudo-Isidorian, 184–85
Decretum of Gratian, 151
Defiance, feudal, 99, 123, 128
Dictatus papae of Gregory VII, 189–90
Diocese, 155, 156
Diocletian, Roman emperor (284–305), 2
Dniester River, 3
Dominican order, 175, 223
Donatus, 204
Dreux, county of, 18
Dry farming, 38
Duchies, German, 11, 13, 106, 118
Durand of Le Puy, 109

Edward the Confessor, king of England (1042–1066), 24
Edward I, king of England (1272–1307), 21
Egbert, archbishop of York, 210
Egypt, 11, 166, 167
Elbe River, 28, 30
Eleanor of Aquitaine, 19, 117
Elton (Huntingdonshire), 46

Enclosures, 47
England, 20, 21, 23–8, 40, 43, 45, 46, 48, 49, 66, 74, 75, 76, 81, 96, 109, 117, 122, 123–34, 142, 143, 144, 145, 146, 147, 148, 205, 210, 216
Ennodius, St., bishop of Pavia, 190
Euclid, 216
Eugenius IV, pope (1431–1447), 198–99

Fairs, 61, 63–5, 67
Fallowing, 37
Felix V, antipope (1439–1449), 199
Ferrara, council of, 199
Fertilizers, 37–8
Fief, 92–7, 99, 106, 110, 114
Fisc, Carolingian, 105
Flanders, county of, 21, 64, 65, 71, 74, 75, 76
Florence, 18, 76, 81
Florence, council of, 199
Foliot, Wido, 141
Fondi, 196
Forfeiture, feudal, 99
France, 3, 4, 8, 9, 10, 11, 12, 18–23, 25–6, 40, 43, 63, 64, 65, 74, 75, 76, 81, 87, 96, 99, 106, 108, 114–18, 122, 132, 142, 148, 149, 158, 192, 209, 214, 216, 228
Franciscan order, 175, 229
Franconia, duchy of, 12
Franks, 4, 8–12, 30, 89, 102, 138, 182
Fraxinetum, 12
Frederick I Barbarossa, king of Germany, emperor (1152–1190), 16, 17, 115, 121, 122, 131, 149
Frederick II, king of Germany and Sicily, emperor (1212–1250), 17, 21
Frisians, 9
Frontiers, medieval, 28–33
Fulda, monastery of, 211

Gaeta, 53
Gaiseric, king of the Vandals (d. 477), 4
Galileo, 224

Garigliano River, 12, 185
Gascony, duchy of, 19, 26, 32, 66, 117
Gaul, see France
Geneva, Lake, 4
Genoa, 32, 53, 54, 63, 81
Geoffrey, count of Anjou (d. 1151), 25 116–17
Gerbert, see Sylvester II
German law, 129, 130, 136–42, 143, 144, 145, 146, 149, 217
German tribes, 2–9, 23, 202
Germany, 10, 12–18, 28, 29, 63, 65, 76, 95, 96, 102, 109, 114, 115, 118–22, 132, 148, 156, 171–72, 186, 191, 216, 224
Gerson, Jean, 197
Gibraltar, Straits of, 4, 11
Gilds
    craft, 71–3, 77, 80, 83
    merchant, 61, 67, 73–4, 75, 76
    student, 218–19, 224
    teacher, 219, 222–23, 224
Gorze, monastery of, 171
Gratian, 151
Gregory I the Great, pope (590–604), 23, 180, 204, 205, 208
Gregory II, pope (715–731), 182
Gregory V, pope (996–999), 15
Gregory VI, pope (1045–1046), 14, 15
Gregory VII, pope (1073–1085), 15, 21, 26, 188–90, 191, 192, 228
Gregory IX, pope (1227–1241), 151
Gregory X, pope (1271–1276), 194
Gregory XI, pope (1370–1378), 23, 196
Gregory XII, pope (1406–1415), 197
Guienne, see Aquitaine
Guiscard, Robert, 16

Hadrian I, pope (772–795), 150
Hadrianople, battle of (378), 3
Harold of England, 24
Henry I, king of England (1100–1135), 25, 27, 123, 124
Henry II, king of England (1154–1189), 19, 20, 25, 27, 117, 126, 127, 128

Henry V, king of England (1387–1422), 26
Henry I the Fowler, duke of Saxony, king of Germany (918–936), 13, 28
Henry II, king of Germany, emperor (1002–1024), 14, 118, 186
Henry III, king of Germany, emperor (1039–1056), 14, 118, 187, 188
Henry IV, king of Germany, emperor (1056–1106), 14, 15, 21, 119, 120, 188, 228
Henry V, king of Germany, emperor (1106–1125), 16
Heribert of Hildesheim, 216
Hincmar, archbishop of Reims, 139–40
Hippo, 162
Hohenstaufen dynasty, 121–22
Holy Land, 21, 31–2
Homage, 88, 94, 97
Honorius III, pope (1216–1227), 221
Hospital, knights of the, 32
Hugh Capet, king of France (987–996), 11, 18, 19
Humanism, 224, 226
Humbert, cardinal, 188–90
Hundred Years War, 23, 26, 66
Hungary, 4, 30, 32
Huns, 3, 4

Iconoclasm, 182
Immunities, 104, 105, 106, 159
Incardination, 192–93
Inger of Faldingthorpe, 141
Innocent III, pope (1198–1216), 17, 27, 140, 214, 222
Innocent VII, pope (1404–1406), 197
Investiture, 94
Investiture controversy, 15, 16, 21, 27, 120, 186–91
Irnerius, 217
Isidore of Seville, 184, 210
Islam, 11
Italy, 3, 4, 5, 8, 10, 12–18, 22, 53, 54, 61, 62, 65, 74, 78, 79, 81, 82, 99, 102, 115, 120, 122, 132, 146, 147, 149, 150, 158, 172, 178, 180, 182, 185, 186, 187, 191, 192, 199, 207, 208, 209, 216, 217–21, 223, 224
Ivo of Chartres, 150, 151

James, St., 31
Jarrow, monastery of, 209
Jerome, St., 204
Jerusalem, 31
Joan of Arc, 26
John X, pope (914–928), 185
John XI, pope (931–935), 170
John XII, pope (955–964), 14, 186
John XIX, pope (1024–1032), 14
John, king of England (1199–1216), 26, 27, 127, 128
John of Salisbury, 124–26, 131
Just price, 55–7
Justinian, Roman emperor (527–565), 5, 8, 12, 146, 147, 150, 217, 218
Jutes, 23
Juvencus, 205

La Ferté, monastery of, 173
Lagny, 64
Lanfranc, archbishop of Canterbury, 27
Laon, 216
Lateran Council, Second (1139), 162
Lateran Council, Third (1179), 222
Lateran Council, Fourth (1215), 140
Lateran palace, 185
Lechfeld, battle of (955), 13
Leo I, pope (440–461), 55, 180
Leo IV, pope (847–855), 185
Leo IX, pope (1049–1054), 192
Leon, 30
Liege homage, 97
Lincoln, 224
Loire River, 40, 103
Lombards, 5, 8, 9, 53, 138, 146, 180, 182, 208
Lombardy, 15, 16
Lorraine, 10, 119, 158, 171, 172
Lothair I, emperor (840–855), 10, 12, 13
Louis the German, king of the East Franks (840–876), 10

Louis the Pious, king of the Franks, emperor (814–840), 9, 10, 158
Louis II, emperor (855–875), 12
Louis V, king of the West Franks (d. 987), 18
Louis VI, king of France (1108–1137), 19
Louis VII, king of France (1137–1180), 19, 25
Louis IX, St., king of France (1226–1270), 20, 21, 26
Louis XIV, king of France (1643–1715), 131
Lowlands, 10, 65, 66
Lucca, 81

Magna Carta, 128, 129
Magyars, 11, 13, 28
Mahdia, 54
Main River, 4
Maine, county of, 20, 25, 117
Mancipia, 43
Manor, 44–7
Markets, 63–4, 65
Marling, 38
Marozia, 186
Martin V, pope (1417–1431), 198
Mathilda of England, 25, 124
Mayor of the palace, 9
Mediterranean Sea, 4, 10, 11, 12, 53, 54, 63, 66, 74, 79, 154, 167
Melun, county of, 18, 19
Mendicant orders, 175
Merovingian dynasty, 8–9, 90, 182, 209
Meuse River, 79, 103
Milan, 18, 81, 207, 217
Mining, 30, 76–7
Ministeriales, 119, 120, 121
Minting, 104
Missi dominici, 103, 142
Monasticism, 30, 31, 166–75, 191, 207, 208–9, 213, 214
Money changers, 60, 65
Money economy, 59–60
Mongols, 66
Monte Cassino, 167, 207
Montfort, *see* Amaury, Simon

Morimond, monastery of, 173
Moslems, 9, 11, 12, 30–2, 53, 54, 227
Mundeburdum, 87

Naples, 53
Nations, in the university, 198, 199, 218, 223, 224
Natural economy, 59–60
Navarre, 30
Nicaea, council of (325), 195
Nicholas I, pope (858–867), 183, 184
Nicholas II, pope (1059–1061), 187, 192
Nicholas IV, pope (1288–1292), 194
Nîmes, 161
Norbert, St., 174
Normandy, duchy of, 15, 20, 24, 25, 26, 43, 116, 117
North Sea, 10, 52, 65
Northmen, *see* Vikings

Odo of Paris, king of the West Franks (887–898), 10, 11, 18
Odofredus, 219
Odovacar, 5
Ordeal, 139–41
Orleans, 19, 216, 223
Ostrogoths, 3, 4, 5, 8
Otto I the Great, king of Germany, emperor (936–973), 13–14, 28, 171
Otto II, king of Germany, emperor (973–983), 14, 171
Otto III, king of Germany, emperor (983–1002), 14
Otto IV, king of Germany, emperor (1198–1215), 17
Ovid, 204
Oxford, 224

Padua, 223
Palestine, 11
Paris, 18, 19, 114, 221
Paris, university of, 197, 198, 216, 221–24
Parish, 156, 165–66
Parliament, 132–34
Parochia, 155, 156, 165

Patrimony, 168, 191
Patronage
  ecclesiastical, 161
  Roman, 87
Paul, St., 31, 155, 178
Paul the Deacon, 204
Pavia, 208, 217
Pavia, council of, 198
Peace of God, 108–9
Penitentiary, papal, 194
Pepin, king of the Franks (751–768),
  9, 182, 183, 185
Persia, 11
Peter, St., 31, 178–79, 182, 183, 184,
  185, 190
Peter the Hermit, 140
Peter's pence, 26
Peterborough, monastery of, 45–6
Petrarca (Petrarch), Francesco, 224
Philip I, king of France (1060–1108),
  21
Philip II Augustus, king of France
  (1180–1223), 20, 25, 26, 116,
  117, 122
Philip III, king of France (1270–
  1285), 22
Philip IV, king of France (1285–
  1314), 21, 22, 23, 132
Piccolomini, Aeneas Sylvius, see Pius II
Pilgrimages, 31
Pisa, 32, 53, 54, 81, 197
Pius II, pope (1458–1464), 199–200,
  227
Plow, 38
Po valley, 5
Poitiers, 117
Poitou, county of, 19, 20, 117
Poland, 30
Policraticus of John of Salisbury, 124–
  26
Politics of Aristotle, 144
Pontigny, monastery of, 173
Population, 36, 37, 66, 67, 74
Praemunire, Statute of (1353), 28
Prebends, 163, 164, 169
Precaria, 92–3
Premontré, monastery of, 174
Primogeniture, 96

Principalities, French, 106–11, 116–
  18
Provins, 64
Provisions, papal, 27, 165, 192, 194,
  198
Provisors, Statute of (1351), 28
Ptolemy, 216
Pyrenees, 12, 30, 117

Quadrivium, 207, 214

Ravenna, 2, 53, 185, 207, 217
Recceswinth, king of the Visigoths
  (649–672), 137
Reims, 159, 216
Relief, feudal, 96
Representation, 129–34
Rhetoric, 203–7, 212
Rhine River, 4, 79, 103
Rhone River, 117
Richard I Lionheart, king of England
  (1189–1199), 20, 25, 26, 127
Robert Curthose, son of William the
  Conqueror, 24, 25
Robert Guiscard, 16
Robert the Strong, 103
Roger of Sicily, 16
Roman Empire, 2–8, 23, 36, 41, 42,
  86, 87, 88, 112, 138, 150, 154,
  155, 156, 180, 182, 185, 205–6
Roman law, 47, 56–7, 115, 124–25,
  129, 130–31, 136, 137, 139, 143,
  144, 146–49, 150, 152, 217–21,
  230
Rome, 2, 3, 4, 5, 9, 14–17, 22, 31, 53,
  150, 178–95, 204, 207, 208, 217
Rota, 194

Saale River, 28
St. Gall, monastery of, 213
St. Genevieve, church of, 221
St. John Lateran, church of, 192
St. Lawrence, church of, 192
St. Mary Major, church of, 192
St. Paul Outside the Walls, church of,
  192
St. Peter, church of, 192
Saintes, 117

Salerno, 53
Salian dynasty, 14–15, 118–21
Saracens, 15, 170, 185
Sardica, council of (343–344), 179
Sardinia, 54
Savoy, 4
Saxon dynasty, 13–14, 118, 121
Saxons, 9, 23
Saxony, 43, 119
Saxony, duchy of, 13
Scabini, 104
Scheldt River, 79
Schism, papal, 194, 196–97, 228
Sea loan, 62–3
Seigneury, 43–7
Seine River, 103
Senlis, 19
Sens, 159
Serfdom, 43, 80, 230
Services, common, 194
Shipping, 63
Sicily, island of, 4, 12, 16, 204
Sicily, Angevin kingdom of, 18, 194
Sicily, Norman kingdom of, 15, 16, 17, 122
Siena, council of, 198
Siete Partidas of Alfonso X, 148
Silesia, 30
Simon de Montfort, 20
Simony, 187, 189, 195
Siricius, pope (384–398), 180
Slavs, 28
Soissons, 216
Spain, 3, 4, 8, 9, 12, 18, 30–1, 63, 64, 65, 74, 81, 132, 148, 192, 208, 216
Stephen III, pope (752–757), 182
Stephen of Blois, king of England (1135–1154), 25, 27, 124, 126
Sueves, 3
Switzerland, 10
Sylvester I, pope (314–335), 184–85
Sylvester II, pope (999–1003), 14
Symmachus, St., pope (498–514), 190
Syria, 11, 31

Taxation, Carolingian, 103–4
    manorial, 47
    parliamentary, 133

Temple, knights of the, 32
Tertullian, 203
Teutonic knights, 32
Theobald, archbishop of Canterbury, 216
Theodora, 186
Theodoric, king of the Ostrogoths (d. 526), 5, 8, 207
Theodosius I, Roman emperor (379–395), 3, 179, 181
Theodosius II, Roman emperor (408–450), 146, 217
Theophylact, 186
Thessalonika, 181
Tithes, 104
Tithes, papal, 22
Toulouse, 20, 32, 117, 161, 223
Touraine, county of, 20, 117
Tours, 159, 212
Towns, 78–83, 120
Trenchebof, William, 140–41
Trial by combat, 139, 141
Trivium, 207, 214, 217
Troyes, 64
Truce of God, 109–9
Turks, Ottoman, 32, 66, 227
Tuscany, 17, 81
Tusculum, counts of, 14
Tyrrhenian Sea, 53

Universities, 217–24
Unstrutt River, 13
Urban II, pope (1088–1099), 31, 191
Urban V, pope (1362–1370), 196
Urban VI, pope (1378–1389), 194, 196, 197
Usury, 57–8, 61, 64, 195

Valens, Roman emperor (364–378), 3
Valentinian I, Roman emperor (364–375), 181
Vallombrosa, monastery of, 172
Vandals, 3–4, 5, 8, 12
Vassalage, 88–99
Vatican, 185
Venice, 18, 32, 53, 54, 81
Verdun, treaty of (843), 10
Verona, 217

Vicenza, 223
Vienna, 30
Vienne, 204, 208
Vikings, 10, 11, 24, 74
Villages, 39–41, 44–5
Virgil, 204, 205
Visigoths, 3, 4, 8, 12, 137, 138, 144, 148
Vivarium, monastery of, 207

Walter of Henley, 38
Wardship, feudal, 95, 127, 143
Wearmouth, monastery of, 209
Wessex, kingdom of, 24

William of Aquitaine (d. 918), 170
William I the Conqueror, king of England (1066–1087), 24, 25, 26, 27, 123, 124
William II Rufus, king of England (1087–1100), 24, 25, 27
William II, king of Sicily (1166–1189), 16
Worms, Concordat of (1122), 15, 16, 17

York, 209, 210

Zeno, Roman emperor (474–491), 5